Adam Smith's Pragmatic Liberalism

Lisa Hill

Adam Smith's Pragmatic Liberalism

The Science of Welfare

palgrave
macmillan

Lisa Hill
University of Adelaide
Adelaide, SA, Australia

ISBN 978-3-030-19336-2 ISBN 978-3-030-19337-9 (eBook)
https://doi.org/10.1007/978-3-030-19337-9

This Palgrave Macmillan imprint is published by the registered company Springer Nature Switzerland AG
The registered company address is: Gewerbestrasse 11, 6330 Cham, Switzerland

Dedicated to Stephen Sinclair

Acknowledgements

The author thanks the Australian Research Council for the generous funding that made this book possible. She also thanks her research assistants Veronica Coram, Max Douglass, Kelly McKinley and Mollie Hohmann for their able assistance.

Contents

CHAPTER 1

Introduction: The New Science of Welfare and Happiness

Introductory Comments

Adam Smith's importance as a political thinker has been underestimated, due, in part, to the misplaced perception that his political project lacked coherence and even the belief that he evinced no interest in politics. A key aim of this book is to challenge those perceptions and show that Smith does have a politics but that it has been obscured by his attempts to make the art of governing less ideological, more social-scientific and, most of all, more productive of good effects. Although he showed some interest in conventional political science topics, his main concern was to reconfigure the art of governing according to a new set of methods, values and concerns. It is no use trying to read into the text what we ourselves might expect to discover but to try and allow Smith himself to come through. What he offers is a rich, subtle and original edifice well worth the trouble.

Adam Smith (1723–1790) was a leading figure of the 'Scottish Enlightenment' and, among other things, Chair of Moral Philosophy at the University of Glasgow. He is best known as a pioneer of political economy but he was also a moral philosopher with a deep interest in social theory and human psychology. Smith's first major work was the *Theory of Moral Sentiments* (1759) (hereafter referred to as *TMS*) but he is better known for *An Inquiry into the Nature and Causes of the Wealth of Nations* (1776) (hereafter referred to as *WN*), which secured his reputation as the parent of modern economics. Smith's most influential ideas relate to his theory of 'natural liberty' and the free market and his belief

L. Hill, *Adam Smith's Pragmatic Liberalism*,
https://doi.org/10.1007/978-3-030-19337-9_1

in the positive effects of self-interest. There is enormous and unabated interest in Smith's thought partly because he remains—rightly or wrongly—the most important touchstone for the liberal, free market project. But it is also because his work is so rich and therefore capable of bearing multiple interpretations.

This book is about Smith's political thought and especially his 'political economy'—'the science of a statesman or legislator'—an important and hitherto underdeveloped 'branch' of statecraft that was not an enterprise separate from politics but the most important aspect of it (*WN*, IV: 428). Not only could politics not be siloed off from economics, it could not be siloed off from all the other human 'sciences' either; it was inextricably intertwined with his ethics, his social science, his historiography, his realist model of human psychology, his proto-sociology and even his deistic theology.

Although Smith's politics has been described as 'radical' (McLean 2006) and even 'revolutionary' (Himmelfarb 1985: 46), particularly in its attitude to commercialism and the poor, his politics was not radical in the technical sense; for example, his critique of 'capitalism' and class privilege was not radical insofar as he in no way thought either should be transcended. But his politics *was* radical in the context of how political science was approached in his time. It was a call for government to radically shift its attention from the fortunes of economic, political and military elites to those of the people more generally and especially the poor. It was also a protracted diatribe against elite manipulation of the state, against corruption, Mercantilism, crony capitalism, prejudice, 'enthusiasm', blind nationalism and a preference for glory over welfare. He also asked people to think of the wealth of nations, not in terms of gold, a favourable balance of trade or the extent of conquered territory, but in more human terms: did the people enjoy sufficient freedom, security and social and political stability? Was everyone 'tolerably well fed, clothed, and lodged'? Was the population growing or declining? Had infant mortality rates risen to unconscionable levels? Were people paid enough? Were they enabled to live with dignity? Most of all, were they happy? The latter was, Smith insisted, a perfectly legitimate question for a political economist to pose and he repeatedly came back to that question as his standard.

In prosecuting his political economy Smith believed that he was engaged in an enterprise so noble and absorbing that its successful execution embodied an aesthetic dimension:

> The perfection of police, the extension of trade and manufactures, are noble and magnificent objects. The contemplation of them pleases us, and we are interested in whatever can tend to advance them. They make part of the great system of government, and the wheels of the political machine seem to move with more harmony and ease by means of them. We take pleasure in beholding the perfection of so beautiful and grand a system, and we are uneasy till we remove any obstruction that can in the least disturb or encumber the regularity of its motions. (*TMS*, IV.i.11: 185)

This is exactly how Smith regarded the system of 'natural liberty' that was at the very centre of his political thought: as a beautiful system or machine that badly needed to be untangled from its myriad 'obstructions'. However, in what reads like a pointed reminder to himself, Smith concludes this reflection with a caution that the single-minded pursuit of beauty, perfection and system in the context of a project that was more or less constituted by the human element could end in tears if one wasn't careful. Perfection is all very well but, at the end of the day, 'all constitutions of government' are only as good as their tendency 'to promote the happiness of those who live under them'. Indeed, '*[t]his is their sole use and end*' (*TMS*, IV.i.11: 185; emphasis added). So, let us by all means make the system of government beautiful but, most of all, we should ensure that it is actually capable of promoting human flourishing and happiness.

Smith's Purpose in Writing

Not all scholars have perceived in Smith's thought a well-defined political project. Due to the cautious and sceptical strains in Smith, Èlie Halevy once decreed that Smith was interested neither in a science of politics nor in 'the political bearing of his economic doctrines' (Halevy 1934: 142). For John Robertson, Smith's interest in social and economic progress and individual choice were not 'particularly political goals' (Robertson 1997), while E.G. West suggests that there is no 'explicitly coherent analysis of political behaviour in Smith's work' (West 1976: 55). Other scholars have argued that Smith sought to subordinate, elide or 'displace' politics in order to make way for a fuller understanding of society and the economy (e.g. Wolin 1960; Singer 2004; Minowitz 1994). Some of these statements are partly true but none really captures completely what Smith was trying to achieve.

The political material that is found throughout all Smith's major works was written to mesh with the concerns of his major published works, namely, economics, jurisprudence and moral philosophy. Since these disciplines are all cognate with political science (and were conceived by Smith himself as subfields of it), Smith had multiple occasions to introduce political themes, often discoursing at great length and in fine, practical detail.

For Smith, politics was not just about ideas: it was an *activity* as well. He was more than a scholar but was actively involved in framing government policy and was frequently called on to offer advice to government ministers. Apart from his years as a customs commissioner,[1] he enjoyed friendships with MPs on both sides of the House—including Edmund Burke—and was closely associated with successive Prime Ministers of Britain (Ross 1995: xxxiv and *passim*). His economic doctrines were 'adopted by leading politicians of both parties'; for example, William Pitt the Younger was a 'known admirer of Smith' and, on the basis of Smith's published advice, 'had promoted commercial treaties in order to bring about free-er trade' (McLean 2006: 24, 22). All of this gave him ample scope to either sound out his ideas at the coal face or else apply his political ideas to practice. Smith's advice was not limited to domestic concerns; for example, he was asked to advise the British government on the best course of action with regard to America. Smith saw himself as a public intellectual who wrote to influence governments and shift the political prejudices of the public. It is in these efforts and his interaction with many of the influential political figures of his day that he left behind vivid traces of his politics and where we discover that he was a political realist who understood all too well the constraints of real-world politics.

Smith's political interests were broad and far more focused on the welfare of the poor, the disenfranchised and the 'middling ranks' of people than is commonly allowed: he was an important influence on successive reform movements for taxation, free trade, food security, mass education, labour laws, defence and the management and retention of the colonies. He was also a vociferous critic of many entrenched—but, to Smith's mind, maladaptive—practices such as the poor laws, the corn laws, the low wages of the working poor, religious interference in politics, political corruption and the archaic laws controlling inheritance and workers' rights. He was particularly vocal on the problem of public debt and worried that it would 'in the long-run probably ruin all the great nations of Europe' (*WN*, V.iii.10: 911). Smith himself saw a dominating theme of his social and economic writings—the 'very violent attack upon mercantilism'—as politically controversial (*The Correspondence of Adam Smith*, Smith 1987, hereafter referred to as *Corr.*: 251), with its condemnation of arbitrary restrictions, profligacy, corruption and class privilege.

It is not that Smith's goals weren't highly political ones; it was just that he was attempting to start afresh and redefine what the political consisted in. He sought to reinvent the art of governing and, along the way, effect some progress in the 'science of politics' which, to his mind, had so far been 'inconsiderable ... in comparison of what may be yet expected' (Stewart 1980, vol. 2: 309–10). In order to offer his reconstructed science of public management, Smith had to move away from traditional, classical, normative and constructivist accounts of statecraft to a more social-scientific approach. He wrote that the 'science of politics' gains little 'from the speculations of ancient philosophers' who considered the matter only from the perspective of elites and 'confined their attention' to such relatively worthless concerns as regime taxonomy and means for 'perpetuating' the power and 'extending the glory of the state', no matter the cost (Stewart 1980, vol. 2: 309).

In his attempt to reinvent political science and to focus on previously neglected aspects of public management, Smith rejected not only classical approaches but also the more recent Machiavellian and Hobbesian approaches, first, because they inevitably led to endless, destructive war and ultimately national debilitation; and, second, because they took no account of commerce and its interactions with politics. So, along with the other Scots, Smith sought to reassess human activity 'against the rise of modern trade and manufacture, consumerism and material refinement, as *the* distinctive attributes of modern states' (Oz-Salzberger 2003: 165). Commerce now took centre stage as a natural development to be understood and embraced: Locke had been wrong to conceive commerce as a threat to liberty. Rather, commerce meant progress and had therefore effectively helped to create 'modern liberty' (Hont 2009: 149).

Smith wanted to produce a political science for 'modern times' that embodied 'universal principles' not only of 'justice' but also—and significantly—of more prosaic 'expediency'; principles that any 'form of government' could safely adopt in order 'to regulate the social order' and to ensure that the advantages of living in 'political union' were distributed as evenly as possible 'among all the different members of a community' (Stewart 1980, vol. 2: 309). By this he meant that statecraft should shift its perspective from that of elites to that of the people; it was no longer about extent of territory, military capacity or gold stocks but was all about economic growth, prosperity, food security, order, liberty, human flourishing and social and political stability, all of which could be achieved via sound principles of politico-economic management and a better understanding of human psychology. Political science involved detecting the laws governing human interaction and history and drawing out their political and legal implications. Smith wished to learn what Nature might be trying to tell us and he discovers that 'nature speaks to history in the language of economics' (Cropsey 1975: 151) and so economics is where he directs his attention first. But the politics isn't merely an artefact of the economic theory for Smith; rather, *both* politics and economics are artefacts of his social science and, being artefacts of the same 'scientific' system, are intimately implicated with each other.

Fully understanding Smith's politics lies in an appreciation of the fact that, as a 'spontaneous order' theorist, he was both anti-utopian and anti-ideological; the latter might seem a curious claim given Smith's actual tendencies but, in his own mind, he was simply promulgating objective social science. Because his politics seeks to break free of classical political science and is wary of the traditional left-right dichotomy (such as it existed in the eighteenth century),[2] he has perplexed many of those who wish to classify his political thought. There has been debate over whether he was a Whig or a Tory (Mossner and Ross 1976: 18–19); whether he is a 'real' liberal (e.g. Haakonssen 1988) or else a 'civic humanist' (Brown 1994; Winch 1978); whether or not he was egalitarian (McLean 2006) or stood for 'social justice' (Sen 2009; Fleischacker 2004); and whether he was genuinely a free marketeer (Hewins 1903). The problem with these kinds of debates is that they ask the wrong questions: despite his 'Whiggish' tendencies, Smith does not seem to have been on any particular ideological side, except the side aligned with the laws of nature as he conceived them. Nevertheless, he 'cherry-picked' from competing systems, including the Whig and the Tory, to create his own (see Chap. 2) and this has, understandably, caused confusion.

The other thing to appreciate about Smith's politics is that he is no defender of abstract principle except to the extent that it serves a useful end. Smith was more interested in positive results than principle, because on his account the laws of nature and the system of natural liberty always lead us to adaptive ends. Political controversies could be determined social-scientifically because it is 'science' that directs us to the best welfare-optimising outcomes. For Donald Winch, Smith's 'work marks an important watershed in the history of liberal political thought' in which 'a "scientific" conception of a self-regulating social and economic realm assumed dominance over what, for better or worse, had previously been an exclusively moral and political domain' (Winch 1978: 7). Political economy was, in Smith's mind, a scientific and descriptive enterprise, not a normative one. This is why his liberal credentials have sometimes been questioned because he often abandons liberal principles for the sake of such practical and observable ends as prosperity, welfare, order and security. Contrary to the common perception, liberty was not the be-all and end-all for Smith. Yet, as I will show, this is to be expected in a spontaneous order theorist (to be discussed further in Chaps. 3 and 7).

Smith was interested in the proper management of people and mass societies as they really were and he did not care much about classical virtues or even national greatness. What the legislator should not seek to do is to unduly control or enlist the people in programmes of national virtue or aggrandisement, or to direct their morality (except where it interferes with public order and commutative justice), but to provide the right conditions for their naturally self-interested self-management, including any infrastructure necessary to support and encourage this self-management. It was a social-scientific exercise in pragmatic 'expediency' and law, both positive and natural (*WN*, IV.ix.51: 687). Well aware that the 'realist' conception of human behaviour, upon which he built his entire system, would elicit moral outrage among some members of the public, he reminded his reader that the 'present inquiry is not concerning matter of right' but 'a matter of fact' (*TMS*, II.i.5.10: 77).

That he was attuned to political realities is reflected in the regular uptake of Smith's ideas into policy (see Ross 1995: *passim*). It should not surprise us, therefore, that his approach to political problems and the art of governing was generally highly pragmatic. A good example is seen in the eight years he spent as a Commissioner of Scottish Customs where we might have expected him to attempt some reforms given his attitude to free trade. But he never sought to innovate; nor is there even any evidence that he used free-trade rhetoric in the conduct of his various duties. Since the Commission was, in reality, a purely policing and enforcement entity, this is perhaps unsurprising. But it also points to Smith's pragmatism, realism and strong streak of conservatism. Having understood the limits of his powers, he evidently decided to devote himself entirely and exclusively to his interest in organisational efficiency (Anderson et al. 1985: 754).[3] Another example is the type of liberal internationalism he espoused: rejecting both moral and political cosmopolitanism as untenable, utopian and naïve, he could only avow a highly realist form of economic cosmopolitanism (Chap. 7). Smith was not only a realist and pragmatist, but also quite conservative about change, as will be shown. Consequently, there were many tensions in his thought.

Smith as Opinion Shaper

Despite his popular reputation, Smith was not so much a high theorist of liberty as a public intellectual whose self-appointed task was to try to shift wrongheaded elite and public opinion about important issues of the day. He once confessed that, although he was often at odds with 'the opinion of the public', he was well aware that he was obliged 'to have some regard' for it (*Corr.*, 9: 5). He certainly did have regard for it and worked diligently on changing attitudes at all levels of society. Although he does not seem to have been a very enthusiastic democrat, Smith's constant refrain is that shifts in public policy should 'never be introduced suddenly, but slowly' and 'after a very long warning' to the public (*WN*, IV.ii.44: 471). In a sense, his publications were a lifelong attempt 'to change society by public consent', as Emma Rothschild so aptly puts it (Rothschild 1992: 91).

Smith pioneered a tradition whereby the scholar takes it upon himself or herself to deliver more than just the facts of the matter; Smith seems to have attributed to himself 'the right and duty to shape and judge public policies, to lead public opinion, to define the desirable ends'. This entailed a belief that economics should be taught to both leaders and the public alike.[4] Smith took this self-appointed task very seriously, opining that a 'just, reasonable and practicable … political disquisition' was just about the 'most useful' kind of scholarly project he could think of; at the very 'least' it might 'animate the public passions of men, and rouse them to seek out the means of promoting the happiness of the society' (*TMS*, IV.i.11: 186).

Evidently assuming that most of the politicians of his day cared not a jot about 'the interest of [their] country', he mused on how he might stir that interest in the nation's leaders. Cynically —or perhaps sensibly—surmising that it would be a waste of time to point out that 'a well-governed state' means that the people 'are better lodged … better clothed [and] … better fed', he decides that his best strategy is to appeal to the amateur engineer inside every political actor. Rather than advert to the public benefits, better to write of a polity as though it were an exquisitely complicated machine that needed explaining and then fixing:

> You will be more likely to persuade, if you describe the great system of public police which procures these advantages, if you explain the connexions and dependencies of its several parts, their mutual subordination to one another, and their general subserviency to the happiness of the society; if you show how this system might be introduced into his own country, what it is that hinders it from taking place there at present, how those obstructions might be removed, and all the several wheels of the machine of government be made to move with more harmony and smoothness, without grating upon one another, or mutually retarding one another's motions. It is scarce possible that a man should listen to a discourse of this kind, and not feel himself animated to some degree of public spirit. He will, at least for the moment, feel some desire to remove those obstructions, and to put into motion so beautiful and so orderly a machine. Nothing tends so much to promote public spirit as the study of politics, of the several systems of civil government, their advantages and disadvantages, of the constitution of our own country, its situation, and interest with regard to foreign nations, its commerce, its defence, the disadvantages it labours under, the dangers to which it may be exposed, how to remove the one, and how to guard against the other. (*TMS*, IV.i.11: 186)

This strategy seems to have worked. Jeremy Bentham observed that there had been 'an evident change in public opinion … on all points of political economy' due, in large part, to 'the circulation of Smith's book [*Wealth of Nations*]' (*Corr.*, App. C: 386). Smith influenced government policy on a whole range of issues, from those relating to free trade, international relations, the internal corn trade, customs and tax reform (Ross 1995: 416; see also Coats 1971) to wages policy and British colonialism. This influence was felt both at home and abroad, particularly in America where, as Glory Liu notes, 'Smith became the embodiment of an entire ideology that started with basic economic logic and concluded with a set of maxims about what government ought or ought not to do, especially on matters of trade and taxation' (Liu 2018: 218).[5] Although the impact of Smith's ideas in his own time has been debated and possibly even exaggerated (Teichgraeber 1987: 339), it is fair to say that, regardless of how much influence they had upon initial publication, subsequently that influence has proved to be a slow, steady and enduring burn that has intensified progressively in the centuries after his own.

Irrational prejudice, self-defeating 'national jealousies', unrestrained self-interestedness, *hubris* and stubborn pride were, to Smith, the main impediments to sensible public policy in the Britain of his day. The question of

American Independence was a prime example and the only real impediment to a good outcome, as Smith saw it, was the British government's preposterous fear of losing face both at home and in Europe due, in turn, to the British public's equally preposterous inability to understand what really mattered (*Corr.*, App.B: 383). Exposing these craven and useless motives and laying out the more rational response[s] to problems of national import galvanised much of Smith's efforts. His goal, ultimately, was to influence government policy on a whole range of issues and according to a new set of values about what welfare really consisted in.

He was often successful in his attempts (Ross 1995: 418; Coats 1971), partly because of his determination and ability to sway the public first but also because his ideas were novel and attractive. This, in turn, was a function of the fact that, as an astute sociologist of social and economic change, he could see what would no longer work on the social-systems level and so he tended not to be rigid. He was also a skilled marketer of ideas. James Morrison's characterisation of Smith as an 'ideas entrepreneur' is apt. Smith, writes Morrison,

> cultivated personal relationships with leading statesmen in an effort to promote his proposals within influential circles. His interactions with policymakers prompted him to refine and repackage his ideas to make them more politically relevant. Framing contemporary events as a crisis, he provided converts with the ammunition they needed to further his revolution. (Morrison 2012: 405)

Donald Winch has observed that Smith saw public opinion as 'the fluid and sometimes volatile medium within which governments operated', acting 'as a constant constraint on their actions though never as a creative influence'. Opinion could be 'synonymous with mere prejudice and ignorance; it could also be swayed by more pathological conditions of "terror", "rage" and "enthusiasm"' (Winch 1978: 170). Smith was ever aware of the potential for 'mobbish opposition' (*WN*, IV.ii.17: 460) to the kind of ideas he wished to promulgate, so he wrote in a style that he hoped would be accessible and persuasive to everyone. Further, he made policy suggestions for the education and civilisation of populations so that they would be better judges of public affairs and therefore no hindrance to these sorts of sensible measures. These included a plan for a state-funded compulsory school education and public diversions to offset religious fanaticism.

Smith clearly felt that he had his work cut out for him; no one who has read his works can fail to notice his exasperation at the manner in which the prejudices of the public affected public policy or else were cynically manipulated by interested parties like merchants and politicians for their own ends. In the case of the former, these interests were almost always at variance with 'and even opposite to, that of the public', since they sought at all times to 'widen the market' yet 'narrow the competition'. Consequently, Smith strongly cautioned that any legislative proposals advocated by mercantile interests 'ought always to be listened to with great precaution' and 'ought never to be adopted till after having been long and carefully examined, not only with the most scrupulous, but ***with the most suspicious attention***' (*WN*, I.xi.p: 267; emphasis added).

An Elusive Author

Writing about Smith's political thought is not as straightforward as might be hoped. He had long promised to write a treatise on 'natural jurisprudence' or the 'science' of 'law and government', declaring at the conclusion of the *Theory of Moral Sentiments* that

> I shall in another discourse endeavour to give an account of the general principles of law and government, and of the different revolutions they have undergone in the different ages and periods of society, not only in what concerns justice, but in what concerns police, revenue and arms, and whatever else is the object of law'. (*TMS*, VII.iv.37, 341–42)

In a letter to Rochefoucauld written in 1785 he referred to this project ('a sort of theory and History of Law and Government') as one of 'two … great works' that was still 'upon the anvil' (*Corr.*: 286–87). Not much had changed by 1788 when he wrote to his publisher Thomas Cadell that he considered his 'tenure of this life as extremely precarious' and felt 'very uncertain whether' he would 'live to finish' the unfinished 'works' upon which he had, nevertheless, 'made some progress'. He had put his 'political science' project aside to concentrate on perfecting the latest edition of the *Theory of Moral Sentiments*, lamenting that he was 'a slow, a very slow workman', apt 'to do and undo everything … at least half a dozen times' before he could be 'tolerably pleased with it' (*Corr.*: 310–11). His strategy in postponing the new manuscript—given the limited time he believed he had left to him and the slow pace of work—was to 'leave' his 'already published' books 'in the best and most perfect state behind' him (*Corr.*: 310–11) rather than attempt to finish the new work first. Therefore, the manuscript that had been eagerly anticipated by scholars and the public alike never saw the light of day because Smith died before it could be published. His readers' disappointment was compounded when it emerged that the draft manuscript had been destroyed along with fifteen other manuscripts he ordered burned upon his death.

To exacerbate matters, Smith notoriously kept his personal political convictions to himself and was discreet to the point of secretiveness, with one observer describing him as 'one of the most elusive modern authors of distinction that ever a biographer and historian of ideas set himself to cope with' (Mossner 1969: 5). Rothschild notes that Smith 'is extraordinarily cautious and elusive when he writes about current policies in the *Wealth of Nations*'. She even suggests that in 'his letters and conversations, he seems to have several more or less distinct personalities' (Rothschild 1992: 89).

Smith wrote few letters and was teased for being a poor correspondent. To make matters worse, only 193 of the letters he did write have survived, while only 129 letters *to* him are still with us. More than half of these belong to the later period of his life and it is assumed that Smith ordered the missing letters destroyed along with his notes, to preserve his privacy (Phillipson 2010: 136). For Nicholas Phillipson, the 'trouble with this act of archival self-concealment is that it was an attempt to cap a life that was already badly documented' (2010: 4). As a consequence, we know 'next to nothing' about the early part of Smith's life and it is not until 1787—when James Tassie made two medallions of him—that we even have any idea what he looked like (Phillipson 2010: 4–5).

There is not much point in speculating on what Smith *might* have written in the lost manuscript (and other material) but there is a good deal of rich political content in the work he actually published on jurisprudence, moral philosophy, public affairs and political economy; in the extremely detailed sets of lecture notes later published as his *Lectures on Jurisprudence* and in the policy documents he wrote for government and government advisers. After all, Smith made it clear by his actions that he wanted to be understood only through the work and opinions he deemed fit to publish. Given the meticulous care he took to revise and refine these opinions (the *Theory of Moral Sentiments*, for example, saw six editions in Smith's own lifetime) and his determination to show the public only fully realised work, we should expect to find a fairly high degree of coherence in them. There is also much to be learned from the records and biographical material relating to his various political activities, including his advice to government and his time spent as a Commissioner of Scottish Customs towards the end of his life (1778–1790). So, while it is true that Smith provides no aggregated account of politics, he did leave us with a wealth of material on and related to politics. This material embraced a wide range of political subjects that we would today identify as political economy, political theory, public administration, ethics, moral psychology, public law, philosophy of law, comparative politics, political sociology, diplomacy, statecraft and international relations. Notably, some of it was not intended for public consumption, enabling a further layer of understanding about how Smith operated on the political level.

This political material is not merely vestigial or subservient to the economic content of Smith's writings; he was, after all, a *political* economist who insisted that 'political economy' was but a sub-discipline of statecraft or 'the science of the legislator' (*WN*, Intro., IV: 428): in other words, he regarded political science—not economics—as the master social science. But there is an important qualification here. Statecraft had for too long ignored political economy, which was the most important thing to consider where Smith was concerned. As Fania Oz-Salzberger has observed, Smith (along with other thinkers within the Scottish Enlightenment) wanted political economy to become the modern 'alternative to Aristotelian politics as a high science of government' (Oz-Salzberger 2003: 164). So, he brought economic statecraft and economic citizenship front and centre into the realm of political science and here lay, arguably, his most important contribution to the Western political tradition. The impact of this reconfiguration was profound, in part because his alternative embodied a more social-scientific approach to the business of governing nations.

The Welfare of the People

Political economy, Smith tells us, has two key and urgent 'objects': first, to enrich and provide for the people ('or more properly to enable them to provide such a revenue or subsistence for *themselves*'); and, second, to supply the 'commonwealth with a revenue sufficient for the publick service', specifically, those necessary public works and offices that the market does not deliver well or spontaneously. The state's main tasks are therefore to provide the conditions for negative liberty but also to provide the conditions of positive liberty via 'public services' (*WN*, IV.Intro.I: 428).

The indicators Smith used to test how well states were governed did not include traditional markers like the extent of conquered territory or the amount of stockpiled gold, but referred to factors that directly impacted the lives of the average person: available food supply, population levels, productivity and employment levels, general living conditions, education standards, wages, mortality rates and even the ability to live with social dignity. Smith's idea of welfare was thus very broad and concerned with more than just material welfare. What he ultimately hoped for was a society that could deliver human flourishing, 'promote happiness and guard against misery' (*TMS*, III.5.7: 166). The people should be numerous, clothed, fed, housed, properly paid, independent, pacific, industrious, free from arbitrary interference, secure, educated and happy, with the wherewithal for a little luxury, frivolity and pleasure and, regardless of social location, able to hold their heads up in society.

Smith defined human needs quite broadly as things that not only serve the needs of the body, but that also contribute to the dignity, respectability and social survival of a person (*WN*, V.ii.k.3: 869–70). He appreciated our deep social and emotional needs for recognition and respect and understood that a person's economic and social desires were intimately enmeshed (*TMS*, I.ii.1.6: 29; Hill 2012).

No one should have to beg for a living or be dependent on others for their needs. In fact, most people were perfectly capable of securing most of their needs for themselves, if only they were allowed to get on with it. What Smith wanted most was for everyone to practise full *economic* citizenship in a manner that served the interests of society in an indirect and impersonal fashion. As Lisa Herzog puts it: 'Smith's vision is one in which all members of commercial society are sufficiently well off, pursue their interests in socially beneficial ways, and have an independent standing as citizens' (Herzog 2016: 56). I refer to this way of life in later chapters as 'commercial strangership'. But this could only happen on full stomachs.

Food Security and Population Growth

Smith's preoccupation with food security has not always been well appreciated as arguably the key motivation for his aversion to monopoly and concomitant advocacy of free trade (*WN*, IV.v.b.6: 527; see also Firth 2002). It should be borne in mind that the major economic sector of his time was still agriculture and food was the major expenditure item for the vast bulk of the population. Yet this most vital sector was unavoidably subject to fluctuations in both output and price; therefore, during the eighteenth century 'the achievement of a low and stable price for grain' was perhaps the most urgent political problem facing European governments. Smith thought that the best way to encourage domestic production while ensuring ready access to 'an international market in foodstuffs'—especially grain—was via free trade.[6]

In England, from the Middle Ages onwards fears of poor harvests inspired pamphlets attacking hoarders and speculators for driving up the price of corn. Parliament responded with laws that prohibited the practices of 'forestalling, regrating, and engrossing' grain (Rashid 1980: 493). Smith strongly opposed such laws, insisting that '[t]he unlimited, unrestrained freedom of the corn trade … is the only effectual preventative of the miseries of a famine' just as 'it is the best palliative of the inconveniencies of a dearth' (*WN*, IV.v.b.6: 527; *WN*, IV.v.b.39: 538–39). But the greed of merchants and corrupt unwisdom of sovereigns blocked the path to this solution, thereby occasioning misery and death for many (*WN*, IV.vii.c.107–108: 641).

Smith indicates that the main point of political economy is to find ways of improving the per capita consumption of the labouring classes: 'The whole benefit of wealth and industry', he wrote, 'is that you either employ a greater number or give those already employed a more comfortable subsistence.' He felt sure that there was 'no trade which, carried on properly' could not achieve this (*Lectures on Jurisprudence A*, Smith 1978, hereafter referred to as *LJ[A]*, 161–62: 390–91; see also *Lectures on Jurisprudence B*, Smith 1978, hereafter referred to as *LJ[B]*, 262: 511). Mercantilism is wrong in its perception of non-consumables like gold as the source of wealth. As he wrote, in presciently (and unwittingly) Marxist tones, about the difference between use and exchange value and the superiority of the former:

> Tis true indeed that the gold lasts for a long time and the claret is very soon consumed, but this makes no odds. For to what purpose do all those things which a nation possesses serve? To no other but the maintaining the people? And how is it that this end is answered? By being consumed. It is the *consumptibility* of a thing which makes it usefull. To what purpose does industry serve but to produce the greatest quantity of these necessaries … The production of the necessaries of life is the sole benefit of industry. (*LJ[A]*, 161–62: 390–91; original emphasis)

Smith's opinion here was pre-empted by Bernard Mandeville who had written that regardless of whether 'the Value of Gold and Silver either rise or fall, the Enjoyment of all Societies will ever depend upon the Fruits of the Earth, and the Labour of the People; both which joined together are a more certain, a more inexhaustible, and a more real Treasure, than the Gold of Brazil, or the Silver of Potosi' (Mandeville 1924: 197–98). Contrary to the gold-obsessed Mercantilists, Smith says, '[t]is not in money that opulence consists … it consists in the abundance of the necessaries and conveniences of life (*LJ[A]*, vi.129: 378). A nation's wealth consists 'in the cheapness of provisions and all other necessaries and conveniences of life', whereas poverty consists 'in the uncomeatibleness or difficulty with which the several necessaries of life are procured' (*LJ[A]*, ii.33: 83).

A primary measure of an economy's success is whether the poor are able to maintain a standard of living sufficient not only to keep infant mortality rates low, but to preclude the ghastly practice of infanticide (*WN*, I.viii.15: 85–86; *WN*, I.viii.24: 90; *WN*, I.viii.38: 97; *LJ[A]*, iii.133: 193). A wealthy society is always marked by a growing population and '[t]o complain of it is to lament over the necessary effect and cause of the greatest public prosperity' (*WN*, I.viii.36: 96). Although 'poverty … does not prevent the generation, it is extremely unfavourable to the rearing of children'. The 'scantiness of subsistence' sets 'limits to the further multiplication of the human species … by destroying a great part of the children which their fruitful marriages produce' (*WN*, I.viii.35–39: 97–98; *LJ[A]*, iii.47: 159).

What Smith desired most of all was the prevention of '[w]ant' and premature 'mortality' (*WN*, I.vii.26: 91) and he recoiled at the thought of the 'dreadful horrors of a famine' occasioned by 'disorderly' state management (*WN*, I.xi.e.23: 204). The 'starving condition' of the 'labouring poor' signifies that the economy is 'going fast backwards' (*WN*, I.viii.27: 91). It also leads to social instability (something Smith greatly feared) in driving the poor 'to seek a subsistence either by begging or by the perpetration perhaps of the greatest enormities' (*WN*, I.vii.26: 91). Indeed, 'in times of necessity the people will break thro all laws'; for example, it 'often happens' that the people, in times of famine 'will break open granaries' (*LJ[A]*, iii.143: 197).

Debates about whether governments should interfere in the corn market through laws preventing hoarding and the export of corn during a scarcity intensified from 1750 onwards. Smith entered the debate in 1776 and, largely due to his influence,[7] by 1844 the laws controlling the trade in grain had been abolished. Further, when it was twice proposed to reinstate the laws in Britain towards the end of the eighteenth century, opponents invoked Smith's authority to prevent them from being applied (Rashid 1980: 496).

Because of Smith's profound concerns about food security, it has sometimes been suggested that he thought governments should intervene whenever a famine occurred (see, for example, Rashid 1980; Endres 1995). In fact, Smith says the exact opposite, arguing that interference only makes the situation worse because of inevitable false beliefs about its real causes. He likened the 'popular fear of engrossing and forestalling' to 'suspicions of witchcraft' (*WN*, IV.v.b.26: 534). The 'history of the dearths and famines which have afflicted any part of Europe' in the last three centuries shows that

> a dearth never has arisen from any combination among the inland dealers in corn, nor from any other cause but a real scarcity, occasioned sometimes … by the waste of war, but in by far the greatest number of cases, by the fault of the seasons; … *a famine has never arisen from any other cause but the violence of government attempting, but improper means, to remedy the inconveniencies of a dearth* … When the government, in order to remedy the inconveniencies of a dearth, orders all the dealers to sell their corn at what it supposes a reasonable price, it either hinders them from bringing it to market, which may sometimes produce a famine even in the beginning of the season; or if they bring it thither, it enables the people, and thereby encourages them to consume it so fast, as must necessarily produce a famine before the end of the season. (*WN*, IV.v.b.5–7: 526–27; emphasis added)

Smith does make one exception here in allowing an assize (price control) of bread but this is only to break a genuine monopoly already operating: '[w]here there is an exclusive corporation, it may perhaps be proper to regulate the price of the first necessity of life. But where there is none, the competition will regulate it much better than any assize' (*WN*, I.x.c.62: 158).

Although it appears that most commentators at the time agreed with Smith's advice, he—and those who followed it—did not escape opprobrium. William Wilberforce, for example, wrote of 'the callousness, the narrow and foolish wisdom of servilely acquiescing in Adam Smith's general principles, without allowance for a thousand circumstances which take the case out of the province of that very general principle' (cited in Rashid 1980: 493). It is ironic that, in much of his other advice, Smith was a routine violator of his own 'general principles' but on the question of the internal corn trade, he was inflexible.

The Poor

A major theme of this book is that welfare, not ideology—libertarian or otherwise—should be the decisive criterion for public policy. Whose welfare is Smith most concerned about? According to Martha Nussbaum—and a long line of others before her—Smith seems indifferent to the poor and 'is prepared to let the market do its worst with little constraint, partly because he believes that the poor do not suffer at their very core, retaining a dignity that life's blows cannot remove' (Nussbaum 2000). At the other end of the spectrum, there is a school of thought that posits a left-leaning Smith, suspicious of 'commercialism' and invariably on the side of the poor labourers (see, for example, Rothschild 2001; Fleischacker 2004; Kennedy 2005; McLean 2006; Witzum and Young 2006). Some have argued that Smith is so concerned with the poor that he promulgates a distributive theory of justice, especially where food security is concerned. The grounds for this conclusion are that Smith posits 'the right to subsistence' as a 'natural right' (Witzum and Young 2006: 467, 437). Samuel Fleischacker agrees, arguing that Smith's 'moral egalitarianism' causes him to espouse distributive justice (Fleischacker 2004: 212).

Distributive Justice?

It is true that Smith is usually on the side of workers and consumers (Hanley 2009: 18). It is also true that he wants to create a policy framework that results in 'as equitable a distribution as possible, among all the different members of a community … of the advantages arising from the political union' (Stewart 1980, vol. 4: 309–10). But his advocacy of equality and advertised desire for a diffusion of 'advantages' does not equate to 'equal re-distribution'. This is because, first, it is really equality of ***opportunity*** that he seeks—the removal of all 'systems of preference and restraint' (*WN*, IV.ix.51: 687), rather than ***substantive*** equality. Economic citizenship—the equal right to participate and compete in the market—is something he wanted every member of the population to enjoy and it was the state's job to make sure that they did enjoy it. As he says himself, a government's duty to 'enrich and provide for the people' is strictly and 'properly' understood in terms of '***enabl[ing]*** them to provide such a revenue or subsistence for *themselves*' (*WN*, IV, Intro.1: 428; emphasis added). Further, it has already been shown that even in times of famine government should not interfere with distribution.

This is not to say that Smith never advocates *any* redistributive measures, the most notable of which is a publicly funded school system for the children of the poor (*WN*, V.i.f, 54–57: 785–87) and which is discussed in more detail in Chap. 7. He also points to two cases where the rich should be paying proportionally more tax than the poor, with the explicit proviso that the excess be redistributed. The first is that there should be a higher road toll on 'carriages of luxury … than upon carriages of necessary use, such as carts [and] waggons' in order that the 'the indolence and vanity of the rich is made to contribute … to the relief of the poor' (*WN*, V.i.d.5: 725). Presumably his thought here is that luxury carriages are clogging up a vital piece of publicly funded infrastructure that is really supposed to be facilitating industry. He also proposes a tax on house rents on the grounds that the rich will bear the heaviest burden. This 'sort of inequality' is not in the least problematic, says Smith; it is 'not very unreasonable that the rich should contribute to the public expence, not only in proportion to their revenue, but something more than in that proportion' (*WN*, V.ii.e.6: 842).

This is not a progressive tax but really only a flat tax that the rich would obviously be required to pay more of due to the extreme luxury of their homes. Nevertheless, Smith's avowed purpose in suggesting this tax is to squeeze more money out of the rich for the benefit of the poor. However, these are the only three examples of anything like redistribution in Smith and a thoroughgoing theory of redistribution cannot and should not be inferred from them. Further, Smith nowhere alludes to a 'right to subsistence' as has been imputed to him insofar as it is claimed that the right of subsistence is implied or embedded in two other rights that Smith lists as 'perfect rights': the right to life 'and property rights to the fruits of one's labour' (Witzum and Young 2006: 439).

In his *Lectures on Jurisprudence*, Smith enumerates the perfect rights to which we are entitled and limits them to the rights to 'person', 'reputation' and 'estate' (*LJ[A]*, i.12: 8; Salter 2012: 567). Smith gives no sign that these rights imply a right to subsistence or any redistribution of property that might be required to ensure it. In fact, he says what amounts to the opposite: 'What they call imperfect rights are those which correspond to those duties which ought to be performed to us by other *but which we have not title to compel them to perform*' and it is '*intirely in their power to perform them or not'* (*LJ[A]*, i.15: 9). He gives as his example the 'beggar' who is 'an object of our charity and may be said to have a right to demand it'; however, 'when we use the word right in this way it is not on a proper but metaphorical sense'. By this Smith means it is not a right in the sense of constituting a perfect right. He dilates so as not to be misunderstood:

> The common way in which we understand the word right, is the same as what we have called a perfect right, and is that which relates to commutative justice. Imperfect rights ... refer to distributive justice. The former are the rights we are to consider, the latter not belonging properly to jurisprudence, but rather to a system of morals as they do not fall under the jurisdiction of the laws. *We are therefore ... to confine ourselves entirely to the perfect rights and what is called commutative justice.* (*LJ[A]*, i.15: 9; emphasis added)

Smith's evident and sincere sympathy for the poor does not mean that he saw poverty as a matter of distributive justice; it is only commutative justice that he recommends and defends (see Cohen 1989: 58; Salter 2012). Commutative justice, when properly and impartially administered in the context of 'natural liberty', was enough to ensure that the poor would be able to comfortably subsist and live a dignified life. So long as the law protects equality of opportunity, liberty, property and contracts, economic well-being is secure and there will be no need for redistribution because, for Smith, those rights *are* the rights to subsistence; there was no need to make subsistence a separate right once these other rights were honoured. As Smith put it so simply: '[t]he establishment of perfect justice, of perfect liberty, and of perfect equality, is the very simple secret which most effectually secures the highest degree of prosperity' (*WN*, IV.ix.17: 669).

Commercialism and the Poor

It is agreed that Smith was more concerned with the working poor (and the middle class of small, self-employed makers, traders and shopkeepers) than he was with the wealthy, and he persistently argued that the poor had more to lose or gain from any policy or practice. So, there is a lot of truth to Gertrude Himmelfarb's comment that the *Wealth of Nations* is 'genuinely revolutionary in its view of poverty and its attitude towards the poor' (Himmelfarb 1985: 46). But Smith did not see advancing commercialism or what we might call 'proto-capitalism' as the problem. In fact, his belief in its 'capacity to provide for the poor' is the main reason he defended it (Hanley 2009: 18) just so long as it was allowed to operate naturally.

Smith never shied away from pointing out the downside of commercial progress, was never 'a flat-footed optimist about the effects of commercialism on the texture of human life' (Forman-Barzilai 2010). But overall he had faith in the free market so long as it was appropriately managed, believing it would turn out to be the solution to alleviating poverty—both at home and throughout the globe—and of promoting equality along the way. In some ways, Smith was a typical liberal with his faith in and advocacy of equality; however, there are some important qualifications here that mark him out as a thinker working within his own eccentric tradition. I will return to what these qualifications are presently.

In any case, Smith is extremely sympathetic to the working poor—as well as 'landowners'. But his reasons are far from sentimental and this explains why landowners are viewed with the same degree of sympathy. Smith identifies three productive classes or 'three great orders' of society: 'those who live by rent, those who live by wages, and … those who live by profit. These are the three great, original and constituent orders of every civilized society, from whose revenue that of every other order is ultimately derived' (*WN*, I.xi.7: 26). His preference lay with workers and landowners but not, significantly, with 'employers' or 'those who live by profit' because their interests are always at variance with the interest of society. Of this class he was perpetually suspicious. It wasn't that employers were inherently untrustworthy; rather, their natural self-interest caused them to habitually rent-seek due to a dynamic largely outside their control. As Smith explains: 'The rate of profit does not, like rent and wages, rise with the prosperity, and fall with the declension of the society. On the contrary, it is naturally low in rich and high in poor countries, and it is always highest in the countries which are going fastest to ruin.' As a consequence, unlike wage labourers and landlords the 'interest of this third order … has not the same connection with the general interest of the society' (*WN*, I.xi.10: 266).

Equality: Formal or Substantive?

Smith certainly dislikes poverty and wants the poor to be fed and clothed. He also likes *formal* equality, but these views have been taken to mean that Smith is bothered by *substantive* inequality (provided, of course, that it is not a product of formal inequality). For example, Deborah Boucoyannis has suggested that the policies Smith advocated were intended to 'prevent inequalities from arising in the first place' (Boucoyannis 2013: 1052). From what Smith writes, this is not what he wanted at all. It is true that he did want the poor to be richer and he welcomed the expansion of the middle class. Further, he does not even attempt to disguise his disdain for the indolent rich and regularly gripes that the 'labour and time of the poor is in civilised countries sacrificed to maintaining [them] in ease and luxury' (*LJ[A]*, 26: 340).

But, far from wanting to eradicate inequality, he saw it as serving vital system functions. Smith admits that the ultra-rich strike us as objectionable parasites: 'a pest to society, as a monster, a fish who devours up all the lesser ones'. However, they are, in reality, 'in no way prejudicial to society but rather of advantage to it' (*LJ[A]*, iii.135: 194). This is because, first of all, their consumption habits provide employment for a multitude of workers (*LJ[A]*, iii.138: 195). Second, their conspicuous consumption provides a powerful incentive to the productive efforts of the lower, aspirational classes who wish to imitate them (*TMS*, I.iii.3.7.7: 64); and, finally, they contribute to and are a mainstay of social order (*TMS*, VI.ii.1.20: 226), forestalling the 'confusion and misrule which flows from a want of all regular subordination'.

Notably, that 'want of regular subordination' is found only in nations which have yet to surmount a general 'extreme poverty' (*Essays on Philosophical Subjects*, Smith 1980, hereafter referred to as *Essays*: 51). Smith claims that the state of inequality and even exploitation is peculiar to commercial modernity: in the state of savagery,[8] where the accumulation, maintenance and legal regulation of private property is yet to be developed and where specialisation is uncommon,[9] there exists a state of relative equality where 'every savage has the full enjoyment of the fruits of his own labours'. Here, 'there are no landlords, no usurers, no tax gatherers' to domineer, exploit or subordinate (*LJ[A]*, 26: 340). But in commercial nations 'those who labour most get least' (*LJ[A]*: 564). Therefore this seemingly unfair relationship between classes was an unavoidable externality of progress because wealth inequalities are both desirable and unavoidable in the prosperous state: 'wherever there is great property, there is great inequality' (*WN*, V.i.b.2: 709–10). Inequality was, for Smith, one of the many disconcerting externalities of commercial progress and I say more about it in Chap. 5.

It was *absolute* poverty Smith wanted to eradicate, not relative poverty (Rasmussen 2016: 343). Smith's hope is that the poor will be 'tolerably well fed, cloathed and lodged' with some change to spare for a little 'luxury', which by eighteenth-century standards was quite an ambitious goal. In effect, social welfare will be maximised when, first, the distribution of necessaries is equal, and, second, 'when the indirect effects of unequal wealth distribution are such as to promote economic activity and increase total wealth' which of course makes the necessaries easier to procure (Gee 1968: 293; *TMS*, IV.1.10: 184–85).

Just as Smith asked us to forebear the extreme prosperity of the rich, so he also asked those who grumbled about the relative and increasing prosperity of the poor to look at the situation from the point of view of overall utility: any 'improvement in the circumstances of the lower ranks of the people' is not 'an inconveniency to the society', as some did, in fact claim (see Chaps. 3 and 7). Workers 'make up the far greater part of every great political society' and whatever 'improves the circumstances of the greater part can never be regarded as an inconveniency to the whole'. Surely everyone wants a happy society, Smith surmises, yet '[n]o society can … be flourishing and happy, of which the far greater part of the members are poor and miserable' (*WN*, I.viii.39: 97). 'National opulence', he opines elsewhere, '*is the opulence of the whole people*', not the few (early draft of *WN*; *LJ[B]*: 567, emphasis added).

Commercial Modernity: Friend or Enemy?

Often Smith seems ambivalent about progress and commercial life but he really wasn't; the most one could say is that he had mixed feelings. He basically welcomed progress and commercialism but, as an intelligent observer of a world that was fast changing around him, he could not fail to notice that both trends produced externalities. Smith was aware of the downside of specialisation which, in effect, amounted to worker 'alienation', a condition that could cause 'the almost entire corruption and degeneracy of the great body of the people … in every improved and civilized society' (*WN*, V.i.f.49–50: 781–82). He was also dismayed by the asymmetrical power relations occasioned and exacerbated by the social division of labour, noting that 'in disputes with their workmen, masters must generally have the advantage' (*WN*, I.viii.14: 85). He even acknowledged that the social division of labour entails a certain degree of exploitation:

> The poor labourer who has the soil and the seasons to struggle with, and who, while he affords the materials for supplying the luxury of all the other members of the commonwealth, bears, as it were, upon his shoulders, the whole fabric of human society, sees himself to be buried out of sight in the lowest foundation of the building. (*LJ[A]*: 564)

Yet, overall commercial modernity was good for the poor and Smith's defence of it consisted in its superior capacity over previous economic stages to provide for them. Even as he laments the terrible effects of the refinements in specialisation functions that characterise the commercial age, he concludes that it is this very thing that 'occasions, in a well-governed society, that universal opulence which extends itself to the lowest ranks of the people' and establishes a system in which 'a general plenty diffuses itself through all the different ranks of the society' (*WN*, I.i.10: 22).

Commercial progress is 'the cheerful and the hearty state to all the different orders of the society', but especially so for the poor whose life in a 'stationary' economy is 'hard' and, in a declining one, downright 'miserable' (*WN*, I.viii.43: 99). The commercial state also helps release serfs, women, children, the working poor and every other oppressed group from the kind of dependency relationships that Smith abhorred. It is therefore, on balance, the natural, desirable state for Smith. Committed to freedom, independence, food security and overall welfare yet also committed to commercialism, commutative justice but not distributive justice, formal but not substantive equality and tolerant of the system of rank distinctions, Smith's main task becomes how to make such a system work properly. The first question in working this out was: what role should government play?

The Organised State: Strong, Stable, Perhaps 'Expensive', But Not Extensive

Smith's economic thought has been highly influential in shaping contemporary expectations of the state's proper role in the economic realm. Given his belief in the self-organising character of society and the economy, Smith appears to regard the organised state as, generally, an obstruction to social equilibrium and a thriving economy; conversely, an expanding free market is the main guard of civil society due to its role as a bulwark against the potentially noxious power of the state. But there is an important qualification to be made here: the state Smith lived with was fatally mismanaged. This did not preclude a substantial role in human affairs for a well-run one.

On the belief that the system of 'natural liberty' was capable of delivering economic prosperity, Smith famously advocated a small, unobtrusive state. But it is not as unobtrusive as many tend to believe; indeed, Smith argued that the more advanced commercially and politically a state is, the more complicated and therefore expensive the business of governing is expected to become. There was no use complaining about this because it would be tantamount to complaining that one had to put up with prosperity, development and civilisation:

> [G]overnment in a civilised country is much more expensive than in a barbarous one; and when we say that one government is more expensive than another, it is the same as if we said that the one country is farther advanced in improvement than another ... There are many expences necessary in a civilized country for which there is no occasion in one that is barbarous. Armies, fleets, fortified places and public buildings, judges and officers of the revenue must be supported, and if they be neglected disorder will ensue. (*LJ[B]*, 309–10: 530–31)

Note also that an 'expensive' government in a nation where 'the people are not oppressed' is the same as saying 'that the people are rich'. In other words, a nation cannot be prosperous if the people have no freedoms and a nation cannot be a truly liberal state without a lot of expensive infrastructure and the proper apparatus for justice and police. Finally, Smith is communicating in these few pithy words that commercially advanced nations are always and naturally more complicated to operate (*LJ[B]*, 307–10: 530–31).

One of the reasons governments in advanced states are so expensive is because the complexity of functions means that they need to be managed professionally. If state officials are not remunerated for their time, corruption will soon become a major problem:

> When government becomes so complex as to take up the whole attention of the public magistrate he must undoubtedly have some reward, and if this be not given him by the public he will fall upon some more dangerous method of obtaining it. Few will be so generous as to exact nothing. When applications are made, every one must bring his presant and the man who pays best will be best heard. (*LJ[B]*, 307–308: 530)

Government should be as expensive and extensive as it needs to be in order to be trusted and effective *but no more*. So, not only was Smith not averse to government, neither was he necessarily averse to an expensive and complex system of government but only so long as there was no waste, 'profusion' or corruption; in fact, it can be a sign that things are going in the right direction. Unfortunately, in Smith's time, it generally wasn't, and in some respects his own government was the worst of all governments, namely, a profligate one that ruled in its own interests and was rent-seeking, or else 'captured by rent-seeking interests' (McLean 2006: 80). Therefore a good deal of his discourse is taken up with enumerating the various deficiencies of the British state and laying out in often minute detail how it should really be run and—especially—funded. While he evinced great faith in the constitution, its norms and practices left much to be desired.

The Scientific Legislator

It is sometimes assumed that Smith sees politics as transcended by the market and that he reserved no significant role for legislators in political action. However, Smith saw certain types of leaders—namely, wise ones—as key to a properly functioning, flourishing state. Unfortunately, wise leaders were in short supply, a fact of which Smith was painfully aware when he wrote of 'that insidious and crafty animal, vulgarly called a statesman or politician' (*WN*, IV.ii.39). But the good leader evinces a kind of 'patriot[ic]' devotion to the public good (*TMS*, VI.ii.2.12) and will operate according to 'the science of a legislator', by which Smith means a mode of 'deliberatio[n]' that is informed by 'general' and invariable 'principles' rather than 'momentary fluctuations of affairs' as per the style of the calculating, opportunistic types that tended to dominate politics in his time (*TMS*, VI.ii.2.12). Smith wanted to find a way of 'elevating statesmanship above the politics of interest' (Hanley 2008: 221).

The 'science' to which Smith alludes is not scientific in the purely descriptive, 'hard science' sense but in the sense particular to eighteenth-century usage, namely, as a 'body of systematic knowledge' with normative implications for what, practically, ought to be done, in this case, by legislators. The 'science of the legislator' was 'a system of what might properly be called natural jurisprudence' to serve as the 'foundation of the laws of all nations'. Such principles, being 'general' and natural, were universalisable and 'independent of all positive institutions' (Letwin 1988: 2). But, as will be shown, Smith himself did not find his own principles to be as universally applicable as he might have liked.

Although Smith's promised synthetic account of these 'general principles of law and government' never eventuated, there is no shortage of material in his published works to indicate that it was to be built around the idea of a self-equilibrating universe, or what Smith referred to as the system of 'natural liberty' (*TMS*, VII.iv.36–37). This was an enterprise founded on what he saw as a systematic understanding of universal social and economic laws and an appreciation of the full extent of civil society. Smith's attempt to forge a new, welfare-focused science of politics therefore began with his spontaneous order theory but, as I also show in this book, it certainly did not end there.

A legislator's wisdom consists in knowing why and how to restore the system of natural liberty to its rightful state and in comprehending the proper limits of state action. 'He' understands when the system of natural liberty is working well and when it needs some help. This seems to have been the whole point of Smith's project: to show when reform or removal of any 'obstruction' was necessary; to demarcate the boundaries of proper state action; and to provide advice to leaders on when action was required and when history and the mechanisms of spontaneous order should be allowed to do their steady work (*WN*, IV.v.b.43: 540). The legislator schooled in a thorough knowledge of the laws of society and natural liberty knows the importance of proceeding 'by trial and error and … retain[ing] what experience shows to be valuable'. When 'he cannot establish the best system of laws, he will endeavour to establish the best that the people can bear' and what the 'interests, prejudices, and temper of the times would admit of' (*WN*, VI.ii.2.16, 233). Smith's polity required legislators of uncommonly good judgement and there was much more for the competent to do than is usually acknowledged.

The problem is recognising when social and political arrangements are 'natural' and therefore not in conflict with the natural order and those that have been engineered by interested agents. So, in spite of Smith's admonitions around intrusive government, this only applied to a system ***already corrected*** according to his advice, to a system in which the hundreds of 'impertinent obstructions' imposed by the 'folly of human laws … encumbers [the] operations' of the market and the society itself (*WN*, IV.v.b.43: 540). As George Stigler notes, 'Smith gave a larger role to emotion, prejudice and ignorance [and stupidity] in political life than he ever allowed in ordinary economic affairs' (Stigler 1975: 241) and most of what was wrong with the way the state operated in his time was due to ignorance, knavishness or else a lack of sincere regard for the public good. Once corrected according to his advice, the state could withdraw and provide strong, perhaps even extensive and expensive, but never *intrusive* or *overweening* government.

Smith's ideal legislator exhibits a higher-order form of prudence that is not merely directed towards the care of the self—something he expected and hoped the average person would do—but is exhibited in the conduct of a great 'general ... statesman [or] legislator', where it is 'combined with many greater and more splendid virtues' like 'valour ... extensive and strong benevolence [and] ... a sacred regard to the rules of justice', all of which are 'supported by a proper degree of self-command':

> This superior prudence, when carried to the highest degree of perfection, necessarily supposes the art, the talent, and the habit or disposition of acting with the most perfect propriety in every possible circumstance and situation. It necessarily supposes the utmost perfection of all the intellectual and of all the moral virtues. It is the best head joined to the best heart. It is the most perfect wisdom combined with the most perfect virtue'. (*TMS*, VI.i.15: 216)

The process of reforming the modern state would begin with rulers capable of understanding how humans were really psychologically constituted and the way in which the economy, society and polity naturally interacted. Such rulers would also need the virtue to enable them to resist the importunate demands of rent-seekers as they set in place the appropriate rules and regulations that would allow a system of political economy to operate properly even after they were gone, and regardless of whether their successors were virtuous.

Conclusion

Throughout this book I argue that Smith is best described as a 'pragmatic proto-liberal'. The good life and how to achieve it for the greatest number of people seems to have been his primary preoccupation and ultimate commitment. He never commits to any policy or behaviour that does not conduce to good outcomes, some of which could be construed as enabling what we now call 'positive freedom'. Smith's delineation and defence of the system of natural liberty is not borne of any desire to promote abstract liberal values like individualism, freedom and autonomy as ends in themselves, but is a pragmatist's reaction to the most pressing political problems of his day, namely, political corruption, relentless war and interstate conflict, public debt, political corruption, suboptimal productivity levels, stalled growth and economic—and especially food—insecurity, declining literacy rates and poor public health.

Smith only defends 'liberal' values to the extent that they serve substantive ends and he readily abandons them when the ends demand it. In other words, he often violates negative liberty for the sake of *positive* liberty. It should also be noted here that some of the 'liberal' things Smith liked—liberty and progress—also had a tendency to produce externalities of which he was painfully aware. In such cases, the state should act as a corrector.

Smith does not have a consistent or thoroughgoing proto-liberal agenda as such, unless it is accepted that the achievement of the stable, secure, pacific and prosperous society constitutes a liberal or ideological programme.[10] Smith's politics—and libertarianism—are made to fit around these goals and this explains his inconsistent commitment to (negative) liberty. Sometimes his defence of liberty seems intractable yet at other times it is readily sacrificed to the demands of social science. To complicate matters, there are still other times when liberty and social science are ignored when economic and human flourishing are at stake. I say more about this hierarchy of commitments in Chap. 7.

For the moment it is enough to emphasise that Smith is no high theorist of liberty, partly because he is sceptical about high political theory more generally, but also because liberty becomes a low priority when it is failing to deliver the things Smith really wants: food and military security, innovation and entrepreneurship, economic prosperity and growth, stability, public order, human happiness, order, mobility and the flourishing society, all of which resolve into Smith's idea of 'happiness' (see also Chap. 7). He tended to look to the big picture and the long view; to judge from the perspective of the welfare and stability of the society in general. Sometimes this caused him to reveal a conservative streak born of his great need for order. He did not allow himself to be caught up in the ideology that is often attributed to him as his own invention because he liked results best of all. In other words, he was less libertarian and more consequentialist than is normally allowed.

Notes

1. Smith's appointment as a Commissioner of customs has perplexed many given that the customs service 'functioned basically as an agent of English mercantilism and as a tax collection agency' (Anderson et al. 1985: 745). There have been a number of explanations for Smith's acceptance of this position—which he seems to have actively sought—but the 'most plausible explanation ... is simply that he was tired of scholarly work ... he enjoyed his customs work and found it relaxing' compared to the ardours of research and writing (Anderson et al. 1985: 752).
2. Craig Smith (2013) has addressed the issue of where Smith sits on the left-right spectrum by considering whether he can be associated 'with the modern egalitarian idea of social justice'. Ryan Hanley suggests that he 'cuts a useful new path between "right" and "left" on the issue of the legitimate extent of state action' (Hanley 2014).
3. He is reported to have enjoyed the position and performed his official duties diligently (Anderson et al. 1985: 754).
4. As Joseph Schumpeter wrote in relation to Frank William Taussig, citing Smith as the first of the great economists to think and act this way (Schumpeter 1952: 207).
5. For Smith's influence in America and on government debates in particular, see Liu (2018) and Fleischacker (2002). According to McLean and Peterson (2010: 95), 'Adam Smith is not referred to in the records of the U.S. Constitutional Convention of 1787, but he indirectly influenced the substance of the framers' decisions on several matters, especially the Establishment and Free Exercise Clauses of the First Amendment'.
6. 'Freedom of trade in grains moderated domestic prices and maximised production since producers with access to extensive markets would be confident of sales at reasonable prices' (Tribe 1995: 25–26).
7. Rashid surmises that the 'freedom of the internal corn-trade may well be considered the first major applied field in which principles of the *Wealth of Nations* were tested' (Rashid 1980: 496).
8. Smith defines savage societies as those whose subsistence depends on fishing and hunting.
9. Yet the division labour is not peculiar to commercial nations (*WN*, i.3: 27–28).
10. This would probably apply to most political ideologies anyway.

References

Anderson, G. M., Shughart, W. F., II, & Tollison, R. D. (1985). Adam Smith in the Customhouse. *Journal of Political Economy, 93*(4), 740–759.

Boucoyannis, D. (2013). The Equalizing Hand: Why Adam Smith Thought the Market Should Produce Wealth Without Steep Inequality. *Perspectives on Politics, 11*(4), 1051–1070.

Brown, V. (1994). *Adam Smith's Discourse*. London: Routledge.
Coats, A. W. B. (Ed.). (1971). *The Classical Economists and Economic Policy*. London: Methuen.
Cohen, E. S. (1989). Justice and Political Economy in Commercial Society: Adam Smith's "Science of the Legislator". *The Journal of Politics, 51*(1), 50–72.
Cropsey, J. (1975). Adam Smith and Political Philosophy. In A. S. Skinner & T. Wilson (Eds.), *Essays on Adam Smith* (pp. 132–153). Oxford: Clarendon Press.
Endres, A. M. (1995). Adam Smith's Advisory Style as Illustrated by His Trade Policy Prescriptions. *Journal of the History of Economic Thought, 17*(1), 86–105.
Firth, A. (2002). Moral Supervision and Autonomous Social Order: Wages and Consumption in Eighteenth Century Economic Thought. *History of the Human Sciences, 15*(1), 39–57.
Fleischacker, S. (2002). Adam Smith's Reception Among the American Founders, 1776–1790. *The William and Mary Quarterly, 59*(4), 897–924.
Fleischacker, S. (2004). *On Adam Smith's Wealth of Nations: A Philosophical Companion*. Princeton: Princeton University Press.
Forman-Barzilai, F. (2010). *Adam Smith and the Circles of Sympathy*. Cambridge: Cambridge University Press.
Gee, J. M. A. (1968). Adam Smith's Social Welfare Function. *Scottish Journal of Political Economy, 15*(1), 283–299.
Haakonssen, L. (1988). *Traditions of Liberalism*. St. Leonards: Centre for Independent Studies.
Halevy, E. (1934). *The Growth of Philosophical Radicalism*. London: Faber and Faber.
Hanley, R. P. (2008). Enlightened Nation Building: The Science of the Legislator in Adam Smith and Rousseau. *American Journal of Political Science, 52*(2), 219–234.
Hanley, R. P. (2009). *Adam Smith and the Character of Virtue*. Cambridge: Cambridge University Press.
Hanley, R. P. (2014). The "Wisdom of the State": Adam Smith on China and Tartary. *The American Political Science Review, 108*(2), 371–382.
Herzog, L. (2016). The Normative Stakes of Economic Growth; or, Why Adam Smith Does Not Rely on "Trickle Down". *The Journal of Politics, 78*(1), 50–62.
Hewins, W. A. S. (1903, June 5). The Fiscal Policy of the Empire. *The Times*.
Hill, L. (2012). Adam Smith on *Thumos* and Irrational Economic Man. *European Journal of the History of Economic Thought, 19*(1), 1–22.
Himmelfarb, G. (1985). *The Idea of Poverty: England in the Early Industrial Age*. New York: Faber and Faber.
Hont, I. (2009). Adam Smith's History of Law and Government as Political Theory. In R. Bourke & R. Geuss (Eds.), *Political Judgement: Essays for John Dunn* (pp. 131–171). Cambridge: Cambridge University Press.
Kennedy, G. (2005). *Adam Smith's Lost Legacy*. New York: Palgrave Macmillan.

Letwin, W. (1988). Was Adam Smith a Liberal? In K. Haakonssen (Ed.), *Traditions of Liberalism* (pp. 83–104). St. Leonards: Centre for Independent Studies.
Liu, G. M. (2018). The Apostle of Free Trade: Adam Smith and the Nineteenth-Century American Trade Debates. *History of European Ideas, 44*(2), 210–223.
Mandeville, B. (1924). In F. B. Kaye (Ed.), *The Fable of the Bees or Private Vices, Publick Benefits.* Oxford: Oxford University Press.
McLean, I. (2006). *Adam Smith, Radical and Egalitarian: An Interpretation for the Twenty-First Century.* Edinburgh: Edinburgh University Press.
McLean, I., & Peterson, S. M. (2010). Adam Smith at the Constitutional Convention. *Loyola Law Review, 56*(1), 95–135.
Minowitz, P. (1994). *Profits, Priests, and Princes.* Cambridge: Cambridge University Press.
Morrison, J. A. (2012). Before Hegemony: Adam Smith, American Independence and the Origins of the First Era of Globalization. *International Organisation, 66*(3), 395–428.
Mossner, E. C. (1969). *Adam Smith: The Biographical Approach.* David Murray Lecture, University of Glasgow.
Mossner, E. C., & Ross, I. S. (1976). Introduction. In A. Smith, *The Theory of Moral Sentiments*, D. Raphael & A. L. MacFie, (Eds.). Oxford: Clarendon Press.
Nussbaum, M. (2000). Duties of Justice, Duties of Material Aid: Cicero's Problematic Legacy. *Journal of Political Philosophy, 8*(2), 176–206.
Oz-Salzberger, F. (2003). The Political Theory of the Scottish Enlightenment. In A. Broadie (Ed.), *The Scottish Enlightenment* (pp. 157–175). Cambridge: Cambridge University Press.
Phillipson, N. (2010). *Adam Smith: An Enlightened Life.* New Haven: Yale University Press.
Rashid, S. (1980). The Policy of Laissez-Faire During Scarcities. *The Economic Journal, 90*, 493–503.
Rasmussen, D. C. (2016). Adam Smith on What Is Wrong with Economic Inequality. *American Political Science Review, 110*(2), 342–352.
Robertson, J. (1997). Introduction, to A. Fletcher, *Political Works.* Cambridge: Cambridge University Press.
Ross, I. S. (1995). *Life of Adam Smith.* Oxford: Oxford University Press.
Rothschild, E. (1992). Adam Smith and Conservative Economics. *Economic History Review, XLV*(1), 74–96.
Rothschild, E. (2001). *Economic Sentiments: Adam Smith, Condorcet and the Enlightenment.* Cambridge, MA: Harvard University Press.
Salter, J. (2012). Adam Smith on Justice and the Needs of the Poor. *Journal of the History of Economic Thought, 34*(4), 559–575.
Schumpeter, J. A. (1952). *Ten Great Economists: From Marx to Keynes.* London: George Allen and Unwin.
Sen, A. (2009). *The Idea of Justice.* London: Belknap.

Singer, B. (2004). Montesquieu, Adam Smith and the Discovery of the Social. *Journal of Classical Sociology, 4*(1), 31–57.
Smith, A. (1976 [1759]). In D. D. Raphael & A. L. MacFie (Eds.), *The Theory of Moral Sentiments*. Oxford: Clarendon Press.
Smith, A. (1979 [1776]). In R. H. Campbell & A. S. Skinner (Eds.), *An Inquiry into the Nature and Causes of the Wealth of Nations*. Oxford: Clarendon Press.
Smith, A. (1978). In R. L. Meek, D. D. Raphael, & L. G. Stein (Eds.), *Lectures on Jurisprudence (A and B)*. Oxford: Oxford University Press.
Smith, A. (1980). In I. S. Ross (Ed.), *Essays on Philosophical Subjects*. Oxford: Clarendon Press.
Smith, A. (1987). In E. C. Mossner & I. S. Ross (Eds.), *The Correspondence of Adam Smith*. Oxford: Oxford University Press.
Smith, C. (2013). Adam Smith: Left or Right? *Political Studies, 61*(4), 784–798.
Stewart, D. (1980 [1793]). Account of the Life and Writings of Adam Smith, LL.D, I.S. Ross (ed.). In W. P. D. Wightman & J. C. Bryce (Eds.), *Adam Smith: Essays on Philosophical Subjects*. Oxford: Oxford University Press.
Stigler, G. (1975). Smith's Travels on the Ship of State. In A. S. Skinner & T. Wilson (Eds.), *Essays on Adam Smith* (pp. 237–246). Oxford: Clarendon Press.
Teichgraeber, R. F. (1987). 'Less Abused Than I Had Reason to Expect': The Reception of the *Wealth of Nations* in Britain, 1776–90. *The Historical Journal, 30*(2), 337–366.
Tribe, K. (1995). Natural Liberty and Laissez-Faire: How Adam Smith Became a Free Trade Ideologue. In S. Copley & K. Sutherland (Eds.), *Adam Smith's Wealth of Nations: New Interdisciplinary Essays* (pp. 23–44). Manchester: Manchester University Press.
West, E. G. (1976). Adam Smith's Economics of Politics. *History of Political Economy, 8*(4), 515–539.
Winch, D. (1978). *Adam Smith's Politics*. Cambridge: Cambridge University Press.
Witzum, A., & Young, J. T. (2006). The Neglected Agent: Justice, Power and Distribution in Adam Smith. *History of Political Economy, 38*(1), 437–471.
Wolin, S. (1960). *Politics and Vision*. Boston: Little, Brown and Company.

CHAPTER 2

Adam Smith on Conventional Political Themes

Introductory Comments

I have suggested that Smith sought to reinvent the art and study of statecraft; but before looking more closely at his attempts to do that, I want to show that he also contributed to traditional debates in political theory, albeit in his own eccentric way. He wrote on political topics ranging from the basis of political obligation, the grounds for right of resistance, suffrage reform and the pros and cons of democracy to his preferred constitution. The latter topic embraced the constitutional principles that he valued most as well as the proper relationship between the different parts of government. The discussion begins by exploring where Smith might have located himself in terms of the political currents of his day.

Progressive Whig or Conservative Tory?

What is the best way to classify Smith politically, if at all? The most obvious question here is, was he a Whig or a Tory? There has been some debate on whether Smith's sympathies lay with the Tories or Whigs, partly because he enjoyed friendships 'with MPs on both sides of the House' (Ross 1995: xxiv). Although most commentators have labelled him a Whig of one form or another,[1] he has struck others as more Tory in inclination. For example, his intense aversion to radical reform and innovation has led to the conclusion that in his later years he developed into a kind of Tory (Mossner and Ross 1976: 18–19). Other evidence invoked for Smith's supposed Toryism

L. Hill, *Adam Smith's Pragmatic Liberalism*,
https://doi.org/10.1007/978-3-030-19337-9_2

is his advertised view that respect for rank distinctions engenders social stability (*TMS*, VI.ii.1.20: 226; *TMS*, VI.ii.2.9–10: 230–31). Certainly, this put him at the conservative end of Whiggism but is far from making him a Tory as the example of Edmund Burke has amply shown. Like Burke, he revered 'law and order' and, despite his Whiggish tendencies,[2] had no hesitation in rejecting Whig principles when they conflicted with his social science or threatened order and stability. Key among the tenets of Whiggism with which Smith dispensed was the Lockean notion of a social contract and its accompanying conception of consent (*LJ[B]*, 14–17: 402–403). He also saw the system of rank distinctions as adaptive and was conservative in his attitude to abrupt social change and the importance of order (I will say more about this presently). On the other hand, he was typically Whiggish in insisting on religious toleration (*WN*, V.i.g.8: 792; see also Bradley 1975), denying the doctrine of the divine right of kings and resisting any 'attempt to increase the power of the crown' (Dunn 1941: 335, 345). He was also committed to the principles of the supremacy of Parliament and had a general preference for the principle of 'utility', which he identified as a Whig prejudice (*LJ[A]*, 122–23: 319).

Like any good Whig he was (in theory at least—see Chap. 7) opposed to slavery (*WN*, III.ii.9: 387–88),[3] partial to any government that protected commerce and economic rights and had a typically Whiggish love of liberty. However, as I seek to show here, he often compromised these values, particularly liberty, for the sake of order and stability, values we might normally think of as Tory-ish. Smith saw value in both Tory and Whig ideas and believed the world needed a political theory that was able to reconcile the Whig principle of 'public utility with the allegedly opposed Tory principle of authority' (Hont 2009: 139–40). He saw himself as providing that theory in expounding his spontaneous order/natural liberty[4] theory because it embraced both progressivist and conservative elements.

Smith's desire to sidestep existing ideological categories and to meld the best of Whig and Tory ideas is demonstrated in his excursus on the basis of political obligation and the right of resistance. His discussion of the topic also reflects an impatience with both high political theory and political theology in favour of a more grounded, social-scientific approach.

Obligation and Right of Resistance

Smith says that there is 'no doubt … but that the power of the king may be resisted'; but the real question is 'when is it lawfull or allowable to resist the power of the king and Parliament'? (*LJ[A]*, v.1.13: 315). His answer to this question is neither entirely Whig nor entirely Tory; instead, he absorbs elements of both sides while firmly rejecting the intellectual methods used to arrive at them. The Tory conception of obligation was based on a belief in the divine right of kings which Smith characterises as the 'authority' principle; it vests absolute and indefeasible authority in the king and therefore precludes resistance. On the other hand, the eighteenth-century Whig position entailed a rationalistic dependence on Lockean notions of natural law, pre-political individual rights and a social contract (*LJ[A]*, 134: 323). Smith characterises this position as the 'utility' principle and it allows for resistance on the grounds that government was established for the 'benefit of the ... people', not the rulers (*LJ[A]*, 123: 319).

While Smith finds some Tory and Whig conclusions acceptable, he takes issue with the methods used to arrive at them. On the one hand, he finds the Whig notion of utility attractive but poorly defended because it attempts awkwardly 'to reconcile it' with contractarianism. On the other, the Tory account is even more suspect because of its reliance on theological sophistry. Smith's solution is to make an argument for obligation that incorporates both the authority and utility principles but without relying on improbable premises. In fact, unlike both Whigs and Tories, he makes it clear that he is not that interested in discovering the moral 'foundation' of obligation; instead, he wants to determine what factors have the 'effect' of bringing obligation about (*LJ[A]*, 120: 318). It is not a question of morality, rationalistic argumentation, ideology or belief, but of social science and careful observation.

Smith begins by attacking the Whig notion of an explicit contract. If you were to ask the average person 'why [s]/he obeys the civil magistrate' he or she never answers that they were contracted to do so. The answers are generally along the lines of 'it is right to do so'; that he or she 'sees others do it' or that he or she does so to avoid punishment (*LJ[B]*, 14–17: 402–403). There are a number of reasons why Smith considers the contract theory implausible. First, it is peculiarly Anglocentric so it cannot possibly be rated a universal social law. As Smith observes, somewhat prosaically: 'government takes place where it was never thought of'. To those who would insist that 'by remaining in the country you tacitly consent to the contract and are bound by it' he replies that no one was ever 'consulted whether [they] should be born in it or not'. Furthermore, unless you are rich and well-versed in other languages, 'how can you get out of it?' (i.e. exit). It is implausible to claim that a duty can be founded upon 'a principle with which mankind is entirely unacquainted' (*LJ[B]*, 14–17:

402–403) because '[e]very morall [sic] duty must arise from some thing which mankind are conscious of' (*LJ[A]*, 128: 321).

The same objection applies to the idea of a tacit contract: we all 'have a notion of the duty of allegiance to the sovereign, and yet no one has any conception of a previous contract *either tacit or express*' (*LJ[A]*, 128: 321; emphasis added). Further, if there were 'such a thing as an original contract', foreigners who choose to settle elsewhere 'preferring it to others' surely 'give the most express consent to it'; and yet everyone knows that 'a state always suspects aliens as retaining a prejudice in favour of their mother country' and are always less trusted than 'freeborn subjects'.[5] Finally, with regard to the native population, if such a contract already exists, surely the required 'oath of allegiance whenever a man enters on any office' is superfluous? (*LJ[B]*, 14–17: 402–403). As for the idea that consent is conferred—and a contract established—by democratic elections, Smith retorts that this is a ridiculous notion and could only supply 'a very figurative metaphorical' form of consent where 'so few have voting rights' (*LJ[A]*, 134–35: 323; see also *LJ[B]*, 94: 435).

And yet, Smith also notes that the average person generally *is* obedient to 'civil authority'. How can this be explained? Smith finds that we submit out of a combination of two considerations: the first is 'utility' and the second is 'authority'. Smith's notion of authority is somewhat eccentric and distinct from the Tory notion of divine right. It does not denote a moral claim but relates to a peculiar psychological disposition in humans 'to respect an established authority and superiority in others, whatever they be' (*LJ[A]*, 119–21: 318). This disposition is both reflected in and reinforced by unconscious habits and norms rather than by conscious reasoning (*LJ[B]*, 12–13: 401–402) (and this is presumably why foreigners who become naturalised are required to swear an oath of allegiance). We are 'bred up under the authority of the magistrates'; we recognise the superior 'power' of the magistrate and notice that others routinely respect and obey the established authority. Therefore, to resist would be to find ourselves in the minority (*LJ[A]*, 119–21: 318). As Smith notes elsewhere, it is really 'custom, which sanctifies every thing' (*LJ[B]*, 321: 536).

The strength of the authority argument, from Smith's point of view, lies in the fact that it is founded on 'scientific' psychological principles rather than on political ideology or, worse still, political theology. Our tendency to defer to superiors (in age, power and tenure) is psychogenic rather than rationalistic. 'Mankind' has a natural 'disposition … to go along with all the passions of the rich and the powerful' and it is upon this disposition that is 'founded the distinction of ranks, and the order of society'. Significantly, 'our deference to' the 'inclinations' of the powerful is not 'founded chiefly, or altogether, upon a regard to the utility of such submission, and to the order of society, which is best supported by it' but originates in an urge that no 'doctrine of reason or philosophy recognises'. It is 'Nature' who teaches 'us to submit to them for their own sake, to tremble and bow down before their exalted station, to regard their smile as a reward sufficient to compensate any services, and to dread their displeasure, though no other evil were to follow from it, as the severest of all mortifications' (*TMS*, I.ii.2.3–4: 52–53; *LJ[A]*, 12: 401). This peculiar urge to defer to the powerful is then overlaid with custom. In this way our natural tendency to be habitual reinforces another natural inclination.

Obligation is further cemented by a consideration of its 'utility', by which Smith means its public benefits. We recognise the 'propriety of obeying and the unreasonableness of disobeying' those who rule because there is great general (and even some private) benefit in doing so (*LJ[A]*, 120: 318). '[E]very one sees that the magistrates not only support the government in generall [sic] but the security and independency of each individual' (*LJ[B]*, 14–15: 402; *LJ[A]*, 119–20: 318). Although '[i]t may sometimes be for my interest to dissobey [sic], and to wish government overturned … I am sensible that other men are of a different opinion from me and would not assist me in the enterprise. *I therefore submit to its decision for the good of the whole*' (*LJ[B]*, 14–15: 402; emphasis added). If 'perfection' of authority *could* ever be found, it would not be where the populace has explicitly consented to it, nor where the sovereign claims to be God's representative on earth, but simply where 'government has been of long standing … supported by proper revenues … and in the hands of a man of great abilities' (*LJ[B]*, 14: 402); in other words, where legitimacy is conferred and obligation secured by long tenure and a history of ruling competently in the public interest.

Is there no right of resistance at all in Smith then? Although he dislikes any kind of civil disturbance, Smith is unimpressed by the Tory 'preten[ce]' that 'kingly authority is of divine institution … and that therefore it must be an impiety to resist'. Instead, he is sympathetic to the Whig idea that resistance is proper when rulers rule only in their own interests. It must be obvious, even to a 'Tory' that 'there are some things which it is unlawfull for the sovereign to attempt' and which therefore 'entitle the subjects to make resistance'. Regardless of whether obedience is derived from 'authority' or utility, it is always destroyed by '[a]bsurdity and … great perverseness' (*LJ[A]*, 123–29: 319–21; see also *LJ[B]*, 94: 434) and under 'gross, flagrant and palpable abuse', as it was in the case of Nero, Caligula and Domitian (*LJ[A]*, 141: 326; *LJ[A]*, 126: 320). Subjects are also entitled to resist where the sovereign is beset by 'lunacy, nonnage or ideotism [sic]' (*LJ[A]*, 125: 320). On a more practical note, 'exorbitant taxes no doubt justify resistance, for no people will allow the half of their property to be taken from them' (*LJ[B]*, 95: 435). In mixed monarchies the king may not do 'anything' without the 'permission' of the Parliament, in which case it has 'a right to oppose him', by 'force' if necessary (*LJ[B]*, 96: 435). Note that Smith does not found this 'right' upon anything more secure than that this is the way mixed monarchies have historically—and adaptively—operated.

Yet, Smith's prescriptions carry some important conservative qualifications relating to his insistence that the public peace should not be taken lightly. We must not be too hasty to revolt against the established power and the people should show some forbearance towards the inevitable follies of government. Among the 'many' things over which the people are not entitled to 'rise in arms' are the enactment of 'foolish laws', the imposition of 'improper taxes', the waging of 'imprudent wars' and the making of 'foolish peaces' (*LJ[A]*, 141: 326). After all, '[n]o government is quite perfect' and 'it is better to submitt [sic] to some inconveniences than to make attempts against it' (*LJ[B]*, 95: 435). Yet, Smith makes the important qualification here that even if the people do not rise up on account of burdensome taxes they should always retain 'the liberty of remonstrating against them'. He also warns governments to be careful where taxes are concerned since the state was 'established to defend the property of the subjects' not to divest them of it (*LJ[A]*, 134: 324).

Smith is unapologetically unsure about what really is the moral 'foundation' or 'principle' of the obedience of subjects'(*LJ[A]*, 125: 320; *LJ[A]*, 127: 321) but he *is* sure about the conditions for its existence, namely, where it is supported by habit and a perception of its utility and legitimacy. He is also sure that 'it must have some limits' (*LJ[A]*, 128: 321). These limits cannot be determined definitively according to some rule or principle because they will vary with circumstances and must be weighed up in each case and against the utility and authority values. As Smith notes without any apparent sense of discomfiture or embarrassment: 'how far the sovereign power may go with safety can not be said' (*LJ[A]*, 141: 326). But if, on balance, utility or 'the good of the publick is the price of obedience' and where there is less 'mischief' in overthrowing 'the established government' (violating the authority value) than in 'allowing it to continue ... resistance is proper and allowable' (*LJ[A]*, 126: 320–21; see also *LJ[A]*, 134: 324).

Here we see Smith attempting to find a balance between order and innovation by partly buying into but also partly sidestepping the existing Whig-Tory debate on the subject. The sidestepping is achieved by avoiding the normative and ideological justifications for obligation and adopting instead a pragmatic, social-science perspective in which conclusions are drawn from observation rather than a priori premises. This case-by-case approach to assessing political problems within what he believed to be a social-scientific framework and according to its empirical effects lends Smith's political thought an ad hoc appearance that belies its underlying—albeit 'fuzzy'—logic.

Utility and the Impartial Spectator

The claim that Smith's approach is substantially utilitarian requires some further explanation, given the common perception that he is some kind of natural rights advocate (which is also true to a degree). Smith's device of an impartial spectator and its dynamic relationship with the 'sympathetic imagination' is central to understanding why his moral reference point seems to shift about so much, vacillating unpredictably between natural law and natural rights, deontology, virtue theory and consequentialism, with the latter generally emerging as dominant.

In mass societies of individuated strangers, where total states, theocratic forms of power and absolute moral codes are rapidly losing their hold over subjects, sympathy becomes a key method of social control. Sympathy (positive identification) works in concert with the judgements of the impartial spectator, to reduce conflict and bring forth order, 'tranquility' and 'concord' (*TMS*, I.i.4.8–10: 22–23). We all wish to attract the 'sympathy' or approval of others but, as spectators, others are never fully able to sympathise with our own feelings. Therefore we sympathise with the spectator so as to imagine how he or she would perceive our behaviour: 'We suppose ourselves the spectators of our own behaviour, and endeavour to imagine what effect it would, in this light, produce upon us' (*TMS*, III.1.5: 112). The impartial spectator allows us to see ourselves as others see us; it perpetually monitors and corrects the 'strongest impulses of self-love' (*TMS*, III.3.38: 153–54; *TMS*, III.3.4: 137; *TMS*, VI.3.18: 244–45). The impartial spectator ensures that our behaviour is never unsociable and protects us from losing the sympathy, and therefore approval and cooperation, of those around us (*TMS*, II.ii.2.2: 83; *TMS*, III.5.5: 165). We possess a 'natural disposition to accommodate and to assimilate, as much as we can, our own sentiments, principles, and feelings, to those which we see ... in the persons whom we are obliged to live and converse a great deal with' (*TMS*, VI.ii.1.17: 224). Making sympathetic judgements from the standpoint of the impartial spectator allows us to be 'more disciplined, in "command" of ourselves, proper, sociable and polite' (Forman-Barzilai 2005: 207). By this process, we are continually 'weeding out' behaviour that 'is incompatible with social life' (Haakonssen 1981: 58).

John Rawls adopts this device in his own, much later, explanation of how we maximise social utility:

> Endowed with ideal powers of sympathy and imagination, the impartial spectator is the perfectly rational individual who identifies with and experiences the desires of others as if these desires were his own. In this way he ascertains the intensity of these desires and assigns them their appropriate weight in the one system of desire the satisfaction of which the ideal legislator then tries to maximise by adjusting the rules of the social system. (Rawls 1971: 27, 184)

One could not say, of course, that Smith ever offers his reader 'a properly defended utilitarian *theory*'; as Knud Haakonssen has rightly noted (1981: 97; original emphasis) and as I show throughout this book, he is not always and consistently utilitarian in his judgements.[6] I will return to this theme in subsequent chapters but for the moment I should signal my agreement with Edward Cohen's more general observation that the 'judgements of the impartial spectator, in effect, provide the content of Smith's Science' because it is the source of 'those principles that ought to run through and be the foundation of the laws of all nations'. While accounting for order in the moral sentiments, 'sympathy links this order with the full variety of human motivations and virtues'. Cohen concludes that 'much of *TMS* is an attempt to develop a theory of virtue that combines the best of a variety of ethical systems' (Cohen 1989: 58, n. 13 and 14.). These laws are 'independent of all positive institutions' and therefore have higher moral authority (*TMS*, VII.iv.36–37: 341). The apparent messiness and dissonance of Smith's theoretical and moral framework is really a function of his belief that no one ethical system is sufficient to cover all cases in the increasingly complex realm of human existence;

sometimes the impartial spectator finds utility the best principle; sometimes deontology fits best; at other times, virtue does the job. The common thread running throughout is that the impartial spectator decides, case by case and after weighing up the pros and cons and in light of observable effects, hence the bias towards utility.

Preferred Constitution?

Nevertheless, it is still possible to detect some political prejudices and leanings in Smith's thought. He has sometimes been described as 'leaning towards republicanism',[7] or as 'always theoretically a republican' (Rae 1895: 124) but this does not tell us much since the meaning of the term was 'fairly elastic' in the second half of the eighteenth century. As Donald Winch has observed: '[f]or bolder spirits it might mean the replacement of the Crown by some kind of elected magistrate', whereas for 'others it simply denoted those who were opposed to specific policies or developments which appeared to be shifting the balance within the mixed constitution too heavily in favour of the monarchy' (Winch 1978: 42).

Duncan Forbes argues that, rather than being a republican, 'the evidence suggests that Smith subscribed to the commonplace Blackstonian view' of the British constitution as a well-balanced 'mixture of all the different forms of government' (Forbes 1976: 195; *LJ[B]*, 61–64: 420–22). Yet the two positions are not mutually exclusive since Smith regarded both democracy and mixed government as variants of republicanism. He adopts Montesquieu's tripartite division of polities—monarchy, aristocracy and democracy—noting that since the 'last two forms may be called republican', the two main types are 'monarchical and republican' (*LJ[B]*, 18–19: 404).

Nevertheless, it is true that the mixed constitution appeals most to Smith, partly because it embraces and expresses the two motives for obligation and obedience towards the state. As already discussed, Smith tells us that the 'duty of allegiance' stems from two principles; first, the principle of authority, which consists of an innate 'disposition to respect an established authority and superiority in others, whatever they be', which is afterwards reinforced by custom. The second principle is that of 'utility', whereby 'every one sees that the magistrates not only support the government in generall but the security and independency of each individuall, and they see that this security can not be attained without a regular government'. They therefore find it 'advisable to submitt to the established government' even if they are not necessarily 'disposed' to do so. This principle is reinforced by the first (*LJ[A]*, V.1201: 318). Smith says that the monarchical form of rule emphasises the principle of authority whereas the republican form stresses the principle of utility (*LJ[A]*, V.121–23: 318–19); although 'each of these principles takes place in some degree in every government ... one is generally predominant' (*LJ[A]*, V.121: 318). In the mixed monarchy they are well balanced, hence his endorsement of it. Authority is a Tory principle, while utility is a Whig principle; it is wrong to try and erect a system that only accommodates one half of the human drives for order; therefore, a system that is at once Tory and Whig is not only desirable, but natural. The good constitution has all elements. House of Lords and king satisfy the authority principle, while the Commons serves the Whig utility principle.

The need for order is consistently emphasised in Smith's discussion of this topic: the hereditary monarch is tolerated by Smith, not because he or she rules by divine authority (which Smith ridiculed) but because hereditary monarchies carry greater authority and are therefore better at engendering order than 'elective ones'. Further, because succession is smoother and less uncertain in them, they are better able to forestall social instability (*LJ[A]*, iv.162–63: 263–64; *LJ[A]*, V.130–31: 322). As the Earl of Buchan characterised Smith's position: 'hereditary succession in the chief magistrate [is] necessary ... to prevent the commonwealth from being shaken in ambition, or absolute dominion introduced by the consequences of contending factions' (Buchan 1791: 165).

In sum, the 'respect which is paid to the persons in power in every country makes the wheels of the government go on more smoothly' (*LJ[A]*, v.124: 319). It is not this or that constitutional form that attracts Smith's attention; rather, it is the tendency of particular constitutions to engender order and stability. This was so extremely important to Smith that his desire for it sometimes caused tensions in his prosecution of other important values like liberty, progress and commercial growth. He does not wish to favour any political class of people within a constitution, only to advise on what is necessary to make a commercialising economy like Britain work properly. As he wrote, the sovereign owes 'equality of treatment ... to all the different orders of his subjects' (*WN*, IV.viii.30: 654).

The other advantage of the mixed monarchy, to Smith's mind, is that it is resistant to the Polybian precept that simple forms of rule are unstable, more susceptible to corruption and generally doomed to collapse.[8] Smith agrees that complex systems are more stable than simple ones. They are less apt 'to fall into [an] absurdity than a single person' (*LJ[A]*, V.123–27:

319–21) whereas 'revolutions ... are much more frequent in absolute monarchies than anywhere else' (*LJ[A]*, V.133: 323). Smith's friend and colleague Adam Ferguson also approved of mixed constitutions on the grounds 'that constitutions framed for the preservation of liberty, must consist of many parts; and that senates, popular assemblies, courts of justice, magistrates of different orders, must combine to balance each other, while they exercise, sustain, or check the executive power' (Ferguson 1792: 498, 1996: 252). Pure or unitary forms of rule can lapse into either tyranny or anarchy (Ferguson 1996: 124–25). The main strength of the mixed constitution, Ferguson opines, is that 'it can withstand many evils without being overthrown' (Ferguson 1995: 292); in it is found a 'counterpoise ... in which the public freedom and the public order are made to consist' (Ferguson 1996: 158). This is exactly what Smith sought: a 'counterpoise' between freedom and order.

But there is an important qualification here: for Smith, there can be no fixed or absolute ideal constitution or plan of government within his system because government is an unintended consequence of subrational processes. It has evolved gradually, without design, out of complex and multidirectional moral sentiments and a dialectic that has taken place over millennia; and certainly not in a fixed moment in time via a contract. Technically then, although Smith avows a prejudice towards mixed monarchy, his opinion was open to change. Mixed monarchy is preferred *in this time and place* because it has evolved gradually; wrought by many hands and multiple generations it is therefore suited to the times, but only for so long as it is suited. Smith's relative silence on the question of his ideal constitution is therefore a function of his prior social-scientific commitments: his aversion to political and ideological 'system' and the utopian schemes of self-important legislators (*TMS*: 234).[9] Our institutions, when not interfered with, developed naturally, insensibly and by degrees, embodying the collective genius of generations through time. I say more about this in the following chapters.

What Is the Relationship Between Different Parts of Government?

What seems most important to Smith, above all, is that sovereignty should not be absolute or absolutely vested in one person. There should not be a situation 'wherein the power of making laws and regulations, of trying causes or appointing judges, and of making peace or war, are all vested in one person' (*LJ[A]*, iv.1: 200), who 'can do what he pleases, make peace and war, impose taxes, and the like' (*LJ[B]*, 18–19: 404). The separation of powers was of paramount importance. In order for a system to function properly, there must be a clear separation of powers between each branch of government and none should trespass on the rights and privileges of another. If either the 'Parliament or king should act in the legislative way without the consent of the other, if the Parliament should make war or the king endeavour to raise taxes' this should not be tolerated. For example, the king has the power to 'prorogue' Parliament for any 'unjust proceedings' while the different parts of government are entitled to 'defend themselves ... by force' if their powers are trespassed upon (*LJ[A]*, v.142: 326–27).

The separation of the powers of administering 'Justice' from 'conducting publick affairs and leading Armies' is, according to Smith, 'the great advantage which modern times have over antient, and the foundation of that greater Security which we now enjoy both with regard to Liberty, property and Life' (*LJ[B]*: 176). Especially important is the independence of the judiciary for '[w]hen the judicial is united to the executive power, it is scarce possible that justice should not frequently be sacrificed to, what is vulgarly called, politics' (*WN*, V.i.b.25: 722).

Smith is also keen to impress upon his reader the importance of impartial and predictable rule of law. While '[t]he judge is necessary' it 'is of all things the most terrible'. In order to manage this problem, 'laws and rules' must be established 'which may ascertain his conduct; for when it is known in what manner he is to proceed the terror will in great measure [be] removed'. Indeed, Smith surmises that the 'growth of the judicial power was what gave occasion to the institution of a legislative power' so as to restrain the fearful 'power of judicial officers' and secure the people from the 'absolute' and 'arbitrary' rule of 'judges'. Such 'was the case at Athens, Sparta and other places where the people demanded laws to regulate the conduct of the judge' (*LJ[A]*, V.114: 314–15).

At the same time, for the sake of the 'liberty' of the people the judiciary should be 'intirely independent of the king'. To this end, Smith recommends 'that all judges hold their office[r]s for life' in order to ensure that 'everyone ... is tried by a free and independent judge' who is, nevertheless, 'also accountable for their conduct' (*LJ[A]*, v.5: 271). This independence is secured from abuse by Smith's further qualification that the judges should be significantly constrained in their capacity 'in explaining, altering, or extending or correcting the meaning of the laws'—a function Smith reserved to the Parliament. Further, courts must apply the laws of Parliament with 'great exactness ... according to the literall meaning of the words' (*LJ[A]*, v.16: 275).

How Powerful Should Be the Parliament Within a Mixed Constitution?

Is the Parliament supreme in the manner asserted by so-called 'vulgar Whigs' (Bradley 1975)? According to the Earl of Buchan, Smith 'considered a commonwealth as the platform for the monarchy' (cited in Winch 1978: 7); however, Forbes is sceptical of this view suggesting that 'it was not a question of a commonwealth forming a platform for monarchy'. The English government was a mixed government and it was a question of maintaining the balance between 'the influence of the crown' and the 'force of the democracy'; between the 'monarchical and democratical parts of the constitution' (Forbes 1976: 195; *WN*, IV.vii.c.78: 625). At times Smith seems to prefer it when the monarchical and democratic aspects of the constitution are in balance with neither exerting too much influence over the other (*WN*, IV.vii.c.78: 625). But he does express more concern at the idea of the Monarch overstepping 'his rights' than of the Parliament doing so and he reserves the all-important right to tax to the Parliament. It might be thought that, in reserving the right to 'wage war' to the king, he is delegating more authority to the latter. But in practical terms that right is severely circumscribed by the king's inability to raise taxes for any proposed wars. So, in effect, Parliament has ultimate control over the two most important powers of the state.

So, if Smith leans any way at all it is towards parliamentary dominance. This is also reflected in his approval of the fact that, in both England and America 'the authority' of the Commons 'over-awes the executive power' (*WN*, IV.vii.b.51: 585) and his suggestion that '[u]pon the power which the greater part of the leading men, the ***natural aristocracy*** of every country, have of preserving or defending their respective importance, depends the stability and duration of every system of free government' (*WN*, IV.vii.c: 621–22). The House of Commons is essential to the preservation of liberty, especially in its 'sole right of imposing taxes' (*WN*, IV.vii.b.51: 585).

Democracy and Representation

Should the People Be Having More Say?

Smith seems to be well aware of the value and effects of voting rights. He recognises the link between suffrage and liberty, noting also that the right to vote provides secure protection for economic rights: the possession in England by 'certain lease holders a right of voting for Members of Parliament' makes landlords 'very cautious of attempting to raise his rents, or of demanding any other oppressive exactions of the latter'. Smith also alludes to the 'superior liberty of the English' compared to the Scots, due the fact that the franchise in England is broader (early draft of *WN*, 47: 581). He further stipulates that '[t]he frequency of elections is … a great security for the liberty of the people' to prevent neglect of the peoples' interests (*LJ[A]*, v.8–9: 273). Yet Smith never calls for any widening of the franchise or for greater levels of public input into the business of governing. Despite owning some of their publications, it is significant that there is no mention in any of Smith's published works of suffrage reform or of any of its protagonists like John Wilkes (1725–1797) and Christopher Wyvill (1740–1822).[10] Richard Price is the exception, but even he only gets a passing mention. Price, a dissenter who was part of the Yorkshire reform movement and who supported the French and American Revolutions, was described by Smith disparagingly as 'a factious citizen, a most superficial Philosopher and by no means an able calculator'. He predicted and hoped that 'Price's speculations' would 'sink into the neglect that they always deserved' (*Corr.*: 251).[11]

It should be remembered that in Smith's time only 2 per cent of the population had the right to vote (West 1976: 531). Smith seems disapproving of this fact when he observes that 'the number of voters is nothing to that of the people' (*LJ[B]*, 94: 435)[12] and that 'the house of commons [is] not always a very equal representation of the people' (*WN*, IV.viii.b: 585). But he gives no sign that he thinks this should change any time soon; he only admits that is at least better than any other European system where elections are non-existent (*LJ[A]*, 13, 134–35: 323–24; *LJ[B]*, 94: 435). Overall, Smith does not seem that interested in making government more representative and he seems not to have identified either liberty or equality very strongly with democracy.

Smith's apparent lack of interest in the character and conduct of democratic elections has been attributed to the manner in which they were conducted in Britain, namely, via the simple plurality or majoritarian method of voting.[13] Pre-empting the complaints of modern detractors of this method, Smith outlines how under such a system the successful candidate might actually be 'the most obnoxious of all' to 66 per cent of the electors. Such an objectionable outcome was not uncommon in Britain, he opines, and it 'is without doubt a very great grievance' (*LJ[A]*, 51: 290). Smith was later made aware of Condorcet's solution to the majoritarian problem, namely, some variant of a preferential system, since 'Condorcet … forwarded to Smith a copy of his seminal work of 1785 on mathematical analysis of social groups and majority decision-making' (Ross 1995: 363).

There are several other likely reasons for Smith's apparent lack of interest in democracy. First, he was far more interested in economic citizenship than the political variety since he saw poverty and economic insecurity as the most urgent problems of his time. Second, in line with his general approach to social change, he would have regarded suffrage reform as something to be brought about slowly and by degrees. Third, he was likely doubtful that the average person was equipped for the responsibilities of full suffrage rights. He famously described how, under a system of production dominated by the division of labour, the average detail worker becomes 'as stupid and ignorant as it is possible for a human creature to become' and is soon bereft of any capacity to exercise his or her moral sentiments or to judge his or her own best interests (*WN*, V.i.f.50: 781–82). This lack of judgement also made the average worker easy to incite to civil unrest (*LJ[B]*, 329–30: 539–40). Hence Smith was sceptical about how much public input a constitution could safely accommodate:

> [Although] the interest of the labourer is strictly connected with that of the society, he is incapable either of comprehending that interest, or of understanding its connection with his own. His condition leaves him no time to receive the necessary information, and his education and habits are commonly such as to render him unfit to judge even though he was fully informed. In the publick deliberations, therefore, his voice is little heard and less regarded. (*WN*, I.xi.9: 266)

The fourth likely reason for Smith's neglect of the topic of a broadened franchise has been posited by E.G. West, who suggests, plausibly, that, although Smith was friendly to 'some degree of representation in the law-making authority ... his criteria of representation were not fully democratic ones'. For West, Smith was not especially opposed to constitutional democracy; it is just that he was 'more concerned with the establishment of general laws of procedures that laid down the permanent limits to the coercive power of government than with the precise voting rules within it'. Above all, the discretionary and arbitrary power of kings 'had to be ruled out' (West 1976: 527).

The general drift of Smith's thought here is that the average worker should fix 'his' attention on feeding himself and his family and let his social superiors make the decisions for 'him'. Smith seems content with a representative institution operated by a 'natural aristocracy' and co-terminous with an upper house of nobles, a constrained monarchy and an independent judiciary. Dugald Stewart seems to sum up accurately Smith's attitude to suffrage reform and the role of the working classes in law-making:

> [*T*]*he happiness of mankind depends*, not on the share which the people possesses, directly or indirectly, in the enactment of laws, but on the equity and expediency of the laws that are enacted. The share which the people possesses in the government is interesting chiefly to the small number of men whose object is the attainment of political importance; but the equity and expediency of the laws are interesting to every member of the community: and more especially to those whose personal insignificance leaves them no encouragement, but what they derive from the general spirit of the government under which they live. (Stewart 1980: 310. Emphasis added)

Smith's seeming indifference to suffrage rights may also have been related to the possibility that he regarded other democratic freedoms as more important than the right to vote. Indeed, he identifies free speech as 'a great test of the liberty of the people' signifying that government is neither 'absolute' or 'arbitrary'. Britain is identified as rare among nations in its toleration of political speech (*LJ[A]*, ii.i.142–44: 124–26).[14] Freedom of religious thought was also a vitally important right for Smith, who averred that 'every man' could 'chuse his own priest and his own religion as he thought proper' (*WN*, V.i.g.8: 792).

It is sometimes said that Smith did not indulge in the vulgar Whig conceit that the English constitution alone was 'capable of achieving and guaranteeing liberty' (Winch 1978: 39–40; Forbes 1976: 182–83).[15] However, he does seem to think that, on balance, the English constitution is able to do this better than any other, a theme upon which he occasionally waxed with pride (e.g. *WN*, IV.v.b.43: 540). On top of this, the mixed monarchy was extremely stable. While absolute monarchy can degenerate into tyranny, simple or 'uniform' democracies are equally bad since they tend to be riven with 'rancorous and virulent factions' which divide 'the affections' of the people, disturb 'the tranquillity of their governments' and frequently 'break out into open violence and bloodshed' (*WN*, V.ii.90: 945).

To be sure, he perceived all the shortcomings of the English constitution: he was well aware of the unrepresentativeness of Parliament; how the House of Commons often served sectional interests at the expense of the public and he was alert to political corruption, complaining of judicial bribery, political graft and government profligacy (see Chap. 5). But his desire for order and stability was almost as strong as his desire for liberty and it was certainly stronger than his desire for equality. He thought that the British system was doing a reasonable job of bringing order, stability and liberty, declaring it to be 'a happy mixture of all the different forms of government properly restrained' and therefore 'a perfect security to liberty and property' (*LJ[B]*, 61–64: 420–22). Here was a constitution where 'the sovereign power' was aptly divided between 'the king ... the people, and ... the nobles' (*LJ[A]*, V.123: 319), a 'system of government under which the subjects of a great empire have enjoyed, perhaps, peace, security, and even glory, during the course of several centuries together' (*TMS*, VI.ii.2.13: 232). Although it could do with some reform (of which his work is replete with suggestions), there were many admirable features about it, the most important being its relative stability, its possession of a representative 'assembly' with 'the sole right of imposing taxes' and it being powerful enough to enjoy an ascendancy over 'the executive power', the latter of which had no means by which to 'corrupt' it (*WN*, IV.vii.b: 584–85). Therefore, any proposal to abruptly 'new-model the constitution' and 'alter' its 'essential parts' is seldom a 'plausible plan' (*TMS*, VI.ii.2.13: 232).

Conclusion

Where mainstream political life was concerned, Smith displays both Whig and Tory tendencies (erring more on the side of Whiggism) but his loyalty is really to social science, welfare and overall utility. His prejudice towards mixed monarchy with an ascendant commons is partly because that is the system that had evolved and was still evolving in Smith's time. It is also because the mixed constitution was doing a good job of forestalling social conflict by admitting each sector of society into the business of governing. It was also an effective bulwark against injustice and arbitrary rule because of the separation of powers. Smith certainly does not preclude any alteration to that constitution in the future since he was, after all, a cautious progressivist. So while he does not advocate representative democracy as it is understood now, neither is he particularly against it. He likely just thought it would come in its own time if it was needed.

Smith does show some interest in the topic of political rights but he is far more interested in the neglected topic of *economic* rights so this is where he turns his attention. He wanted to focus on the rights to live and work as one saw fit, to be free from famine and exploitation and to be able to achieve these goals within a stable polity free from arbitrary interference. It is possible that he planned to say more about political rights and institutions in his promised treatise on politics but there is a good chance that this treatise would have simply filled out the themes and conclusions already adumbrated in his published works. I now turn to his thoughts in this welfare-focused direction.

Notes

1. Duncan Forbes refers to Smith as a 'skeptical Whig' (Forbes 1976). This is apt but is not the same as my preferred term 'pragmatic proto-liberal'.
2. As Mossner and Ross suggest, 'Smith believed in a careful balance between order and innovation' (Mossner and Ross 1976: 18–19).
3. Note, however, that the reasons Smith gives for opposing slavery tend to relate to efficiency and practicality rather than justice. See Chap. 7 for more detail on this topic.
4. Smith does not, of course, use the term 'spontaneous order' (a term coined in the twentieth century), but refers instead to a self-equilibrating system of 'natural liberty' and, at one point 'the liberal system' (*WN*, IV.v.b.39: 538).
5. Presumably Smith makes this assumption because of his faith in unconscious habits (in this case for a prejudice towards our country of origin) over rationalistic processes.
6. For excellent discussions of Smith's use of utilitarian ideas see Witzum (2013) and also Rosen (2000).
7. The Earl of Buchan, cited in Winch (1978: 7).
8. Smith refers to Polybius' exposition of the 'civil constitution of the Romans' as 'not only instructing but agreeable' (*Lectures on Rhetoric and Belles Lettres*, Smith 1983, hereafter referred to as *LRB*, Lecture XIX, ii.54: 108).
9. Hume likewise rejected all large-scale 'plans of government' such as Plato's *Republic* and Thomas More's *Utopia* as 'plainly imaginary' though he makes an exception in the case of Harrington's 'Commonwealth of Oceana', which he describes as 'the only valuable model of a commonwealth, that has yet been offered to the public' (Hume 1987: 514).
10. However, two items written by Wilkes are found in Smith's library: 'A letter to the worthy electors of the borough of Aylesbury in the county of Bucks' (1764) and *The North Briton*, Volume I [-III] (1763) (Mizuta 2000: 270).
11. No less than seven works by Price are found in Smith's library, including those that dealt with the American Revolution, the war with America and the nature of 'civil liberty'. Some of them were confined to economic questions about debt and public spending (see Mizuta 2000: 205). Price welcomed the American Revolution and his sermon on 'The Love of our Country', which was preached on 4 November 1789, also celebrated the French Revolution. Provoked by it, Edmund Burke responded with his *Reflections* (1790).
12. 'It is in Britain alone that any consent of the people is required, and God knows it is but a very figurative metaphoricall consent which is given here' (*LJ[A]*, v.134: 323).

13. This, indeed, is Edward West's view. According to West, who uses a different example, Smith thought simple majority voting was conducive to monopoly and 'statutory protectionism' (West 1976: 526; see also *WN*, I.x.c.30: 145–46).
14. This is partly 'because the government is now so well established that there is no reason to take notice of those who write or speak against it' (*LJ[B]*, 52: 429).
15. Even an absolute monarchy like France was able, 'at least to a certain degree', to offer some degree of liberty by keeping 'justice and politics separate' (Haakonssen 1981: 132).

References

Bradley, J. E. (1975). Whigs and Nonconformists: "Slumbering radicalism" in English Politics, 1739–89. *Eighteenth-Century Studies, 9*(1), 1–27.

Buchan, D. E. (1791, June 8). *The Bee or Literary Weekly Intelligence.*

Cohen, E. (1989). Justice and Political Economy in Commercial Society: Adam Smith's "Science of the Legislator". *The Journal of Politics, 51*(1), 50–72.

Dunn, W. L. (1941). Adam Smith and Edmund Burke: Complementary Contemporaries. *Southern Economic Journal, VII*(2), 330–346.

Ferguson, A. (1792). *Principles of Moral and Political Science: Being Chiefly a Retrospect of Lectures Delivered in the College of Edinburgh, in Two Volumes.* Edinburgh: Printed for A. Strahan and T. Cadell, London, and W. Creech, Edinburgh.

Ferguson, A. (1995). *The Correspondence of Adam Ferguson*, V. Merolle (Ed.), with an Introduction by J. B. Fagg, in Three Volumes. London: William Pickering.

Ferguson, A. (1996 [1767]). *An Essay on the History of Civil Society*, edited and with an Introduction by F. Oz-Salzberger. Cambridge: Cambridge University Press.

Forbes, D. (1976). Skeptical Whiggism, Commerce, and Liberty. In A. S. Skinner & T. Wilson (Eds.), *Essays on Adam Smith* (pp. 194–201). Oxford: Clarendon Press.

Forman-Barzilai, F. (2005). Sympathy in Space(s): Adam Smith on Proximity. *Political Theory, 33*, 189–217.

Haakonssen, K. (1981). *The Science of the Legislator.* Cambridge: Cambridge University Press.

Hont, I. (2009). Adam Smith's History of Law and Government as Political Theory. In R. Bourke & R. Geuss (Eds.), *Political Judgement: Essays for John Dunn* (pp. 131–171). Cambridge: Cambridge University Press.

Hume, D. (1987). *Essays Moral, Political and Literary*, E. F. Millar (Ed.). Indianapolis: Liberty Classics.

Mizuta, H. (2000). *Adam Smith's Library: A Catalogue*, edited and with an introduction and Notes by H. Mizuta. New York: Oxford University Press.
Mossner, E. C., & Ross, I. S. (1976). Introduction. In A. Smith, *The Theory of Moral Sentiments*, D. Raphael & A. L. MacFie, (Eds.). Oxford: Clarendon Press.
Rae, J. (1895). *Life of Adam Smith*. London: Macmillan and Co.
Rawls, J. (1971). *A Theory of Justice*. Cambridge, MA: Harvard University Press.
Rosen, F. (2000). The Idea of Utility in Adam Smith's *The Theory of Moral Sentiments*. *History of European Ideas, 26*(2), 79–103.
Ross, I. S. (1995). *Life of Adam Smith*. Oxford: Oxford University Press.
Smith, A. (1976 [1759]). *The Theory of Moral Sentiments*, D. D. Raphael & A. L. MacFie (Eds.). Oxford: Clarendon Press.
Smith, A. (1978). *Lectures on Jurisprudence (A and B)*, R. L. Meek, D. D. Raphael & L. G. Stein (Eds.). Oxford: Oxford University Press.
Smith, A. (1979 [1776]). *An Inquiry into the Nature and Causes of the Wealth of Nations*, R. H. Campbell & A. S. Skinner (Eds.). Oxford: Clarendon Press.
Smith, A. (1983). *Lectures on Rhetoric and Belles Lettres*, J. C. Bryce (Ed.). Oxford: Clarendon Press.
Stewart, D. (1980 [1793]). Account of the Life and Writings of Adam Smith, LL.D, I.S. Ross (ed.). In W. P. D. Wightman & J. C. Bryce (Eds.), *Adam Smith: Essays on Philosophical Subjects*. Oxford: Oxford University Press.
West, E. G. (1976). Adam Smith's Economics of Politics. *History of Political Economy, 8*(4), 515–539.
Winch, D. (1978). *Adam Smith's Politics*. Cambridge: Cambridge University Press.
Witzum, A. (2013). Utilitarianism and the Role of Utility in Adam Smith. *The European Journal of the History of Economic Thought, 20*(4), 572–602.

CHAPTER 3

The System of Natural Liberty and the Science of Welfare

Introductory Comments

This chapter explores the framework Adam Smith used to approach the political issues that concerned him. The underlying foundation for—and dominating theme of—his political, social and economic thought is, of course, his belief in the system of 'natural liberty'. He regarded his disclosure and explanation of this self-ordering system as an exercise in social science that not only comprehended how societies, economies and polities operated in their natural state, but also included a unique and complementary faculty psychology, historiography and Deistic theology, all of which are unpacked in the following discussion. In laying out the full complexity of Smith's social science we are enabled to reconcile some of the tensions and apparent contradictions of his political thought and to appreciate that it is more coherent than is commonly believed. It also helps us to understand that his economics is less a function of ideology than it is of his own social science. Specific topics included in this chapter are the proper role of the state, the existence of market failures, the fair wage debate, the problem of an established church and the standing army debate.

As was discussed in Chap. 1, Smith's political economy was an attempt to address real-world problems associated with food security, national defence, taxation, public debt, declining standards of education and the proper management of the colonies. He sought to reform many entrenched—but, to Smith's mind, maladaptive—practices such as the

L. Hill, *Adam Smith's Pragmatic Liberalism*,
https://doi.org/10.1007/978-3-030-19337-9_3

poor laws, slavery, religious interference in politics, monopolies, political corruption, imperialism, chronic public debt, the abject conditions of the working poor, puritanical and outdated attitudes to (and taxes on) consumerism and luxury and the archaic laws controlling inheritance and workers' rights. The solution, for Smith, lay in working out exactly what role an organised state should play within the system of natural liberty. What did the 'proper state' look like and how much reach into the lives of private people should it have?

For Smith, good governing began with a social-scientific understanding of universal social and economic laws and an appreciation of the full extent and character of civil society. This, in turn, would help us to know what the proper relationship between the state and the civil society of independent, self-governing, self-regarding actors was. Notably, although his framework seems, at first sight, to be highly secular, it was firmly rooted in the design principle. It also requires a subtle appreciation of human faculty psychology in order to understand how best to accommodate and harness human motivations within social, economic and political arrangements.

For Smith, the realm of un-coerced collective action was naturally very large: beneath the complicated structure of arbitrary social arrangements and artificially imposed institutional constraints on human behaviour, there was a system of spontaneous social and economic relations which, when left to itself, would function more or less harmoniously. But this qualification 'more or less' is important; Smith is no high theorist of liberty and no perfectionist either. The system of natural liberty could solve some problems, but some could only be solved by a well-regulated state operated by actors who understood and respected the proper relationship between market and state. Such actors would know that state interference was wholly justified if it served to expand or protect liberty, either directly or indirectly or else promoted happiness.

Spontaneous Order and the System of 'Natural Liberty'

Although Smith is commonly conceived as a key architect or inventor of modern economics, from his own point of view, he was not inventing anything: only carefully delineating a solution that already existed and was readily available. However, due to ignorance, it was being ignored, stifled or subverted by legislators and the economic elites who held them in thrall. This solution was, of course, the market, which, as Lisa Herzog puts it, was 'a natural "problem solver"' as far as Smith was concerned (Herzog 2013: 11 and ch. 2). Although there were times when the market failed to solve a particular problem, nevertheless, on the whole, market solutions should always be the problem-solver's first port of call.

Smith's theory of the system of natural liberty is perhaps his most important contribution to the Western political and economic tradition. The idea and its implications continue to exert great power even today and might be thought of one of the most important 'unit ideas'[1] of modernity. The existence of this self-organising social and economic system is defended in Smith's anti-rationalist account of the manner in which the general equilibrium of society emerges spontaneously from the seemingly random behaviours of individual actors. Order is the product, not of intentional design and planning, but of unconscious or subrational, internal processes played out at the micro level of individual human action. Smith rejects the historiographic 'fictions' that dominated up to and during his time, namely, contractarianism, Great Legislator myths ('Kings and Queens' type histories) and the diffusionist theory of civilisation promulgated by the authors of the *Encyclopedie*.[2] During the seventeenth century it was commonly held that the Greeks adopted most of their knowledge from the Egyptians, a doctrine that remained popular even into the early part of the nineteenth century. But for Smith, cultural borrowing, rationality and long-term, deliberate planning play only a secondary role in the generation of knowledge and the unfolding of human history. The entire universe is a vast equilibrium generated and upheld by divinely orchestrated natural laws while the human universe is regulated by laws that inhere in our species' constitution. These laws—expressed mainly as drives and dispositions—create social structure, order and motion.

In the system of 'natural liberty', each person is by nature the best judge of his or her own interest and should therefore be left unhindered to pursue it in their own way. When maladaptive 'systems either of preference or of restraint' have been eradicated, 'the obvious and simple system of natural liberty establishes itself of its own accord' (*WN*, IV.ix.51: 687). Once this happens, agents are enabled to secure, not only their own best advantage, but that of society as well. As Smith famously put it, each individual is 'led by an invisible hand to promote an end which was no part of his intention', namely, the general welfare and prosperity of the nation (*WN*, IV.ii.9: 456).

The world was full of the unintended social-systems consequences of individualised and self-regarding behaviours that are good both for the individuals who enact them and for society as a whole; conversely, our innate urges dissuade us from actions that have bad consequences. Smith offers the following examples of this dynamic: the desire for material advancement inadvertently produces universal abundance (*TMS*, IV.1: 183–84; *WN*, IV.ii.9: 456); the emergence of private property—and the inequalities in property that are occasioned by it—unintentionally gives rise to formal government and systems of legal justice (*LJ[A]*: 5; *WN*, V.i.b.2, 715); our innate 'resentment', desire to avenge injustice and natural aversion to 'unmerited and unprovoked malice' leads to a system of positive justice (*TMS*, II.i.5.5–10: 75–77; *TMS*, II.ii.3.8–11: 89–90); spontaneous sympathy minimises vice and moderates all form of human interaction in order to render human action benign and useful; the division of labour, which is responsible for so much of human progress and material abundance, emerges as an incidental by-product of the instinct 'to truck barter and exchange' while specialisation, in turn, leads to amazing and infinite technical advancements (*WN*, I.i.9–10: 21–22). Further, wealth inequalities are beneficial due to the trickle-down effect and their tendency to incentivise the poor (*TMS*, IV.i.10: 184–85); the 'gradual improvements of arts, manufactures, and commerce' destroy the undesirable system of feudalism and the power of the medieval church (*WN*, III.iv.10: 418–19; *WN*, III.iv.17: 422; *WN*, V.i.g.25: 803–804; *WN*, V.i.g.24: 802–803); the consumer's natural preference for domestic over foreign goods benefits their own country (*WN*, IV.ii.9: 456); well-regulated government is the incidental effect of a peculiar aesthetic desire for 'love of art and contrivance' (*TMS*, IV.i.11: 185–86) and wealth stimulates population growth (*WN*, I.viii.40: 98; *WN*, IV.vii.b.3: 566).

Other unintended consequences are that 'sympathy' and the need for approbation leads to spontaneous justice (*TMS*, II.ii.31; 130; *TMS*, III.5.6: 165); the natural deference we feel towards the prosperous and great maintains the system of rank distinctions and generates appropriate authority values, thereby preserving social order (*TMS*, I.Iii.2.5: 55; *TMS*, VI.ii.1.20: 225–26; see also *LJ[B]*, 12–13: 401–402)[3]; people are 'compelled by their nature to act with justice' but not benevolence; the inability of the majority of humankind to form sound moral judgements 'is compensated by the emergence of an authoritative code of social mores', while 'agents are induced to express that precise degree of every different kind of sentiment which is most to their benefit' (Kleer 1995: 281–82). Finally, the rich

> are led by an invisible hand to make nearly the same distribution of the necessaries of life, which would have been made, had the earth been divided into equal portions among all its inhabitants, and thus *without intending it, without knowing it*, advance the interests of the society, and afford means to the multiplication of the species. (*TMS*, IV.i.11: 185; emphasis added)

Everywhere he looks Smith sees the law of unintended consequences at work: '[e]very individual … neither intends to promote the public interest, nor knows how much he is promoting it', because 'he intends only his own security' and 'gain' (*WN*, IV.ii.9: 456). Indeed, it is best that we act from ignorance of the social-systems effects of our actions because 'those who affected to trade for the public good' rarely, if ever, achieve their intended aims (*WN*, IV.ii.9: 456). Although Smith is better known for his *economic* conception of the 'invisible hand'—or, his preferred phrase, 'system of natural liberty'—we can see from these examples that the idea of an invisible hand runs throughout every aspect of life and every part of his system of thought, including his moral and political theory, his historiography, his sociology of norms, institutions and human interaction and his faculty psychology or model of human motive forces.

Smith is commonly understood as hostile to grand theory, but careful readers will notice that he limits his critique to the products of *mortal* rationalistic constructivism, to the *hubris* of the 'man of system [who] is apt to be very wise in his own conceit and is often so enamoured with the supposed beauty of his own ideal plan of government' (*WN*, IV.ix.50–51: 687; *TMS*, VI.ii.2.17: 233–34). Smith clearly accepted the existence of an ultimate overarching plan for humanity as laid out by 'God' or the Divine Architect; the 'invisible hand' is his shorthand for the operations of the law of the heterogeneity of ends,[4] and his ideal system of 'natural liberty'.

A beneficent pattern orchestrated by Providence and geared towards human happiness and material prosperity is formed by the uncoordinated, self-regarding acts of individuals. We often attribute the order secured by our instincts to temporal rationality simply because their effects are so commodious, orderly and felicitous but this is far from being the case (*TMS*, II.ii.3.5: 87). Smith describes a two-tiered model where the first tier is represented by the individual goal level and the second by the social-systems level. There is a clear line of demarcation between the individual and social-systems realms (see, for example, *WN*, IV.ix.51: 687). Because the social-systems benefits are generated from the bottom-up by the self-regarding actions of individuals, neither private individuals nor the state should seek to interfere in the latter sphere of activity which is the realm of final causes and therefore reserved for the Author of Nature, who has 'from all eternity contrived and conducted the immense machine of the universe' (*TMS*, II.ii.3.5; see also Hill 2001). A signal example of how this works is found in Smith's explanation for how population levels grow and self-regulate.

Population Levels

A key *telos* of the Creator for humans (later picked up by F.A. Hayek and used as a measure of order success) is population growth. Smith describes in Malthusian tones[5] how population increases are a spontaneous by-product of productivity and material prosperity (*WN*, I.viii.39, 44: 97, 99; *WN*, I.xi.c.6: 180; see also *LJ[A]*, iii.47: 159). He invokes the law of the 'heterogeneity of ends' here in observing that the propagation of the species is wisely based on the often seemingly 'ridiculous' passion that unites the sexes (*TMS*, II.i.5.10: 77–78). The baseness of this method might obscure the Providential character of this dynamic but it bears the clear marks of design. This natural method is far superior to any measures on the part of the state to encourage population growth since such 'regulations' do not always produce the desired 'effect' (*LJ[A]*, iii.47–48: 158–59). Rather, population levels are self-equilibrating, subject to the basic laws of supply and demand: 'the demand for men, like that of any other commodity, necessarily regulates the production of men; quicken it when it goes on too slowly, and stops it when it advances too fast' (*WN*, I.viii.40: 98).

Because human reason is unreliable, efficient causes (in this case sexual desire) do all the survival legwork. This seemingly profane and carnal arrangement in no way denotes a Godless world; rather, it testifies to the Creator's love for us and speaks of our destiny to thrive in prosperity and happiness. At first sight Smith seems to be committing the naturalistic fallacy[6] but his insistence here on the benevolence of the social order would only constitute a commission of this error were his system genuinely profane. But it is not, and his economic and social thought is full of examples where social systems', 'happiness' and prosperity result from the free play of avarice and other self-regarding and even voluptuous desires.

A Designed Universe

Although the preservation and perpetuation of the species is ensured through inwrought laws of nature and seemingly base instincts, in reality this behaviour is both condoned and intended by the 'Divine Architect. By acting on these urges, we unwittingly co-operate with the Deity and serve to advance "His" ends, namely, "the support of the individual and the propagation of the species"' (*TMS*, II.ii.3.5: 87). The motivations of individual agents may seem morally suspect at times yet, overall, the *system* of nature is self-evidently benign, however, because in creating us, God's 'original purpose' was not to make us good but to preserve us, 'to promote happiness, and to guard against misery' (*TMS*, III.5.7: 166; see also Hill 2001).

Living a virtuous life is certainly commendable but it is really 'self-preservation, and the propagation of the species' that 'are the great ends which Nature seems to have proposed in the formation of all animals' (*TMS*, II.i.5.10: 77). God's benevolent ambitions are manifested in the worldly and self-interested aspects of human life; for example, the rather prosaic 'principle in the mind' that prompts us 'to truck, barter and exchange ... is not marked with anything amiable' and yet it is this principle that is, in reality, the 'great foundation of arts, commerce, and the division of labour' (*LJ[B]*, 301–302: 527). Those 'whining and melancholy moralists ... who regard as impious the natural joy of prosperity' (*TMS*, III.3.9: 139) misinterpret God's purposes when they condemn our worldly ambitions. Humans often evince motives and attitudes that appear vicious, but this misses the point that comprehending the dynamics of the human universe in an authentically social-scientific way is not about 'matter[s] of right' but rather of 'fact' (*TMS*, II.i.5.10: 77). Smith admits that his reasoning, at first sight, seems counter-intuitive because those 'principles of the human mind which are most beneficial to society are by no means marked by nature as the most honourable'. It is unfortunate that '[h]unger, thirst and the passion for sex' wrongly 'excite[s] contempt' in moralists when, in reality, these are the very drives that 'are the great supports of the human species' (*LJ[B]*, 300: 527). Moreover, they are signs of God's benevolent regard for humanity.

Design, the System of 'Natural Liberty' and Human Faculty Psychology

That Smith's system embodies the design principle requires some explanation given his insistence on social science as the best guide for action. Although Smith describes a world operated by secondary or 'efficient' causes, this is not incompatible with a Providentialist view of creation; his 'God' is a 'General' rather than 'Special' Providence whose order ***appears*** to derive exclusively from efficient causes whereas these causes are actually triggered by first and final causes (*TMS*, III.5: 165–66). Within the Smithian system, individual agents act as efficient causes of social, political and economic order and they are invested with immutable, uniform instincts and even defects in order to achieve these effects and thereby trigger the disclosure of the divine blueprint through time. Smith optimistically perceived all of our psychological apparatus as Providential and therefore in no way vicious (*TMS*, III.3.10: 140).[7] Indeed, those who renounce or disown our self-regarding drives misguidedly 'obstruct ... the scheme which the Author of nature has established for the happiness and perfection of the world, and ... declare ourselves ... the enemies of God' (*TMS*, III.5.7: 166). The hubristic designs of 'Great Legislators' are heresies against an already perfect, divine order; therefore truly pious agents will imitate the 'perfect confidence' in God of the Stoics and concern themselves only with the 'propriety' of their own restricted 'endeavours' while trusting in the Creator's 'superior power' to '[turn] it to that great end, which he himself was most desirous of promoting' (*TMS*, VII.ii.1.21: 277; see also *TMS*, III.5.6–7: 164–65; *TMS*, VI.ii.3.4: 236).

Smith is a worldly philosopher but this is not to say that there are no metaphysics within his system since it is firmly grounded within the principle of design. As Athol Fitzgibbons has observed:

> Certainly Smith rejected the unworldly tradition that the soul should be cultivated at the expense of the body and mind. However, Smith also thought that society would be lasting only if it conformed to the laws of Divine Nature. The proper approach to God was not through transcendence of the worlds, which was the wisdom of [Greek and Christian] man, but via the world through respect for those rules of Nature, which Smith called the wisdom of God. (Fitzgibbons 1995: 29–30)

Smith's system is manifestly teleological; that is to say, purposeful and designed, yet order is secured by profane means at the human, biogenic level. The distinction between human and divine agency is consistently emphasised. On the one hand, there are our basic urges and, on the other, their tendency to produce 'beneficent ends which the great Director of nature intended to produce by them'. Nature has always 'endowed mankind with an appetite for the end which she proposes but likewise with an appetite for the means by which alone this end can be brought about, for their own sakes and independent of their tendency to produce it' (*TMS*, II.i.5.10: 77–78).

Our powerful drives are conceived, not as evolutionary adaptations to external exigencies, but as purposive, contrived, designed and teleological. There is no sense of open-ended adaptation or evolution. For example, Nature 'formed man for society' and therefore equipped 'him' with the instincts that make social life possible (*TMS*, II.i.5.10: 77; *TMS*, II.3.1: 85; *TMS*, III.2.6: 116; *Essays*: 136); humans were destined for progress therefore they are endowed with progressive drives (*WN*, II.iii.31: 343); humans are destined to command their physical world, hence 'the benevolent purpose of nature in bestowing upon us the sense of seeing' (*Essays*: 156); to improve and develop the physical environment by cultivating the ground 'was the original destination of man' (*WN*, III.i.3: 378); to ensure that the species perpetuates itself the Creator has endowed humans not only with a powerful sex instinct but with a second irresistible urge to care more tenderly for the young than the old. It is willed that 'parental tenderness' is always stronger than 'filial piety' because the 'continuance and propagation of the species depend altogether upon the former and not upon the latter' (*TMS*, III.3.13: 142; see also *TMS*, VI.ii.1.1: 219); the natural school for the moral sentiments is the nuclear family, hence nature has ensured that the 'affection of the sexes ... is constant and does not cease' (*LJ[A]*, iii, 4–5: 142). Even the urge for a positive system of justice is biogenic: humans are endowed with dispositions expressly designed to 'enforce the observation of justice', namely, 'resentment' of 'the mischief which is attempted to be done to us, and to retaliate that which is already done' (*TMS*, II.ii.3.4: 86).

Self-Interest

The most important and consequential set of drives for Smith are of the self-regarding variety. Smith endorses the Stoic idea that self-preservation is the first task ascribed to us by nature (*TMS*, VII.ii.1.15: 272), reflecting God's concern for us and 'His' desire for our physical safety, security, prosperity and perpetuation. Such an important task must be entrusted to our completely reliable 'original and immediate instincts', in other words, the self-regarding passions (*WN*, I.Ii: 26–27; *LJ[B]*, 300–301: 527). Indeed, self-regarding acts are far more likely to protect the interests of others than other-regarding acts: 'By pursuing his own interest [the economic actor] frequently promotes that of the society more effectually than when he really intends to promote it' (*WN*, IV.ii.9: 456). Benevolence is very commendable and may be the 'sole principle of action in the Deity' but it could never be relied upon to secure the welfare of a being so utterly dependent on external supports (*WN*, VII.ii.3.18: 304).

Benevolence, altruism and acts of charity are superfluous in the Smithian universe because of the 'universal benevolence' that inheres in the 'Divine Masterplan'. The apparent coldness and secularity of Smith's portrait of human affairs is really a product of his faith in a divine order that is benign and geared to deliver prosperity and 'happiness' for all. Smith readily admits that this arrangement is apt to 'shock all [our] natural sentiments'; nevertheless, he is keen to reassure his reader that it was 'established for the wisest and best purposes' (*TMS*, III.5.10:168). We ought to put our moralising aside in favour of the observable facts *(LJ[B]*, 300: 527). So, while Smith insists on a benevolent and moral deity, he perceives God's affectionate action in the mundane, bodily and self-regarding dynamics of daily life; in physical and social survival, the perpetuation of the species, the pursuit of pleasure and the avoidance of pain and the pursuit of the 'natural joy of prosperity' (*TMS*, III.3.9: 139).

Smith's Theodicy

The darker and apparently vicious aspects of Smith's explanation of the spontaneous social, moral and economic physics of commercial societies is best appreciated in relation to his adaptation of Stoic theodicy for social-scientific purposes. Theodicy is any attempt to reconcile a belief in an omnipotent, benign God with the apparent evils of life; in other words, it is an attempt to explain the puzzle: if God is good, why evil? A.M.C. Waterman expands:

> Every religion that acknowledges a God who is all-powerful, all-wise, all-knowing, and perfectly good faces the so-called problem of evil. How is the abundant evidence of unwilled suffering in sentient beings (physical evil), and of human wickedness and its consequences (moral evil) to be reconciled with the divine attributes ... Answers that diminish any of the attributes are rejected as heterodox ... An inquiry that seeks to demonstrate the possible co-existence of all the divine attributes is known as *theodicy*. (Waterman 2002: 916)[8]

Like many thinkers of his time, Smith accepted that the world is the product of design and the observable order of regularity in human affairs is a direct result of this design and benign purpose in nature. Smith discovers in our base tendencies a positive latent function. The imperfections of the created universe, even its seemingly destructive and maladaptive aspects, are accommodated within such a framework. Since everything exists for a reason, nothing in the universe is truly evil since all of creation performs some positive role in the Divine scheme. Marcus Aurelius, one of the earliest promulgators of theodicy, and whose thought was familiar to Smith, allowed for a universe simultaneously 'perfect' yet sometimes 'harsh' and 'unpalatable' (Marcus 1964, V.7: 80–81). He wrote that even 'roguery' and 'impudence' are 'necessary to the world' (Marcus 1964, IX.42: 148),[9] just as 'sickness, death, slander, intrigue, and all the other things that delight or trouble foolish men ... are normal' (Marcus 1964, 4.44: 73). Although Smith denies that *all* vices are useful (*TMS*, I.ii.3.4–5: 36–37), he, nevertheless, endorses the general Stoic view that since

> the world was governed by the all-ruling providence of a wise, powerful and good God, every single event ought to be regarded as making a necessary part of the plan of the universe ... that the vices and follies of mankind, therefore, made as necessary a part of this plan as their wisdom or their virtue; and by that eternal art which educes good from ill, were made to tend equally to the prosperity and perfection of the great system of nature. (*TMS*, I.ii.3.4: 36; *TMS*, II.3.3: 105–106)

An intriguing example of apparent vices working to produce benign effects is found in Smith's discussion of our love of social recognition and 'natural' esteem of trinkets, which he portrays as a deliberate 'deception' engineered by God in order to secure 'human progress' and keep 'in continual motion the industry of mankind' (*TMS*, V.i.7–10: 181–83). This example bears closer examination because the theological logic it reflects confirms the Providentialism of Smith's system.

Theodicy, Recognition and Designed Defects

Smith starts by informing his reader that it is not basic material needs that lead people to create a distinctively human existence, because the needs of subsistence are relatively few and easily satisfied (*TMS*, I.iii.2.2: 50). The rich and the poor are subject to the same physical limitations, so in terms of basic requirements there can be little difference between them (*TMS*, IV.i.10, 184–85; *WN*, I.xi.c.7: 180). Nor are we led to pursue wealth and social distinction from the utility to be derived from them. What really induces individuals to labour beyond the satisfaction of basic needs originates in a uniquely human preoccupation with aesthetics, conspicuous consumption and vainglory. 'The pleasures of wealth and greatness', says Smith, 'strike the imagination as something grand and beautiful and noble, of which the attainment is well worth all the toil and anxiety which we are so apt to bestow upon it' (*TMS*, IV.i.8: 182–83; see also *LJ[A]*: 334–35). The desire 'to be observed, to be attended to, to be taken notice of with sympathy, complacency, and approbation and to emulate the rich … first prompted [mankind] to cultivate the ground, to build houses, to found cities and commonwealths, and to invent and improve all the sciences and arts, which ennoble and embellish life' (*TMS*, I.iii.2.2: 50; *TMS*, IV.i.10: 183). Translated to the economic sphere, these factors give rise to the unremitting 'desire of bettering our condition', which 'comes with us from the womb, and never leaves us until we go into the grave' (*WN*, II.iii.28: 341).

Our entirely natural urge to lord it over our neighbours is satisfied via the accumulation and consumption of material goods, a process that is the very engine of progress in the human condition and which is partly responsible for the transition from one historical period to the next. Significantly, Smith states that any thoughtful person will apprehend that, in reality, the objects of material ambition are 'in the highest degree contemptible and trifling'. In fact, our 'natural' esteem of trinkets, baubles and 'frivolous objects' is a deliberate 'deception' engineered by God in Nature. Yet, it is just 'as well', Smith suggests, 'that nature imposes upon us in this manner' because 'it is this deception which rouses and keeps in continual motion the industry of mankind' (*TMS*, V.i.7–10: 181–83). Without this Providential sleight of hand, our species would never have advanced beyond the age of hunters, when a basic subsistence was readily obtained. In other words, it is not adaptive necessity that has brought progress, but the providentially implanted desire to better one's condition and acquire fundamentally useless consumer goods. Rather than being dismayed at this shocking piece of trickery, Smith tells us that we ought to 'admire the wisdom of God even in the weakness and folly of man' (*TMS*, ii.II.Iii.3.2: 105–106).[10] Smith's pragmatic and realist observations are deceptive; they do not denote a profane outlook but rather a sincere commitment to Deistic theodicy. Smith routinely depicts human defects, morally suspect urges and even erstwhile vices in explicitly teleological terms as ***deliberately endued*** by the Creator for the express purpose of securing the latter's ends for us, namely, our happiness, prosperity and perpetuation.

Smith's theodicean Providentialism is key to understanding a number of tensions in his work; between, on the one hand, his evident belief in a dependable system of natural liberty that ultimately delivers good effects, and, on the other, the market failures, knavish acts and other maladaptive phenomena that accompany progress and to which he routinely draws attention. I say more about these in other chapters but for the moment my point is that Smith never insisted upon a perfect world, in which nothing went wrong, where disruptive behaviour never occurred, where markets never failed and where externalities were non-existent. However, he showed a general faith that the system would find ways of correcting itself.

The Self-Correcting Universe

Free will, human error, accident and chance are all acknowledged as factors in Smith's historiography. The laws of nature, though broadly ineluctable, are, nevertheless, moderated by the actions of individuals, especially powerful ones. Accident frequently plays a role in changing human history[11] and humans *do* exercise free will within the broad scheme of history, hence Smith's constant injunctions to act wisely and specifically to exercise the virtue of 'self-command'. Our innate or 'original' drives are often corrupted by 'levity and inconstancy', 'folly and injustice', 'sloth and intemperance', 'gross ignorance and stupidity' and even cowardice (Waterman 2002: 911). Clearly, humans are the *bearers* of history and legislators will always be required to act either to correct or to restrain vices, address externalities or solve problems of collective action that arise as the by-product of economic growth. Smith could not have believed otherwise for this is the whole point of the *Wealth of Nations* which, in effect, is a kind of handbook on the effects of both good and bad policy. Governments must act but it must be judicious activity and the art of good government should be the object of assiduous study (with Smith himself as instructor) (*TMS*, IV.i.11: 186), informed by an awareness of the laws of spontaneous order.

Human progress is teleological in the sense that the plan for the species' history is roughly determined at the point of creation and fulfilled through human effort. Human beings are the principal bearers of history; they exercise considerable independence, yet they are also engaged in fulfilling the Creator's telic blueprint. It thus differs from the doctrine of teleology expounded by Gottfried Leibnitz, where individuals merely realise a minutely determined programme of development without exercising creativity or volition. Smith is no hard determinist; he takes on board the Christian doctrine of free will (*TMS*, VII.ii.1.44: 292) and fuses it with the modern idea of asymptotic progress. Human development is an infinite upward spiral with its broad outlines planned stadially but with its precise content contingent on human input (and error) and particular climatic and geographical conditions. For example, although most societies will progress through the four stages (hunting, pasturage, agriculture and commerce), some societies never reach the fourth stage because of impediments like 'natural scarcity arising from soil and climate' (*WN*, IV.ii.35: 466) or where the local 'laws and institutions' are too prohibitive (*WN*, I.ix.15: 111–12).

Things are bound to go wrong and off-course sometimes but Smith believes that, at a more fundamental level, and for the most part, the human universe is an organic, self-righting unit able to restore to itself its own 'health and vigour' (*WN*, II.iii.31: 343). Within Smith's historiography, the forces of history are so potent that this will happen even under Mercantilist policies and the myriad 'absurd regulations of commerce' imposed by ignorant or corrupt legislators (*WN*, IV.v.b.43: 540; *WN*, II.iii.36: 345; *WN*, IV.ix.28: 674). Because of their transcendent and eternal nature, natural laws tend to be more resilient than the forces that subvert them. For example, although 'the actions of government' have 'retarded the natural progress of England towards wealth and improvement ... [they have] not been able to stop it' (*WN*, II.iii.36: 345). That Smith is no hard determinist or absolute perfectionist is underlined by his rebuke of Francois Quesnay for his unrealistic expectations about what conditions need to hold before prosperity is possible. According to Smith, Quesnay wrongly imagined that economies 'would thrive and prosper only under a certain precise regimen ... of perfect liberty and perfect justice.' Quesnay's error consists in underestimating the potency of innate drives and overestimating the capacity of legislators to subvert them:

> He seems not to have considered that in the political body, the natural effort which every man is continually making to better his own condition is a principle of preservation capable of preventing and correcting in many respects, the bad effects of a political economy, in some degree, both partial and oppressive. Such a political economy, though it no doubt retards more or less, is not always capable of stopping altogether the natural progress of a nation towards wealth and prosperity, and still less of making it go backward. If a nation could not prosper without the enjoyment of perfect liberty and perfect justice, there is not in the world a nation which could ever have prospered. (*WN*, IV.ix.28: 674; emphasis added)

In the 'political body' 'the wisdom of nature has made ample provision for remedying many of the bad effects of the folly and injustice of man; in the same manner as it has done in the natural body, for remedying those of his sloth and intemperance' (*WN*, IV.ix.28: 674; see also *WN*, IV.v.b.43: 540; *WN*, II.iii.36: 345).

Smith refers to 'the natural progress of things towards improvement' despite individual errors, or perverse policy and institutions. Corrupt and maladaptive institutions like the Catholic 'superstition' (long an impediment to progress) are gradually destroyed 'by the natural course of things' (*WN*, V.i.g.24: 802–803). The 'opulence' of nations is preserved by the 'uniform, constant and uninterrupted effort of every man to better his condition', a drive so 'powerful that it resembles "the unknown principle of animal life, [which] frequently restores health and vigour to the constitution in spite, not only of the disease, but of the absurd prescription of the doctor"' (*WN*, II.iii.31: 343). The whole universe is an integrated, self-righting unit that can therefore readily accommodate error and setbacks.

Government Restraint

Within Smith's irrationalist scheme legislators ought to eschew social engineering and large-scale planning. Smith derided 'systems' and the utopian schemes of the legislator who 'fancies himself the only wise and worthy man in the Commonwealth'. Why should 'his fellow citizens … accommodate [themselves] to him and not he to they'? (*TMS*, VI.ii.2.17: 233–34). Using the analogy of a chess game, Smith rebukes the 'conceit' of any legislator who 'imagine[s] that he can arrange the different pieces' without appreciating that 'in the great chess board of human society, every single piece has a principle of motion of its own altogether different from that which the legislature might chuse to impress upon it' (*TMS*, VI.ii.2.17: 233–34; *TMS*, VII.ii.1.46: 292). Any 'statesman' who presumes to 'direct private people in what manner they ought to employ' their resources and efforts 'would not only load himself with a most unnecessary attention, but assume an authority which could safely be trusted, not only to no single person, but to no council or senate whatever'; indeed, the more fit a statesman fancies himself to direct market actors, the more likely it is that 'he' will be 'dangerous … to the general welfare' (*WN*, IV.ii.10: 456). Everyone, 'so long as he does not violate the laws of justice', should be 'left perfectly free to pursue his own interest in his own way'. The 'sovereign is completely discharged from a duty' of which only the dangerously deluded would consider 'himself' under obligation to perform, namely, 'of superintending the industry of private people and of directing it towards the employments most suitable to the interest of society' (*WN*, IV.ix.51: 687).

Objectionable Obstructions

Smith condemned all monolithic, paternalistic and intrusive forms of governance, including any institutional and legal impediments to the free play of the market and the development of independent moral character. Such impediments included monopolies, poor laws, corporation laws, patronage and nepotism, apprenticeship laws and laws regulating the institutions of entail and primogeniture. These restrictions obstructed individual effort and threatened the prosperity and security of entire nations; they should, therefore, be eliminated or curtailed wherever possible.

With regard to primogeniture, Smith asserted that 'nothing can be more contrary to the real interest of a numerous family, than a right which, in order to enrich one, beggars all the rest of the children' (*WN*, III.ii.4: 384). Meanwhile, the related law of entail is 'founded upon the most absurd of all suppositions', namely 'that every successive generation of men have not an equal right to the earth, and to all that it possesses' (*WN*, III.ii.6: 384). Although they might have made sense in previous stages of history, 'in the present state of Europe' laws of entail are 'contrary to nature, to reason, and to justice' (*LJ[A]*, 115–16: 49). Apart from equity considerations, this system is inefficient due to its tendency to hinder agriculture and development (*WN*, III.ii.7: 385; see also *WN*, III.iv.19: 423); in fact, the comparatively rapid development of parts of America is largely attributable to the absence of such restrictive laws (*WN*, IV.vii.b.19: 572). In a comparable vein Smith attacked the practice of slavery, partly because of its cruelty (*TMS*, V.2.9: 206–207), but equally because it is a gross violation of a person's natural rights and a breach of the laws of natural liberty (*WN*, III.ii.9: 387–88; *WN*, I.viii.41: 98–99; *WN*, IV.ix.47: 684; *LJ[A]*, iii.111–12: 185; *LJ[B]*, 138–40: 453–54; 290: 532; 299: 526). This is demonstrated by its inefficient and maladaptive aspects; slavery is both an impediment to innovation (*WN*, IV.ix.47: 684) and an inhibitor of population growth (*LJ[A]*, iii.131: 192–93), both of which occur naturally in a healthy economy (see also Chap. 7).

Smith thought that the system of natural liberty could only work properly when it was operated and constituted by the right kind of people with the right kind of characters and dispositions: independent, just, self-regarding and ambitious. He valued independence in particular, believing that dependency was both a personal failing and a key corruptor of moral character (see Chap. 4). Ideally, agents will be permitted the free-est possible use of their bodies, minds and properties provided that there are no violations of the system of natural liberty.[12] From Smith's point of view, England's poor laws (and to a lesser degree its corporation laws) were the most pernicious constraint on such freedoms and were detrimental to both individual and public welfare. Poor laws were more destructive than corporation laws because they disproportionately disadvantaged the poor (*WN*, I.x.c.44–45: 152). Similarly, the laws of apprenticeship are egregious not only because they are an impediment to the mobility of labour but also because of their tendency to discourage industry and commercial effort.[13] The 1662 laws of settlement—which enabled parish officials to forcibly remove from the parish any stranger who might be in need of poor relief—are a similar and therefore unjust restriction on mobility (*WN*, I.x.c.58–59: 156–57). The power to 'remove a man who has committed no misdemeanour from the parish where he chuses to reside' and seek work where his labour is likely needed 'is an evident violation of natural liberty and justice'. Smith surmises that '[t]here is scarce a poor man in England of forty years of age … who has not … felt himself most cruelly oppressed by this ill-contrived' and 'abusive' law (*WN*, I.x.c. 59: 157). I say more about Smith's attitude towards these types of state-imposed impediments in Chap. 5.

The Enemy Within

Not only should the state take care to avoid inhibiting the freedom and mobility of agents, so too should private actors. The average actor—whether magnate or poor labourer—should mind 'his' own business, responding only to immediate drives and personal interests. In fact, meddling in other people's welfare and fretting over the 'general good' will produce more harm than good. Smith reminds his reader: 'To man is allotted a much humbler department, but one much more suited to the weakness of his powers and narrowness of his comprehension: the care of his own happiness' (*TMS*, VI.ii.3.6: 237). We should imitate the example of the Stoics who taught 'to interest ourselves earnestly and anxiously in no events, external to the good order of our own minds, to the propriety of our own choosing and rejecting', leaving the rest to the 'great

Superintendent of the universe' (*TMS*, VII.ii.1.46: 292). As Smith reasons, Nature would never leave her 'darling care'—the welfare of human beings—to so flimsy and fallible a faculty as 'the slow and uncertain determinations of our reason' (*TMS*, II.i.5.10: 77; see also *TMS*, VII.ii.1: 44–46).

Although Smith is normally conceived as a thinker suspicious of state interferences alone, in fact he was equally critical of the way in which private interests could interfere with the natural operations of the market. He cautioned against 'the spirit of monopoly', berating the 'mean rapacity' and 'monopolizing spirit of merchants and manufacturers' (*WN*, IV.Iii.c.9: 493). The undue influence of mercantile interests is an enduring and ubiquitous theme throughout Smith's body of work: he adverted to the 'clamorous importunity of partial interests' that prevented the legislature from acting always and only with 'an extensive view of the general good' (*WN*, IV.ii.44: 472) noting that the strength of monopolists had become so great that they had 'become formidable to the government, and upon many occasions intimidate the legislature' (*WN*, IV.ii.43: 471). 'Masters' often collude to keep wages low and do so with legal impunity but when workers push for better wages and conditions they are severely punished (*WN*, I.x.c:61: 158).

The Wage Debate

Smith's objections to collusion between 'masters' and the state to keep wages low should be appreciated against the backdrop of contemporary debates on the topic. Until the mid-eighteenth century, the natural indolence and limited aspirations of the working class were taken for granted. As a result, the 'utility-of-poverty' doctrine dominated economic thinking and 'negative incentives to work' were widely advocated (Marshall 2000; Hundert 1974: 140) both in England and abroad. In France, for example, Cardinal de Richelieu likened the working poor to 'mules' who are accustomed to bearing heavy loads and therefore likely to be spoiled by too much leisure (cited in Rimlinger 1976: 341). As late as 1771, the English thinker Arthur Young averred that '[e]veryone but an idiot knows that the lower classes must be kept poor or they will never be industrious' (Furniss 1920: 118). This doctrine was a standard trope among Mercantilists like William Petty and Josiah Tucker, both of whom believed that high wages meant low production (Brentano 1894: 2–3).

David Hume was the first to contradict this view, disputing that high or even reasonable wages affected the work motivation of labourers. Related to this attack was Hume's scepticism—shared by Smith—that workers would be corrupted and made indolent by their ability to afford luxury goods (Hume 1987: 262). He argued that, contrary to the prevailing view, luxury consumption stimulated both 'the industry of the common people' (*WN*, I.viii.44: 99) and the labour supply (Hume 1987: 272; see also Hume 1987: 256–57). Persuaded by this argument, Smith became the most influential high wages advocate of his time (Marshall 2000: 636). He wrote that 'when wages are high … we shall always find the working-men more active, diligent and expeditious, than when they are low' (*WN*, I.viii.44: 99); further, it is 'not very probable … that men in general should work better when they are ill fed than when they are well fed, when they are disheartened than when they are in good spirits, when they are frequently sick than when they are in good health' (*WN*, I.viii.45: 100–101; Stabile 1997). The 'liberal reward of labour' is a good thing because 'it is the cause of increasing population' (*WN*, I.viii.36: 96), thereby ensuring the supply of labour so vital for an expanding economy.

To those who would complain of the 'high price of labour' Smith retorts that it is nothing to complain of at all since it is encouraging 'proof of the general opulence of society … to be regarded as what constitutes the essence of public opulence, or as the very thing in which public opulence properly consists'. A state is truly opulent when 'opulence is easily come at, or in which a little labour, properly and judiciously employed, is capable of procuring any man a great abundance of all the necessaries and conveniences of life' (early draft of *WN*; *LJ[B]*: 567).

Furthermore, low wages lead to crime and other social disorders. If wages fall below the community standard of decency then there is little incentive for people to work and they will 'be driven to seek a subsistence either by begging' or by criminal means. But under a fair wage system, for most people, a life of crime will be irrational: 'No body', Smith wrote, 'will be so mad as to expose himself upon the highway, when he can make better bread in an honest and industrious manner' (*LJ[A]*, 205: 486–87). Apart from these utility considerations, Smith uncharacteristically tacks on an 'equity' argument for good measure: surely 'they who feed, clothe, and lodge the whole body of the people' are entitled to 'a share of the produce of their own labour as to be themselves tolerably well fed, clothed, and lodged' (*WN*, I.viii.36: 96)

Apart from these equity, utility and public order considerations, the utility-of-poverty doctrine also involved a noxious violation of the system of natural liberty in which Smith posited the existence of a 'natural wage'. He defined the natural wage as a subsistence wage for both the worker and 'his family' in order to ensure that 'the race of … workmen … last[ed] beyond the first generation' (*WN*, I.viii.15: 76). Smith never really explains what he means by 'subsistence' but he does mention that 'necessaries' denote 'not only the commodities which are indispensably necessary for the support of life' but also whatever is necessary to maintain the appearance of 'decency' (*WN*, V.ii.k.3: 869–70; Stabile 1997). In saying this he is recognising that not only is social survival a basic human need on a par with bodily survival, but that this former need could be used to invigorate the economy.[14]

Our drive for recognition when harnessed to a fair wage system and reward for effort thus has enormous productive and creative power; it 'rouses and keeps in continual motion the industry of mankind' and is the source of almost all progress, civilisation and material and cultural accomplishments (*TMS*, IV.i1.10: 183–84). Therefore, the utility-of-poverty doctrine contradicts the system of natural liberty while efforts to artificially depress wages are nothing more than a corruption engineered by a conspiracy of 'masters' aided by legislators. Hence Smith feels confident in concluding that whenever a 'regulation is in favour of workmen, it is always "just and equitable" whereas the reverse is often the case when the law decides in favour of "masters"' (*WN*, I.x.c.61: 157–58).

It is noteworthy that Smith never suggests that the state should intervene to aid workers in this power asymmetry with 'masters'. As Martin has suggested, 'he would simply like to see them treated as legal equals to employers' (Martin 2011: 118). There was no need for the state to interfere because the natural laws of competition, he predicts optimistically, would manage things perfectly well if allowed: 'Experience seems to show that law can never regulate [wages] properly, though it has often pretended to do so' (*WN*, I.viii.34: 95). Smith is confident that wages will rise with demand for when 'the demand for those who live by wages; labourers, journeymen, servants of every kind, is continually increasing … the workmen have no occasion to combine in order to raise their wages' (*WN*, I.viii.17: 86). He also seems confident that the demand will be there once the economy starts to work properly and exponential growth becomes a reality.[15] In addition, fixing the rate of work legally and in a centralised manner would have a deadening effect on commercial effort and innovation. Smith quotes and endorses the opinion of 'Dr Burn', author of *History of the Poor Laws* (1764), that

> the experience of above four hundred years ... seems to lay aside all endeavours to bring under strict regulation, what in its own nature seems incapable of minute limitation: for if all persons in the same kind of work were to receive equal wages, there would be no emulation, and no room left for industry or ingenuity. (*WN*, I.x.c.60: 157)

Therefore, although it is true that Smith was suspicious of 'the political power of merchants and the rich, in the economy of an enlightened and virtuous society' where the market was given breathing space to self-equilibrate and expand, he saw the possibility of a 'tolerable harmony of interests between those who live by wages and the owners of inanimate capital' (Martin 2011: 120). But that could not happen under arrangements as they stood. Smith persistently drew attention to the fact that commercial interests missed no opportunity to pervert the natural workings of the market. Even when '[p]eople of the same trade ... meet together' for the sole purpose of 'merriment and diversion ... the conversation' inevitably 'ends in a conspiracy against the public, or in some contrivance to raise prices' (*WN*, I.x.c.27: 145). Yet, it was obvious that 'competition' tends to 'regulate [prices] much better than any assize' (*WN*, I.x.c.61: 158). Similarly, the entire system of global trade was a kind of sinister conspiracy against the public. Mercantile groups drove British colonial policy at the expense of the interests of both 'the colonies' and 'the mother country' (*WN*, vii.b.49: 584) and their interests were almost always 'opposite to, that of the public' *(WN*, I.xi: 267). I say more about this in Chap. 6.

One of the worst things about Mercantilism lay in the fact that it enabled merchants to better their condition in a manner that did not contribute to the nation's economic welfare and this is not how an economic system is supposed to work according to Smith. Rather, personal interest—when pursued in the proper manner—naturally tended to benefit the society at large. Smith complained that the 'interest of our manufacturers has been most peculiarly attended to [by government]; and the interest ... of the consumers ... has been sacrificed to it' (*WN*, IV.viii.54: 661–62). He particularly objected to the dispensation of monopoly grants and the extension of 'extraordinary privileges' to favoured interests. The East India Company with its powerful, state-protected monopoly of British/Asian commerce was a prime target for Smith, as it was for Edmund Burke and Daniel Defoe (see, for example, *WN*, IV.vii.c.91: 631; *WN*, IV.vii.c.107: 641). I say more on this topic in Chap. 6.

The System of Natural Liberty, Religion and the Established Church

Smith saw markets everywhere and believed competition could and should be setting standards and delivering optimal outcomes in almost every aspect of life. Religion was no exception and Smith was extremely critical of state-sanctioned religious monopolies and saw them as a form of corruption. He disliked the manner in which the civil and religious realms had historically related to each other and he railed against the unseparated state on numerous occasions. No religion, Catholic, Protestant or otherwise, should enjoy the kind of state-protected monopoly that not only enabled it to wield noxious levels of power but also constituted a violation of the laws of natural liberty. One of the worst effects of this relationship was that 'positive law always has been, and probably always will be … influenced by popular superstition and enthusiasm' (*WN*, V.i.g.8: 793).

Established churches are also a perpetual threat to the civil authorities and the general health of the polity. Smith wrote, for example, that 'the Church of Rome' represented 'the most formidable combination that ever was formed against the authority and security of civil government, as well as against the liberty, reason, and happiness of mankind' (*WN*, V.i.g.24: 802–803). Further, political and religious zealotry are mutually exacerbating: '[t]imes of violent religious controversy have generally been times of equally violent political faction' (*WN*, V.i.g.6: 791). Throughout his body of work Smith criticises the 'great incorporation' of the established church and seeks to promote 'science [as] the great antidote to the poison of enthusiasm and superstition' (*WN*, V.i.g.14: 796). Where religion was unavoidable, he sought to 'correct whatever was unsocial and disagreeably rigorous' among its adherents (*WN*, V.i.g.12–14: 796). Indeed, some of Smith's French readers interpreted his work 'as a protracted attack on religious prejudice' (Rothschild 1992: 91).

It is evident throughout Smith's corpus that he hankered for a quieter, tamer world, free from sectarian violence and bloody, seemingly endless war. One precondition for this imagined state was radical reform in the status of established religions. This required, first, that religion be decoupled from government and politics and, second, that it be tamed by the forces of competition. Smith's ideal was not to eradicate organised religion because he could see it met a need in people and also that it could play some role in social stability. But it could only be tolerable under conditions conducive to a free market of religious practise characterised by a multitude of sects competing for members. Such sects would even be useful for maintaining public order in being 'productive of ... philosophical good temper and moderation' (*WN*, V.i.g.8: 792) and ameliorating the isolating and demoralising effects of mass commercial life.[16]

For Smith, the only acceptable religions were those that had been subjected to the trials and rigours of the market. He offers a thought experiment in disestablishment in which he imagines a society divided into hundreds, even 'thousand[s]' of small sects. Competition between this diversity of independent denominations would not only prevent any single one of them from becoming a threat to 'the publick tranquillity' but it would also generate the kind of religious freedom Smith valued; by this Smith meant that now every individual could 'chuse his own priest and his own religion as he thought proper' (*WN*, V.i.g.8: 792).

Under 'natural liberty' or free market conditions, where the intolerant, exclusivistic, monopolistic, institutionalised and obligatory features of religion have been eradicated and 'the natural principles of religion' allowed to hold sway, religion might actually exert positive effects. Where a plurality of sects operated in open competition a culture of tolerance and mutual respect would likely develop and eventually 'the doctrine of the greater part of [the sects would be reduced] to that pure and rational religion, free from every mixture of absurdity, imposture, or fanaticism, such as wise men have in all ages of the world wished to see established' (*WN*, V.i.g.8: 792–93; Levy 1978: 674). However, Smith also thought that even such relatively powerless sects could still be problematic if not checked; therefore, in order to offset their 'disagreeably rigorous and unsocial' tendencies and to prevent them from promulgating 'that melancholy and gloomy humor which is almost always the nurse of popular superstition and enthusiasm', he recommended the state subsidisation of 'public diversions', among them 'painting, poetry, musick, dancing ... [and] all sorts of dramatic representations and exhibitions' (*WN*, V.i.g.12.15: 796).

Therefore, Smith's real concern is not so much about the dangers of organised religion per se but with unseparated, monolithic, monopolising churches that promoted particularistic fanaticism, bigotry and unreason (*WN*, V.i.g.24: 802–803). This attitude meshes with his general ***desiderata*** for the modern world which, ideally, would be governed by increasingly neutral, impartial and predictable positive laws and populated by agents of moderate, tolerant, dispassionate, reasonable and orderly moral disposition. Such agents because largely self-governing, self-regarding and quiescent—would consequently enjoy a vastly expanded realm of privacy.

Priority of Natural Over Positive Laws

Smith seems to have had such a deep faith in the system of natural liberty that he tolerated illegal and seemingly immoral practices like smuggling and the selling of 'dirty degrees' on the grounds that they were merely rational reactions to an obstructive state. His permissive attitude here may have been related to the fact that he had direct experience of the effects and causes of both practices. He was a university professor for much of his career and was also involved in government efforts to manage smuggling. For example, in 1783 a House of Commons Committee set up to deal with the smuggling problem invited Smith to share his views on the subject and there is some evidence that Pitt's Commutation Act of 1784 took heed of Smith's principles (Ross 1995: 324). Smith also had experience of the problem first-hand when in 1778 he was appointed a Customs Commissioner for Scotland.[17]

Smuggling and Liberty

Smith was a well-known critic of high importation duties, not only because they drove up the prices of commodities but also because they encouraged smuggling. This in turn caused the 'ruin' of those who had attempted 'unsuccessfully to evade the tax', which, in turn, 'put an end to the benefit which the community might have received from the employment of their capitals.' High duties were perverse because they created perverse incentives: the 'law, contrary to all the ordinary principles of justice, first creates the temptation, and then punishes those who yield to it' (*WN*, V.ii.b.6: 826–27). Smith argued that 'that if it were possible to defray the expences of government by any other method, all duties, customs, and excise should be abolished' (*LJ[B]*, 269: 514).

Smith does concede that the smuggler is, in one respect, 'highly blameable' for 'violating the laws of his country'; nevertheless, such a person has in no way violated the more sacred laws 'of natural justice' and is probably an otherwise 'excellent citizen, had not the laws of his country made that a crime which *nature* never meant to be so'. In 'corrupted' governments where heavy taxes, debt, profligacy and waste are the norm it is not surprising that 'the laws which guard it are little respected' (*WN*, V.ii.k.64: 898; emphasis added).[18]

Dirty Degrees and Liberty

Smith's attitude to the 'dirty practice' of degree-selling also bears notice here. Rather than condemning it outright, as might be expected, he complacently notes that the poorer universities understandably engage in the practice in order to 'turn the penny' in a market improperly—and therefore *unnaturally*—oligopolised by the richer institutions (i.e. Oxford and Cambridge) (*Corr.*: 174–78). Ian Ross reports that 'St Andrews University put itself in this position by conferring an MD on one Green, who happened to be a "stage-doctor", that is, a quack who practiced medicine on a platform' (Ross 1995: 260).

Although Smith seems sincere in admitting that selling degrees is a 'most disgraceful trade', he, nevertheless, denies that it is in any way 'hurtful to the public' because the 'intolerable nuisance' of exclusive privilege is even more destructive due to its unerring tendency to raise the costs of services to consumers (Letter 143 to William Cullen, 20 September 1774, *Corr.*: 174–78). From a moral point of view Smith undoubtedly felt justified in taking this position on the belief that the laws of natural liberty easily trump those positive laws of frail and imperfectly informed mortals.[19]

The take-home message from these two examples is that Smith's faith in liberty seems to run very deep, so much so that he tolerates certain illegal and apparently corrupt practices. But the story for Smith is much more complicated than this: markets and the system of natural liberty in general are much more fallible than might be imagined; further, a certain degree of state intervention was both necessary and perfectly natural.

The Proper State

Smith's discussion of the proper sphere of state action constitutes—more or less—the classic liberal statement of the night-watchman state. Due to market failures—the existence of which are at first sight hard to fathom given Smith's evident faith in a designing if somewhat distant Creator—and the existence of a number of collective action problems (the causes of which Smith never addresses), he outlines 'three proper duties of government' which, although of 'great importance … are plain and intelligible to common understanding'. These are, first, to protect society from the invasion of other societies (defence); second, to establish and administer a system of justice; and, third, to provide essential public works and infrastructure (*WN*, IV.ix.51: 687–88). However, government does much more than just this, as will be shown in subsequent chapters. Although it is somewhat minimal, it is by no means a weak state. Smith's ideal is a strong, consistent and just state whose first instinct is to forebear but is, nevertheless, ready to interfere when needed. But for the moment I wish to focus on how Smith's attitude to the state was far more flexible than is often allowed.

Standing Armies, Security and Liberty

Smith makes clear that the only plausible solution to the problem of external security comes from the interfering and rationalistic 'wisdom of the state'. That solution is the establishment of specialised standing armies, a controversial position in Smith's time (Sher 1989). Even though he sees increasing specialisation as a spontaneous process, there is one profession in which it cannot occur to the required degree of perfection without some state assistance:

> [I]in order to carry [the art of war] to this degree of perfection, it is necessary that it should become the sole or principal occupation of a particular class of citizens, and the division of labour is as necessary for the improvement of this, as of every other art. Into other arts the division of labour is naturally introduced by the prudence of individuals, who find that they promote their private interest better by confining themselves to a particular trade, than by exercising a great number … A private citizen who, in time of profound peace, and without any particular encouragement from the publick, should spend the greater part of his time in military exercises, might, no doubt, both improve himself very much in them, and amuse himself very well; but he certainly would not promote his own interest. *It is the wisdom of the state only which can render it for his interest to give up the greater part of his time to this peculiar occupation.* (*WN*, V.i.a: 697; emphasis added)

Smith justifies this kind of intervention by appealing to a value he holds dear: liberty. Paradoxically, without some degree of state interference in the realm of 'natural liberty', liberty itself could not be enjoyed and economic activity would be pointless, even impossible. Only when '[t]he natural effort of every individual to better his own condition' is protected and secure will the society be prosperous and flourishing (*WN*, IV.v.b.43: 540).

The natural passions of acquisitiveness and invidious comparison, coupled with the economic success of societies based on highly differentiated labour markets, render the establishment of a professionalised system of national defence against foreign enemies both natural and inevitable. Commercial progress produces a worrying externality that the state must address: increasing specialisation enriches the nation but at the same time leads to the neglect of military valour and skill. The monotony of specialised wage labour corrupts the 'courage' of the labourer's mind, rendering 'him' unfit for military service (*WN*, V.i.f.50: 781–82; *WN*, V.i.f 60: 787–88). Such corruptions were unknown to pre-commercial societies of hunters, shepherds and rude 'husbandmen' who could be relied on as courageous warriors (*WN*, V.i.f.51: 783). Further, in the differentiated labour markets of advanced economies it is highly uneconomical for productive workers to leave off work to fight wars. So, the richer the country, the more attractive it is to plunder but that wealth also means that it is more vulnerable to attack because its inhabitants are less able—and willing—to defend it: 'When a civilized nation depends for its defence upon a militia, it is at all times exposed to be conquered by any barbarous nation which happens to be in its neighbourhood' (*WN*, V.i.a.38: 705). Therefore prosperous nations must professionalise defence and transition from the predominant use of ad hoc citizen militias to the establishment of permanent standing armies (*WN*, V.i.a.15: 697–98).

Although Smith identifies security as a collective action problem to be largely solved by the state, he also notes that it is partly solved by the natural progress of technological refinement that accompanies specialisation. The 'invention of fire-arms', which advanced economies pioneered, 'at first sight' might appear to be 'pernicious' but is 'certainly favourable to the permanency and to the extension of civilization' (*WN*, V.i.a–b.44: 708). The security threat posed to commercial states by the potential 'violence and injustice of other independent societies' is, on the one hand, significantly exacerbated by specialisation but it is also, on the other, resolved by specialisation (*WN*, V.i.a.39: 705; *WN*, i.a.40: 706), albeit with some encouragement from the state. Because standing armies afford 'opulent and civilized' nations a considerable military advantage over the 'poor and barbarous' (*WN*, V.ia–b.44: 708), commercial nations ultimately enjoy a superior capacity to urge and protect the expansion of trade, commerce and prosperity; therefore, the interference is, on balance, warranted.

Curiously Smith was a founder member in 1762 of 'The Poker Club', which led the campaign for the establishment of a Scots militia (Sher 1989. 259; see also Ferguson 1816: 10), partly on the grounds that standing armies were a danger to the liberty of the people. Other members included Adam Ferguson, John Home and Alexander Carlyle.[20] It is odd that Smith should be one of the founder members (remaining so until 1774)[21] given his advertised preference for standing armies which, though more expensive to maintain, were more capable and efficient. Perhaps he attended club meetings to follow the debate and to reassure irritated pro-militia enthusiasts like Ferguson[22] that standing armies were no danger to liberty. He certainly made efforts to reassure his readers.

Standing armies in no way infringed on liberty; on the contrary, they significantly enhanced it. The sovereign who enjoys the 'security' of an extensive, professional and well-armed military is unburdened of 'that troublesome jealousy' which causes less secure governors perpetually 'to watch over the minutest actions' and stand poised to 'disturb the peace of every citizen'. Paradoxically, the militarily insecure state is also the oppressive, stifling state:

> Where the security of the magistrate, though supported by the principal people of the country, is endangered by every popular discontent; where a small tumult is capable of bringing about in a few hours a great revolution, the whole authority of government must be employed to suppress and punish every murmur and complaint against it. To the sovereign, on the contrary, who feels himself supported, not only by the natural aristocracy of the country, but by a well-regulated standing army, the rudest, the most groundless, and the most licentious remonstrances can give little disturbance. He can safely pardon or neglect them, and his consciousness of his own superiority naturally disposes him to do so. That degree of liberty which approaches to licentiousness can be tolerated only in countries where the sovereign is secured by a well-regulated standing army. (*WN*, V.i.a.41: 706–707)

Standing armies were to Smith a very effective way of avoiding the evil of investing the 'sovereign' with 'discretionary power' as a means for ensuring the 'publick safety'. He regarded defence as the first duty of the sovereign (*WN*, V.i.a.42: 707) and therefore would not be bound ideologically in his opinions on how this most important duty might be best met. The standing army was not just the best way of adequately defending a commercially advanced 'civilized' country; it was also the only means by which a 'barbarous country can be suddenly and tolerably civilized' (*WN*, V.i.a.40: 706). But most important of all, it was the surest bet for securing liberty of both the positive and negative varieties. Smith gives numerous other examples of collective action problems that can only be dealt with via paternalistic laws and these are enumerated in Chap. 7.

An Imperfect System

Smith does not properly explain why markets—and the other mechanisms of spontaneous order—sometimes fail, nor does he apparently think it necessary to defend the degree of state intervention he advocates beyond its obvious utility. However, these failures and distortions are partly reconcilable in light of Smith's theodicy, coupled with his advertised view that the 'modern' world was such a complicated and unruly system that states often had to interfere in order to manage it (*LJ[B]*, 309–10: 530–31). A further factor is obviously that markets substantially 'result from interactions of highly imperfect human beings' (Mingardi 2018: 451).

At no point does Smith suggest that markets are infallible mechanisms for achieving perfect equilibrium; indeed, he provides numerous examples of market failure[23] and points to serious conflicts between private and public interests (see Viner 1958: 83). Therefore, it is possible that he saw no glaring tension here. Unfettered by the kind of ideological constraints retrospectively imposed on him by those keen to locate him on the left-right spectrum—or else, at the very least, keen to characterise him as an uncompromising free marketeer—he saw himself as simply working out from observation when the system of natural liberty needed some support. I say more about these tensions in subsequent chapters. But for the moment it is enough to point out that he believes the system of natural liberty is both real and achievable under the right conditions; he simply communicated a realist scepticism about the possibility of completely securing these conditions due to the 'prejudices of the publick', 'the private interests' of others (*WN*, IV.ii.43: 471) and the rarity of the kind of wise lawgivers needed to institute and operate his ideal regime (*TMS*, VI.ii.2.16: 233). He was also painfully aware that nothing in the human universe, even a designed one, can ever work perfectly.

Smith seems to have been a firm believer in the muddling-through school of public administration; he saw that there was much work to be done in order to realise his ideal of a system of natural liberty, and he often evinced a profound pessimism about the possibility of it ever being allowed to establish itself. Yet he made it his personal mission to correct these prejudices and to guide legislators towards policies that were compatible with the natural laws already regulating—or attempting to regulate—human affairs. Importantly, he did not see this advice as utopian or interventionist but as conservative, even revisionist; hence his reference to wishing to '*restore*' rather than institute the system of natural liberty. The system of natural liberty already existed in the invisible physics that governed the human universe; it just needed to be recognised and allowed to operate properly (*WN*, IV.ix.51: 687).

The Natural State

Despite the fact that he never explains why collective action problems exist and why markets fail, Smith apparently regards his insistence on the necessity for state action as consistent with the system of spontaneous order and, moreover, a ***designed*** universe. In other words, the organised state, along with its positive laws, is natural insofar as social systems' maladaptivities have a natural tendency to spontaneously generate their own solutions. While such solutions might look like constructivist tinkering, they are not, strictly speaking, or not strictly speaking as far as Smith was concerned, especially when considered in the light of his theodicy.

From Smith's discussion it is clear that the more mass and prosperous (i.e. the more successful and flourishing) the society, the more do problems of collective action arise and the greater is the need to solve them institutionally. This is how Smith explains the emergence of the formal state, which is natural. Its beginnings are not located in imaginary contracts or the meta-schemes of Great Legislators; rather, they are traced to an evolutionistic process. Where people are able to acquire 'valuable and extensive property' the 'establishment of civil government' becomes necessary because 'avarice and ambition in the rich' and 'the hatred of labour and the love of present ease and enjoyment' in the poor inevitably 'prompt [people] to invade property' (*WN*, V.i.b.2: 709). Such a process has been in train for millennia: the 'age of shepherds' where 'inequality of fortune first begins to take place … introduces some degree of that civil government which is indispensably necessary for its own preservation: ***and it seems to do this naturally, and even independent of the consideration of that necessity***' (*WN*, V.i.b.12: 715; emphasis added).

Adam Ferguson made similar arguments about the inception of government when he wrote that '[a]s the commercial arts originate in the necessity of man's animal nature, the arts which may be termed political originate in the wants and defects of instinctive society (Ferguson 1792, I: 256). The state emerges, not from a conscious desire for political order, but to counter the abuses created by the pursuit of private property. Hume also thought that positive justice emerged in order to protect and regulate the use of private property (Hume 2003, III.ii.4: 323) and he agreed with Smith that laws made to protect individual liberties also indirectly encourage commerce and population growth.

The important point here is that Smith sees the state as both necessary and natural because the 'liberty, reason, and happiness of mankind' can 'flourish only where civil [as opposed to ecclesiastical] government is able to protect them' (*WN*, V.i.g.24: 803).[24] Legislation exists to offset the negative spillovers of the self-interested and specialising drives in the context of an expanding and increasingly prosperous economy. But the need for this kind of offsetting is really just tinkering with the big picture and should be viewed as a symptom of a system's success rather than its failure. As Ryan Hanley puts it, 'state action' for Smith 'is at once necessary for and also properly limited to securing the gains of commercial progress and to mitigating its negative externalities' (Hanley 2014: 381).

Smith observes that '[w]herever there is great property, there is great inequality'. For every 'rich man' there are 'at least five hundred poor' who are often 'both driven by want and prompted by envy to invade his possessions'. Invoking the technological argument for the state, he notes that this is really only a problem for advanced and prosperous societies because 'where there is no property, or at least none that exceeds the value of two or three days labour [as in 'nations of hunters'], civil government is not so necessary' (*WN*, V.i.b.2: 709–10). The problems of internal security exacerbated by development-induced scale, wealth concentration and class inequality are resolved spontaneously and endogenously via a parallel evolutionary process: 'Civil government', says Smith, 'supposes a certain subordination' but 'the necessity of civil government gradually grows up with the acquisition of valuable property' (*WN*, V.i.b.3: 710).

Smith understood that the relentless quest for worldly success was a highly competitive business and only beneficial if there existed fair and transparent rules and norms to play by. As far as norms went, the mechanisms of sympathy and the impartial spectator could go some way towards ensuring that market actors played fair and refrained from harm (*TMS*, II.ii.2.1: 83). But these spontaneous mechanisms were not enough and a society left to regulate itself by the moral sentiments alone was untenable, for it would be riven with conflict and mutual injury (*TMS*, II.ii.3.1–3: 85–86). It is therefore a formal system of justice that ultimately makes social life between self-interested competitors possible (*TMS*, III.6.9–10: 174–75). As Smith decreed, 'upon the impartial administration of justice depends the liberty of every individual, the sense which he has of his own security' (*WN*, Vi.I.ii: 722).

Within his system of natural liberty Smith's conception of justice is strictly commutative and not distributive because it precludes any imperfect obligation of benevolence. The state must and should not attempt to enforce any such supposed obligation. It may justifiably use force to prevent the injury of one person by another, but it can hardly attempt to enforce by legal sanctions the exercise of the benevolent virtues. By contrast, justice is precise and its rules are highly impersonal, impartial and predictable: its 'rules ... are accurate in the highest degree, and admit of no exceptions or modifications ... If I owe a man ten pounds, justice requires that I should precisely pay him ten pounds' (*TMS*, III.6.9–10: 174–75).

Conclusion

Although it has been argued here that Smith sees the state as natural and necessary, the natural state is easily corrupted and converted to an unnatural bloated one, out of tune with the rhythms of markets and the naturally self-organising habits of independent commercial actors. I say more about this in Chap. 5. Smith's detailed analysis of the system of natural liberty was his personal contribution to delivering the British people (and anyone else who might be interested) from the consequences of a weak and malfunctioning state still mired in Mercantilist dogma and beholden to powerful sectional interests. He discovers beneath the mess of artificial legal obstructions a natural, invisible but very real system of non-state, voluntaristic, private, non-monolithic and decentralised means for the self-government of people that was capable of delivering prosperity and exponential improvement. Smith's faith in the system of natural liberty ran deep; indeed, it is a function of an apparently sincere belief in a designed universe where human faculty psychology is teleologically conceived and history has a logical trajectory.

Yet Smith also wanted to show exactly how the organised state and a system of positive laws related to spontaneous civil society and getting that relationship right was an abiding concern for him. He believed that if we can understand the natural laws governing the universe we have an objective standard for detecting when the social system should be left alone or adjusted. This usually came in the form of de-regularisation and the expansion of liberties but it could also entail some state intervention to correct any market failures and human error that obstructed liberty. As far as Smith was concerned, this in no way impugned the workmanship of the 'Divine Architect'.

Notes

1. I use Arthur Lovejoy's term here. Lovejoy (1964) wrote that each age is dominated by a set of implicit or explicit assumptions called 'unit ideas'.
2. According to this account, civilisation was transmitted sequentially from nation to nation from its original source in Egypt (Gascoigne 1991). Rousseau held to this view, as did many eighteenth-century Deists (Emerson 1967: 391).
3. For a discussion of the spontaneous emergence of language in Smith's system see Otteson (2002).
4. Whereby my self-regarding, individualised goals—my ends—contribute inadvertently to positive social-systems effects: 'God's' end (Hamowy 1987: 13–22).
5. Significantly, Malthus's views on population were also of a theological bent (Pullen 1981).
6. Any argument or claim that asserts that 'whatever is, is right'; to assume that what occurs routinely or naturally is also good and ought to occur.
7. Jacob Viner also sees Smith's conception of human motive forces as 'partly providentialist and teleological ... deliberately and repetitively' (Viner 1977: 79–82).
8. He adds: 'The term seems to have been coined by Leibniz but within the Judeo-Christian tradition, the enterprise goes back at least to the Book of Job' (Waterman 2002: 916).
9. Adam Ferguson offers a very similar argument that the follies of rogues and knaves provide better incentive to good conduct than the 'mild and shining examples' (Ferguson 1996: 229).
10. This kind of reasoning is not only found in Stoicism but in the teachings of Smith's most influential mentor, Francis Hutcheson. Hutcheson, in his *System of Moral Philosophy*, had attempted to show that 'Divine Providence ... made provision for the happiness of the human race' via 'the various appetites, affections, senses, and powers of human nature' which all 'conspire and work together to promote human happiness. Even the weaknesses of humankind seem to have been designed to permit the cultivation of affections, abilities [and] powers which are indispensable to our greater good and happiness' (Moore 2000: 241).
11. For example, Smith notes that the post-Civil War restoration of the British monarchy was a matter of 'such a concurrence of accidental circumstances as may not ... ever happen again' (*Corr.:* 384). Another example is the development of independent professional courts of law which 'may be looked upon as one of the most happy parts of the British Constitution though introduced merely by chance and to ease the men in power, that the office of judging causes is committed into the hands of a few persons whose sole employment it is to determine them' (*LRB*, ii.203: 176).

12. As James Otteson has noted, for Smith a free 'market is an opportunity for people to buy, sell, trade, or otherwise dispose of their belongings with other people however they see fit' (Otteson 2002: 277).
13. 'During his apprenticeship the young man perceives [correctly] that there is no connection between his effort and his reward [as would exist under piecework], and habits of slothfulness and laziness are therefore encouraged' (Rosenberg 1960: 561; *WN*, I.x.c.14–16: 139–40).
14. For a more complete discussion of this point see Hill (2012).
15. The demand for labour itself comes from 'the increase of the revenue and stock of every country, and cannot possibly increase without it' (*WN*, viii.32.86–87).
16. According to Smith, people who had moved from small towns to large ones soon became 'sunk in obscurity and darkness' with adverse effects to conduct and moral character. Because the new immigrant's 'conduct is observed and attended to by nobody he is ... very likely to neglect it himself, and to abandon himself to every sort of low profligacy and vice'. Ironically, the problem can be overcome when the person concerned joins a 'small religious sect' (*WN*, V.i.g.12: 795–96).
17. Although Smith performed this role with extreme diligence, as Ian Simpson-Ross notes, it was at odds with his political economy (Ross 1995: 318–19). Curiously, although the third edition of the *Wealth of Nations* was published almost seven years after his appointment, this edition contained no additional 'material concerned with customs organization and operation or smuggling' (Anderson et al. 1985: 754).
18. Smith no doubt objected to the fact that 'in defiance of the terms of the Treaty of Union, Parliament proposed in 1712 to levy the Malt Tax on Scotland'. Further, 'Scotland was brought within the system of English excise and customs regulations, which burdened normal trade links with the Continent. Instead of producing higher tax returns this change pushed more people into smuggling activities'. Eventually 'the younger Pitt took Smith's advice about lowering duties to the point at which the dangers and outlays of smuggling were clearly greater than the yields' (Ross 1975: 7).
19. See, for example, *Essays*: 113. For further discussion of this claim see Hill (2001).
20. The latter also produced a widely read pro-militia pamphlet. It was entitled *The Question Relating to a Scots Militia Considered* (1760) and was edited by Ferguson and William Robertson (Sher 1985: 225).
21. Hume was also a member (Winch 1978: 104–106).
22. When he learnt of Smith's views on the topic Ferguson wrote him the following irate letter: 'You have provoked, it is true, the church, the universities, and the merchants, against all of whom I am willing to take your part; but you have likewise provoked the militia, and there I must be against

you. The gentlemen and peasants of this country do not need the authority of philosophers to make them supine and negligent of every resource they might have in themselves' (Adam Ferguson in a letter to Adam Smith, 18 April 1776, number 154, *Corr.*: 193–94). Alexander Carlyle wrote a pamphlet attacking Smith's views. It was entitled: *A Letter to His Grace the Duke off Buccleuch on National Defence with Some Remarks on Dr Smith's Chapter on that Subject in (A?) Book Entitled 'An Inquiry into the Nature and Causes of the Wealth of Nations*' (Winch 1978: 106, n.2).

23. For a discussion of how such failures are reconcilable within Smith's wider vision of a system of natural liberty see Hill (2004).
24. Further, all of society's 'different orders ... are dependent upon the state to which they owe their security and protection' (*TMS*, Vi.ii.2.10: 231).

References

Anderson, G. M., Shughart, W. F., & Tollison, D. (1985). Adam Smith in the Customhouse. *Journal of Political Economy, 93*(4), 740–759.

Brentano, L. (1894). *Hours and Wages in Relation to Production* (W. Arnold, Trans.). Lindon: Swan Sonnenschein Co.

Emerson, R. (1967). Peter Gay and the Heavenly City. *Journal of the History of Ideas, 28*(3), 383–402.

Ferguson, A. (1792). *Principles of Moral and Political Science: Being Chiefly a Retrospect of Lectures Delivered in the College of Edinburgh, in Two Volumes.* Edinburgh: Printed for A. Strahan and T. Cadell, London, and W. Creech, Edinburgh.

Ferguson, A. (1816). *Biographical Sketch or Memoir of Lieutenant-Colonel Patrick Ferguson Originally Intended for the British Encyclopedia.* Edinburgh: Printed by John Moir.

Ferguson, A. (1996). *Collection of Essays*, edited and with an Introduction by Y. Amoh. Kyoto: Rinsen Book Co.

Fitzgibbons, A. (1995). *Adam Smith's System of Liberty, Wealth and Virtue.* Oxford: Clarendon Press.

Furniss, F. S. (1920). *The Position of the Labourer in a System of Nationalism.* Boston: Houghton Mifflin.

Gascoigne, J. (1991). The Wisdom of the Egyptians and the Secularisation of History in the Age of Newton. In S. Gaukroger (Ed.), *The Uses of antiquity* (pp. 171–212). Amsterdam: Kluwer Academic Publishers.

Hamowy, R. (1987). *The Scottish Enlightenment and the Theory of Spontaneous Order.* Carbondale: University Press.

Hanley, R. P. (2014). The "Wisdom of the State": Adam Smith on China and Tartary. *The American Political Science Review, 108*(2), 371–382.

Herzog, L. (2013). *Inventing the Market: Smith, Hegel, and Political Theory*. Oxford: Oxford University Press.
Hill, L. (2001). The Hidden Theology of Adam Smith. *European Journal of the History of Economic Thought, 8*(1), 1–29.
Hill, L. (2004). Further Reflections on the Hidden Theology of Adam Smith. *European Journal of the History of Economic Thought, 11*(4), 629–635.
Hill, L. (2012). Adam Smith on *Thumos* and Irrational Economic Man. *European Journal of the History of Economic Thought, 19*(1), 1–22.
Hume, D. (1987). *Essays Moral Political and Literary*, E. F. Miller (Ed.). Indiana: Liberty Classics.
Hume D. (2003). *A Treatise of Human Nature*, D. F. Norton (Ed.). Oxford: Oxford University Press.
Hundert, E. (1974). The Achievement Motive in Hume's Political Economy. *Journal of the History of Ideas, 35*(1), 139–143.
Kleer, R. (1995). Final Causes in Adam Smith's "Theory of Moral Sentiments". *Journal of the History of Philosophy, 33*(2), 275–330.
Levy, D. (1978). Adam Smith's 'Natural Law' and Contractual Society. *Journal of the History of Ideas, 39*, 665–674.
Lovejoy, A. O. (1964). *Great Chain of Being: A Study of the History of an Idea*. Cambridge, MA: Harvard University Press.
Marcus Aurelius. (1964). *Meditations*, translated with an Introduction by M. Staniforth. London: Penguin.
Marshall, M. G. (2000). Luxury, Economic Development, and Work Motivation: David Hume, Adam Smith, and J.R. McCulloch. *History of Political Economy, 32*(3), 631–649.
Martin, C. (2011). Adam Smith and Liberal Economics: Reading the Minimum Wage Debate of 1795–96. *Economic Journal Watch, 8*(2), 110–125.
Mingardi, A. (2018). Adam Smith and the Vocabulary of Liberty: Two Views. *Economic Affairs, 38*(3), 447–455.
Moore, J. (2000). Hutcheson's Theodicy: The Argument and the Contexts of a System of Moral Philosophy. In P. Wood (Ed.), *The Scottish Enlightenment: Essays in Reinterpretation* (pp. 239–266). Rochester: University of Rochester Press.
Otteson, J. (2002). *Adam Smith's Marketplace of Life*. Cambridge: Cambridge University Press.
Pullen, M. J. (1981). 'Malthus' Theological Ideas and Their Influence on His Principle of Population. *History of Political Economy, 13*(1), 39–54.
Rimlinger, G. V. (1976). Smith and the Merits of the Poor. *Review of Social Economics, 34*, 333–344.
Rosenberg, N. (1960). Some Institutional Aspects of the Wealth of Nations. *Journal of Political Economy, 68*, 557–570.

Ross, I. S. (1975). Political Themes in the Correspondence of Adam Smith. *The Scottish Tradition, 5*, 5–22.
Ross, I. S. (1995). *Life of Adam Smith.* Oxford: Oxford University Press.
Rothschild, E. (1992). Adam Smith and Conservative Economics. *Economic History Review, XLV*(1), 74–96.
Sher, R. B. (1985). *Church and University in the Scottish Enlightenment.* Princeton: Princeton University Press.
Sher, R. B. (1989). Adam Ferguson, Adam Smith, and the Problem of National Defense. *Journal of Modern History, 61*(2), 240–268.
Smith, A. (1976 [1759]). *The Theory of Moral Sentiments*, D. D. Raphael & A. L. MacFie (Eds.). Oxford: Clarendon Press.
Smith, A. (1978). *Lectures on Jurisprudence (A and B)*, R. L. Meek, D. D. Raphael & L. G. Stein (Eds.). Oxford: Oxford University Press.
Smith, A. (1979 [1776]). *An Inquiry into the Nature and Causes of the Wealth of Nations*, R. H. Campbell & A. S. Skinner (Eds.). Oxford: Clarendon Press.
Smith, A. (1980). *Essays on Philosophical Subjects*, I. S. Ross (Ed.). Oxford: Clarendon Press.
Smith, A. (1983). *Lectures on Rhetoric and Belles Lettres*, J. C. Bryce (Ed.). Oxford: Clarendon Press.
Smith, A. (1987). *The Correspondence of Adam Smith*, E. C. Mossner & I. S. Ross (Eds.). Oxford: Oxford University Press.
Stabile, D. (1997). Adam Smith and the Natural Wage: Sympathy, Subsistence and Social Distance. *Review of Social Economy, 55*(3), 292–311.
Viner, J. (1958). *The Long View and the Short.* Illinois: The Free Press.
Viner, J. (1977). *The Role of Providence in the Social Order.* Princeton: Princeton University Press.
Waterman, A. M. C. (2002). Economics as Theology: Adam Smith's *Wealth of Nations. Southern Economic Journal, 68*(4), 907–921.
Winch, D. (1978). *Adam Smith's Politics.* Cambridge: Cambridge University Press.

CHAPTER 4

Adam Smith's Political and Economic Sociology: A Quiet State for a Quiet People

Introductory Comments

Smith's new science of public management involved attending to conditions as they really were and for Smith that meant understanding how the political and governance needs of the world had changed. He was highly attuned to the sociological shifts that commercial development had brought with it and perceived that the political system needed to adapt to them. So he built his politics around a prescient sociology of change under commercial modernity. This chapter shows how Smith conceived the new social physics of mass market society and draws on his moral psychology to explore what he meant when he referred to the 'natural' behaviour of human beings under ideal conditions of 'natural liberty'.

Smith's new economic citizens were ideally free, independent, pecuniary, consumeristic, self-regarding, specialised, separative, mutually enabling, orderly and politically quiescent. These industrious strangers were determined to get ahead and to get along with each other. The new quiescence of their civil society called for a quieter state. In unpacking his subtle sociology of change and modernity, Smith provides us with a sociological justification for his legislative science as well as the efficient, more reserved night-watchman state he preferred. While it is a stretch to claim that he had so much faith in self-interest and the market that he expected politics itself ultimately to 'withe[r] away' (Rosanvallon 2006: 149–52), as will be shown, he certainly expected politics to be less conspicuous and the state to become more professional, lean, pacific and forbearing. This is partly

L. Hill, *Adam Smith's Pragmatic Liberalism*,
https://doi.org/10.1007/978-3-030-19337-9_4

because market agents are more orderly and better self-governors and partly because commercial progress has resolved many of the security problems that previously required a more obtrusive state.

Many assume that they already know the answer to why Smith preferred the small state, assuming it is easily located within an ideological tradition (i.e. libertarianism). However, there is a far more complicated and subtle rationale found in Smith's highly original sociology of change. I show that, although Smith did not want politics to disappear, he did want it to transform itself radically. The government of people in commercialising societies badly needed reform in order to align itself with the massive social shifts that were accelerating in the eighteenth century. These included the breakdown of archaic political units like the feudal estate and the extended family; the centralisation of government; the regularisation and professionalisation of security and justice; the mechanisation and specialisation of labour; enormous increases in productive output; the geographical concentration of manufacture and the concomitant growth of cities; the division of the manufacturing population into either owners/employers of wage labour or workers; changing consumption habits and an expanding middle class.

In increasingly mass societies of strangers secured by a regular system of justice and police, near-total forms of government that had previously made significant political demands on its citizens had becoming obsolete; the minimal, restrained and impartial state was more appropriate, as was a less politically engaged public. This is partly a function of the fact that commercial modernity brings with it greater quantities of social capital and a public better able to both manage itself and avoid conflict. As will be discussed, Smith's aversion to conflict is key to understanding both his theory of self-equilibration and his conception of the proper role of citizens in his ideal polity.

Contrary to the view of some scholars that Smith is heavily influenced by classical virtue discourses, his vision is basically modern: he describes and endorses a mass society held together by voluntaristic mechanisms, in which the obligatory and total aspects of monolithic institutions like the church, feudal estate, extended family and corporation have been broken down. This necessitates the emergence of a new moral and emotional economy. Increasingly independent agents are now internally regulated by cool virtues and the conventions of friendly 'commercial strangership', while their interactions are ordered and sustained, not by habitual duty and custom, but by the division of labour, exchange relations and a regular, impartial system of justice. Smith embraces the depersonalisation of the commercialising state, and welcomes a society that is increasingly pacific, legalistic and inhabited by moderate, tolerant, dispassionate, orderly and self-governing ***individuals***. The night-watchman state is the natural corollary of this new way of relating and the politically quiescent public of independent producers its economic and social mainstay.

The chapter also explores further Smith's historiography in order to show that he believed that liberal commercialism was natural and historically inevitable; it therefore challenges claims in the secondary literature that he did not welcome commercial progress and was actually rather pessimistic about it. Key to understanding Smith's politics is his sociology of change that he devised to comprehend the effects on social and affective life of the material and economic changes that were rapidly taking place in his time. Like other colleagues within the Scottish Enlightenment, Smith found himself in a unique position to understand the developments brought on by modernisation and commercialisation. Although modernity came later to Scotland than it did to other parts of Britain and Europe, its momentum accelerated in the second half of the eighteenth century when commercialism took off rapidly (Strasser 1976: 53) and 'the Scottish Lowlands' became 'the economic wonder region of Europe' (Eriksson 1993: 251).

Of special interest are Smith's prescient observations on the transition from social arrangements based on what Emile Durkheim would later refer to as 'mechanistic solidarity' and homogeneity to those characterised by organic solidarity and heterogeneity.[1] Key developments here included the erosion of clan and village life, urbanisation, the expansion and reach of markets and increasing refinements in task specialisation, changes that fed into and catalysed each other. Other significant developments were the decline of arbitrary and diffuse forms of rule and the accompanying rise of the modern bureaucratic state. Smith warmly embraced and welcomed the knock-on effects of these trends. The economic benefits were obvious, but less obvious was their positive tendency to wear down the liberty-retarding constraints of sectarian, feudal and clannish social structures, thereby unleashing the tremendous productive power of individual free agents and providing the conditions for a less muscular state.

Social change brought, in turn, a new moral economy to complement Smith's political economy. We might think of this as a novel kind of 'civil society' inhabited by his new economic citizens; superior, in Smith's mind, to earlier forms of social organisation because of its calmer and more predictable rhythms and modes. In an increasingly differentiated society, agents operated outside intensely emotional and exclusivistic units and alliances formed mainly for security purposes and were able to act more freely, voluntaristically and individualistically. These changes in social structure were both enhanced by and hastened technological progress and therefore the prosperity of nations. They also significantly enhanced liberty.

Commercial Strangership

The eclipse of feudal and pastoral alliances based on intense and particularistic 'beneficence' brought with it new patterns of behaviour animated by the cooler, more impersonal and constant virtues of 'prudence' and 'justice'. Intense interactions were increasingly less important than the rapidly proliferating forms of amicable 'strangership' peculiar to commercial society. For Smith 'only a society of strangers, of mediated and indirect social relations', had 'the dynamism to achieve progress' (Ignatieff 1984: 119). Social intimacy was becoming less important to the functioning of mass, commercial society and people would learn to develop better and more sophisticated patterns of social *distance*, a new and better form of strangership in which the powerful drive of self-interest could at last be harnessed and deployed productively.[2]

Smith acknowledges the loss of civic virtue and social intimacy that comes with commercialism but there is little hint of regret because, on balance, he believes that material prosperity has priority. Virtue and citizenship capacity, though laudable, must be sacrificed for the sake of progress and wealth. Smith's was thus a somewhat complacent, at times seemingly enchanted, vision of the new world of commerce and modernity. On his account, the transition towards large-scale commercial society did not jeopardise the social fabric but rather displaced a stressful, conflict-riven, meagre and insecure world with one rich in possibilities for civility, mutual enablement and human flourishing.

Modular Humans

In the new civil society of amiable strangers, immobilising feudal structures have been broken down, permitting the emergence of relatively independent working and 'middling' class agents. Citizens are no longer bound together by total forms of governance, the exigencies of security or the restrictive ties of place and tradition; they move about freely, anonymously and in a more modular fashion. Smith rated highly the value of personal mobility and it is central to his conception of individual liberty. Agents should enjoy the free-est possible use of their bodies, minds and properties provided that there are no violations of either the public interest or the system of natural liberty. Within Smith's ideal universe, the archetypal agent is 'modular'; social links have moved 'from situs to contract' and are now 'flexible, specific [and] instrumental'.[3] Unlike Adam Ferguson or Rousseau, Smith finds little romance in the necessitous and compelled relations of socially intimate societies but embraces instead the possibilities unleashed by interactions unanchored in place or time, impersonal, interchangeable, deracinated, cosmopolitan and mobile and largely regulated by neutral contract and justice.

In contrast to the classical approach—where citizens owe almost everything, including their lives if necessary, to the community[4]—Smith had a comparatively thin conception of what each citizen owed to the other and to the society in general. People in commercial societies owe very little beyond a decent measure of honesty, civility and propriety exercised in the spirit of fair competition. Most importantly, they should respect the autonomy of others and extend reciprocal non-interference. Justice between individuals consists in mutual forbearance, rather than blind loyalty to a sacramental community or the exercise of filial or religious piety or beneficent charity. Similarly, institutions—especially the state—are just if they refrain from interfering with the autonomy and mobility of individual agents. The latter, if left to follow their natural tendencies, will readily secure their own happiness and prosperity as well as that of the society in general (*WN*, IV.v.b.43: 43). As Smith wrote, little else is required 'to carry a state to the highest degree of opulence from the lowest barbarism, but peace, easy taxes, and a tolerable administration of justice; all the rest being brought about by the natural course of things'.[5] In consequence, he advocated government restraint: intrusive and paternalistic forms of governance not only corrupt individual moral character but subvert the prosperity and well-being of nations.

The Age of Independence: Specialisation, Social Breakdown, Changing Consumption Patterns

Smith welcomed the expansion of freedom and individual power brought on by the decline of feudal and aristocratic social arrangements and the breakdown of total and ecclesiastical forms of governance, all of which changes are necessary for commercial society to come into existence. What gave rise to this self-sufficiency? In other words, why do societies naturally tend towards commercialism? Three intimately connected causes can be identified here: first, the increasing refinement of specialisation functions (which also included professionalisation in defence and policing); second, the breakdown of feudal social structures; and, third, the new consumption patterns. I will start with the latter first.

Luxury

During the eighteenth century the topic of luxury was central to debates within political economy and moral philosophy (Berg and Eger 2003: 28–40). Prior to this period luxury had been condemned by both the church and 'oeconomists' as morally and economically destructive. Ancient histories are full of claims that hedonism precipitates the decline of nations and empires by weakening civic and martial virtue (Hill 2006). There was also the concomitant belief that virtue could be recovered via a return to primitive conditions (Reesor 1951: 16). Closer to Smith's time, the Mercantilists, in particular, equated frugality with prosperity, arguing that high levels of savings properly invested was the basis of economic growth. Even Smith's friend and colleague, Adam Ferguson, harped on the pitfalls of prosperity and the 'prodigality, licentiousness and brutal sensuality' (Ferguson 1792, II: 501) that riches engender. But by the beginning of the eighteenth century, it became an increasingly acceptable view that the domestic consumption of luxury items created employment, stimulated the circulation of money and commodities and indirectly encouraged population growth. Smith helped to make this happen.

The production of affordable and ever more ingenious luxury goods became a distinctive feature of mid- to later-eighteenth-century Britain. New goods were constantly being created for consumers who 'valued individuality, variety and accessibility' while the delight 'in ingenuity went with a desire for difference, and the new commercial economy circulated accessible luxuries' (Berg and Eger 2003). From Smith's perspective, all this inventive and productive activity expanded markets and made life more enjoyable and commodious. Although basic human needs are limited, the 'desire of the conveniencies and ornaments of building, dress, equipage, and household furniture' is 'altogether endless'. Limitless productivity, industry and economic growth are thereby assured when this urge is given free rein. In order to provide for their necessities, the poor work to 'gratify [the] fancies of the rich' and in order to gain advantage 'they vie with one another in the cheapness and perfection of their work'. Such perpetual competitive exertion, fuelled by the expectation of reward for effort, increases the 'quantity of food' and therefore stimulates population levels among 'workmen'. It is this dynamic that drives increasing specialisation and innovation, and which, in turn, drives the demand for greater and more various supplies of raw materials (*WN*, I.xi.c.7: 180–82).

Contrary to the claims of some, the ability of workers to afford luxury goods did not disincentivise them or cause their moral corruption; rather, it acted as a spur to industry, preserved law and order and ensured the labour supply (*WN*, I.viii. 36–40: 96–97). As with private property, were luxury to be abolished, acquisitiveness, the driving force of commerce, would be undermined and polished society—not to mention progress itself—would falter. Similarly, the conspicuous consumption of the wealthy inspires the labours of the poor (*TMS*, I.iii.2.2: 50: 256). In so saying, Smith challenged prevailing attitudes about luxury and consumption. He continually emphasised that luxury was benign, more likely to reflect an industrious, flourishing state than one in imminent danger of moral corruption (*WN*, I.i.11: 23–24; *WN*, I.viii.35: 95–96). Challenging the 'popular ascetic doctrines ... which placed virtue in the entire extirpation and annihilation of all our passions', Smith opined that, so long as a person can consume them 'without any inconveniency', it is 'certain that luxury, sensuality, and ostentation are public benefits' for they encourage the vital 'arts of refinement' upon which progress and prosperity depend (*TMS*, VII.ii.4.12: 313).

Critics of the new consumption patterns were misguided in regarding 'as gross luxury and sensuality' anything that 'falls short of the most ascetic abstinence, so that there is vice', Smith remarks sarcastically, 'even in the use of a clean shirt, or of a convenient habitation' (*TMS*, VII. ii.4.11: 312). Smith's definition of luxury was relative because he believed that it was legitimate for anyone, regardless of social location, to indulge in some temperate displays of wealth in order to maintain his or her social status and sense of dignity. Necessities are defined broadly as things that not only serve the needs of the body but also contribute to the dignity, respectability and social survival of a person: 'By necessaries I understand, not only the commodities which are indispensably necessary for the support of life, but whatever the custom of the country renders it indecent for creditable people, even of the lowest order, to be without' (*WN*, V.II.k.3: 869–71). Both necessities and luxuries are defined in relation to prevailing custom and opinion. Although the 'Greeks and Romans' managed 'very comfortably' without linen, in contemporary Europe any sensible person 'would be ashamed to appear in publick without a linen shirt'. Similarly, whereas for every English person, leather shoes are 'a necessary of life', in France, it is acceptable for the poor to appear either bare-footed or 'in wooden shoes' (*WN*, V.II.k.3: 869–71). Smith therefore concluded that the consumption of luxuries could not be dissipating—and was certainly socially productive—provided it was moderate (*WN*, V.ii.k.3: 869–70).

For Smith, interest, luxury and commercial prosperity are natural, basically innocent and a major cause of positive social effects and changes. His defence of luxury was just one aspect of a broader political economy that attempted to leave pessimistic moralising behind, in favour of confronting the material and economic realities of commercial life and attending to the welfare, rather than virtue, of the people. Interest was not vicious, so long as it was exercised properly and the desire for luxury goods was a perfectly natural consequence of specialisation and equally natural vanity, glossed by Smith as the human need for social status and recognition (Hill 2011). In sum, the production, consumption and export of luxuries were both a sign and source of prosperity.

The new consumption patterns are not just symptoms of commercial progress: they also played a vital role in positive social change, such as the re-organisation of class structures into a more adaptive system. The development of exchange and manufactures made it possible for the feudal barons to acquire luxury commodities, whereas under a feudal economy wealth could only be deployed in the maintenance of retainers for the purposes of either hospitality or military security. The availability of luxuries caused the wealth of the barons to be dispersed in new and other ways and for the labour power of the now independent serfs to be employed more productively. So over time, and without ever intending it, the barons destroyed their own social structure and power base. This 'revolution' led, in turn, to the growth of a new class of burghers (the 'merchants and artificers') whose material and moral influence brought about greater liberty and a more even distribution of power (*WN*, III.iv.5: 412–14; *WN*, III.iv.11–18: 419–22). Once the great mass of tenants had attained their independence, feudal proprietors 'were no longer capable of interrupting the regular execution of justice' (Berry 1994: 157–58). As David Hume observed, the nobility's 'taste for elegant luxury' thus disabled 'the great noblemen from resistance' to the sovereign, 'promoted the execution of the laws, and extended the authority of the courts of justice' (Hume 1983, v.4: 246; Hume 1983, v.5: 88; see also Wootton 1993).

The Division of Labour, the New Independence and the Decline of the Extended Family

The other key source of social change and the transition to commercial modernity was the development of the division of labour and the breakdown of the extended family that went hand in hand with that development. As far as Smith is concerned, the best thing about the commercial age is its tendency to permit ever increasing degrees of *independence*. At the same time, it also produces a new form of impersonal *inter*dependence via specialisation and the new, universalistic civility.

Whereas people in pre-commercial orders jealously preserved extended family networks for the purpose of 'common defence', in commercial states, the evolution of an organised system of justice and defence offers adequate protection to even the 'meanest man in the state'. With the exigencies of security solved, families, over time, 'naturally separate and disperse' and 'in a few generations' cease to care for (or even remember) one another (*TMS*, VI.ii.1.12–13: 222–23). Smith notes that the longer a 'civilization' has been 'established', the less intense is its '[r]egard for remote relations' (*TMS*, VI.ii.1.12–13: 222–23). This critical transformation in social structure did not spell the end of community and social cohesion but simply altered the quality and modes of interdependence. Foreshadowing a major theme in classical sociology, Smith explains how an increasing division of labour prompts greater interdependence among people, in ways 'mutually beneficiall to each other' (*LJ[A]*, vi.46–49: 348–49). In the new universalistic society of specialisers, exchange gradually displaces clan and familial displays of loyalty as the paradigmatic social interaction; it is 'by treaty, by barter, and by purchase, that we obtain from one another the greater part of those mutual good offices which we stand in need of' (*WN*, I.ii.1–3: 25–27). Exchange is now the primary form and *purpose* of association (*WN*, VI.1: 37). By this means the equally natural institution of society is held together (*WN*, I.ii.1–3: 25–27). Pursuing self-interest within a complex division of labour promotes exchange relationships and in turn shifts the mechanisms of solidarity away from those generated by necessity, custom and tradition.

Dependency is not only an obstruction to productivity and liberty: it also corrupts moral character; hence, Smith condemns any paternalistic and therefore dependency-generating remnants of pre-commercial economic stages. Women, for example, are kept in dependence by the law of primogeniture which prevents them from inheriting family wealth (*LJ[A]*, i.115: 49), while the antique understanding of marriage is egregious because under law wives are classified as the property of their husbands and therefore effectively slaves (*LJ[A]*, iii.52: 161). Smith's greatest objection to the feudal age is the necessary dependence associated with the pre-commercial system of great landholders and retainers. Dependency is objectionable because it breeds servility and fosters asymmetrical and therefore unhealthy and unproductive social relations (*WN*, III.iv.4–7: 412–15; *WN*, I.ii.2: 27). There is nothing so likely 'to corrupt and enervate and debase the mind as dependency': conversely, 'nothing gives such noble and generous notions of probity as freedom and independency.' (*LJ[A]*, vi.6: 333; see also *LJ[B]*, 205: 486–87 and *LJ[B]*, 326: 538).

Dependency is also a law and order issue: because it promotes poverty and indolence, dependency is the root cause of all the crimes, 'disorder and confusions' that take place in cities. The solution, according to Smith, is the expansion of 'commerce' (*LJ[A]*, v.4–8: 332–33). Due to its capacity to encourage 'independency', the growth of 'commerce and manufactures' is 'the best police for preventing crimes' because a life of crime is risky and unnecessary when the economy is flourishing (*LJ[B]*, 205: 486–87). It is also for the sake of independence that Smith advocated high wages.

The dissolution of the system of great landholders decentralised dependency relations and offered greater security to individual tradespeople: now '[e]ach tradesman or artificer derives his subsistence from the employment, not of one, but of a hundred or a thousand customers'. This is positive because '[s/]he is not absolutely dependent upon any one of them' (*WN*, III.iv.12: 420). A great disadvantage of 'menial' labour performed inside dependency relationships (and therefore outside market relations) is that it is unproductive; in other words, it does not result in 'vendible' or exchangeable commodities (Perelman 1989: 316). Further, because of the 'the waste which attends rustick hospitality', productive labour under commercialism is able to support greater numbers of people (*WN*, III.iv.12: 420).

Finally, the new age of independence, competition and liberty is not only 'conducive to general utility' (Griswold 1999: 294), efficiency and opulence, but it is also congenial to the cultivation of the cool, instrumental, practical and therefore highly desirable virtues of prudence, justice, propriety, self-command, frugality, sobriety, vigilance, circumspection, temperance, constancy, firmness, punctuality, faithfulness, enterprise and industry (*WN*, II.iii. 36: 345–46; *TMS*, VII.ii.3.15: 304; *TMS*, III.5.8:

166). Although Smith lavishly praised those who exercised the higher, other-regarding virtues, his real moral focus is on the pragmatic and more easily attainable forms of virtue that could and should be exercised by every market society actor. Smith's modest ideal is a character who is unlikely to be positively virtuous or beneficent but can, at the very least, be negatively virtuous, industrious, self-governing, self-advancing, law-abiding (*LJ[A]*, v.124: 320) and punctual.

Specialisation not only promotes productivity and wealth, it solves a long-standing obstacle to commerce and modernity itself: the security problem. The internal security of states is solved by the establishment of a formal system of justice and the development of professional, 'well-regulated' standing armies to 'execute and maintain' it. 'A standing army', Smith wrote, 'establishes, with an irresistible force, the law of the sovereign through the remotest provinces of the empire, and maintains some degree of regular government in countries which could not otherwise admit of any' (*WN*, v.i.a.40: 706). As has been shown earlier, an organised system of justice underpinned by regular armies affords 'to industry, the only encouragement which it requires, some tolerable security that it shall enjoy the fruits of its own labour' (*WN*, I.xi.i: 256; WN, I.xi.g: 213–14). When '[t]he natural effort of every individual to better his own condition' is unleashed under conditions of 'freedom and security' the society will be prosperous and happy (*WN*, IV.v.b.43: 540). Smith was happy to note that 'In Great Britain', the most opulent, differentiated and commercially advanced nation in the world, 'industry is perfectly secure ... [and, arguably] freer than in any other part of Europe' (*WN*, IV.v.b.43: 540).

The Big Wide World of Strangers

Although specialisation promotes independence it also, paradoxically, generates unprecedented levels of *inter*dependence and mutuality. Now associations are increasingly voluntaristic, egalitarian, mutually beneficial and purely instrumental (*WN*, I.ii.2: 26). The loss of small-scale, intimate society is not sentimentally regretted because it was, in reality, restrictive, oppressive, precarious, intermittently traumatic but generally 'indolent', monotonous and dull[6] compared to the rich new 'strangership' of the commercial age with its endless possibilities for social and material exchange, personal development, refinement, comfort, prosperity and liberty.

After the new strangership and interdependence has broken down the obligatory and particularistic constraints of rank, sect, clan and treaty, less intense forms of 'friendship' can now extend to almost everybody that one has contact with in the course of the business day. The new voluntaristic civil society is preferred because it is not as intense and exclusivistic as were pre-commercial forms of solidarity (e.g. kinship, fictive kinship and clientage). Further, it embodies the Enlightenment ideal of cosmopolitanism in the sense that commerce progressively enlarges markets and therefore the concentric circles of instrumental friendship.[7]

The Quiet Citizen: Sympathy, Strangers and Social Control

The new commercial world that Smith writes about brings many other changes, not least of which is a revolution in how we should emote and moralise about one another. This is a world that has to be navigated largely by and between strangers; consequently, the ardent passions attendant on village, clan and other feudal alliances will be transcended by tamer and more amiable passions and virtues. The golden mean is emotional equilibrium, not benevolent passion; impartial rationality, not personalism, particularism, philanthropy, charity or nepotism. Since all strangers are now potential contractees or role-pair candidates—for example, seller and buyer, lawyer and client, teacher and pupil or doctor and patient—and not potential enemies, the exchange culture will be calm, open, rational, impersonal, polite, flexible, voluntaristic and rule-governed.

The spontaneous and intimate temper of clan and village life is supplanted by the cool friendships of amiably disposed strangers. Their interactions in business and the workplace depend upon a type of relationship that Smith calls '*necessitudo*', which, 'from the etymology, seems to denote that it was imposed by the necessity of the situation'. 'Colleagues in office, partners in trade' find that '[t]heir good agreement is an advantage to all; and, if they are tolerably reasonable people, they are naturally disposed to agree' (*TMS*, VI.ii.1.15–16: 223–24).[8]

In mass societies of individuated strangers and mere acquaintances, where total states, theocratic forms of power, tradition and absolute moral codes wielded by patriarchs, feudal lords and ecclesiastics are rapidly losing their hold over subjects, spontaneous and portable 'sympathy' becomes the primary method of social control. Sympathy is Smith's term for positive identification; it intersects with the judgements of the impartial spectator to reduce conflict and generate 'concord' between individual agents (*TMS*, I.i.4.8–10: 22–23). To elicit the sympathy of those with whom they have to live and work, whether familiars or strangers, people must constantly attune their dispositions and actions to the judgements of an internal surveillance mechanism or hypothetical observer: Smith's famous 'impartial spectator'. The crowds of nameless strangers become internalised in the moral personality as this 'impartial spectator' who constantly monitors, constrains and adjusts the 'impulses of self-love' (*TMS* III.3.38: 153–54; TMS, III.3.4: 137; *TMS*, VI.iii.18: 244–45).

Smith emphasises our 'natural disposition to accommodate and to assimilate, as much as we can, our own sentiments, principles, and feelings, to those which we see ... in the persons whom we are obliged to live and converse a great deal with' (*TMS*, VI.ii.1.17: 224). This desire to 'accommodate and to assimilate' the sentiments of others represents a desire, not to forge warm friendships, but rather to generate amicable strangership. Strangers are neither friends 'from whom we can expect any special favour and sympathy' nor enemies 'from whom we cannot expect any sympathy at all' (Mizuta 1976: 122).

The spectator offers the vantage point of someone who is not only impartial but also indifferent (Mizuta 1976: 122, n.4). This detached perspective is vital to market societies because they are in a perpetual state of competition and therefore of potential conflict. Regardless of the intensity of competition between agents, the 'sympathy' of the impartial spectator has to be maintained at all times: 'In the race for wealth, and honours, and preferments' we 'may run as hard as [we] can, and strain every nerve and every muscle, in order to outstrip all [our] competitors. But if [we] should justle, or throw down any of them, the indulgence of the spectators is entirely at an end'. Our task is to 'humble the arrogance of [our] self-love, and bring it down to something which other men can go along with' (*TMS*, II.ii.2.1: 82–84). The function or ultimate ***purpose*** of our capacity to sympathise is to achieve social 'harmony' in societies of strangers where complete 'unisons' are otherwise out of the question. We are always ready to moderate our emotional and social responses so as to bring about 'harmony and concord with the emotions of those' around us (*TMS*, I.i.4.8: 22). Commercial societies still need goodwill and civility in order to operate; the difference is that these dispositions are now produced outside obligatory social categories and by internal, psychological mechanisms that allow our affective dispositions to be toned down and depersonalised to generate a kind of generalised social and emotional golden mean (*TMS*, III.3.25: 146–47).

The Pacific Society

A key focus of Smith's sociology is on how large-scale societies of strangers can function with a minimum of conflict. Social harmony and order are extremely important for Smith both in the domestic and in the international realm. In societies affectively regulated by 'constrained sympathy', which Smith distinguishes from spontaneous and sincere 'natural sympathy' (*TMS*, VI.ii.1.18: 224–25), justice is the key virtue and contract, specialisation and exchange the primary mechanisms of association. While justice is the foundation, self-interest, specialisation and exchange are the solidary mediums of commercial society. Together they give rise to an order that generates and evokes instrumental mutual enablement. As Smith famously wrote:

> [M]an has almost constant occasion for the help of his brethren, and it is in vain for him to expect it from their benevolence only. He will be more likely to prevail if he can interest their self-love in his favour, and shew them that it is for their own advantage to do for him what he requires of them. Whoever offers to another a bargain of any kind, proposes to do this. Give me that which I want, and you shall have this which you want, is the meaning of every such offer; and it is in this manner that we obtain from one another the far greater part of those good offices which we stand in need of. It is not from the benevolence of the butcher, the brewer, or the baker, that we expect our dinner, but from their regard to their own interest. (*WN*, I.ii.2: 26–27)

In the emerging 'assembly of strangers' (*TMS*, I.i.4.9: 23), classical and Christian virtues like beneficence and compassion are no longer sufficient to supply its members' increasingly complex and myriad needs. The more temperate and reliable sentiments of prudence, propriety and especially justice are much better suited to that task because they can be regulated. Society may justifiably use force to prevent the injury of one person by another, but it can hardly attempt to enforce by legal sanctions the exercise of the benevolent virtues (*TMS*, II.ii.1.7: 80). Justice is the more solid virtue because it can be treated with precision. Its rules are highly impersonal, impartial and 'accurate in the highest degree' (*TMS*, III.6.10: 175).

The atmosphere of Smith's new civil society is imbued, not with the spontaneous vitality of benevolent warmth, but with the constancy of legal rules and the steady constraints of social decorum (Mizuta 1976: 1459–64). The new 'strangership' of the commercial age is more pacific, orderly and predictable than its stadial predecessors (in the hunting, herding and agricultural stages) partly because its regulating mechanisms are generated *outside* zealously emotional, intimate and exclusivistic social units like the family, the village, the *umma* or the feudal estate. Our social behaviour is now learned more diffusely and impersonally through interaction with the world at large, in less particularistic markets, 'societies', 'associations', 'companies', coffee houses and 'clubs'.[9] Here we learn civility, self-command,[10] politeness, mutual forbearance, independence, 'equality of temper', ideas of liberty and all the other distant modes of interaction required by commercial life (*TMS*, III.3.25: 146; *TMS*, I.i.4.10: 23). As these affects and dispositions are cultivated, so hostility and suspicion are defused and the particularistic alliances generated by sectarianism, 'custom, corporate group, station, and estate ... dissolved' (Silver 1989: 274–79). The lines between out-groups and in-groups, strangers and friends, become blurred and the society becomes increasingly open. Now, we potentially stand in need of everyone (i.e. *anyone*) for purely instrumental reasons; therefore, our suspicion of strangers must inevitably give way to a new openness and amiability.

It is not only the outward signs of civility that undergo radical change: so too must the inner, affective lives of individuals. Archaic emotions like anger, hatred, resentment and the desire for revenge are 'unsocial' passions that 'poison ... the happiness of a good mind' and ought to be reined in and kept within the bounds of civility and justice (*TMS*, I.ii. 3. 7: 37–38). Such ardent passions 'mounted to the highest pitch of fury' might have been useful to small-scale societies where food and military security and the maintenance of intimate loyalties were daily life-or-death matters (*TMS*, V.2.11–13: 208–209),[11] but they were no longer appropriate in mass societies of secure, differentiated strangers[12] where qualities moderated by 'equality of temper' are much more useful to meeting our everyday needs (*TMS*, I.i.4.10: 23).[13]

Politics in the Quiet State

It is within this complex and subtle sociological context that Smith detects and describes so ingeniously that we begin to understand his underlying rationale for the quiet, minimal state and the concomitant demise of the muscular, interfering one. A quieter people need a quieter state. Although Smith endorsed the idea of 'the good citizen', he or she is a somewhat insipid character whose virtue consists mainly in a 'respect' for laws, obedience to 'the civil magistrate' and a generalised, though not particularly energetic, interest in 'the welfare of the whole society' (*TMS*, VI.ii.2.10: 231). 'The prudent man', though not especially lovable or praiseworthy, does not take on any unnecessary public responsibilities, avoids 'meddl[ing]' and 'confines himself, as much as his duty will permit, to his own affairs'. Further, if he is wise, he will be 'averse to enter into any party disputes' (*TMS*, VI.i.13: 215–16).

Smith's ideal polity is a fairly tepid affair, relying as it does on a well-regulated professional and disinterested leadership, a quiescent, orderly, self-governing public and a professional system of justice and military defence (standing armies). While Smith is definite that virtue is the main guard against social and economic corruption, the virtues he valorises and promotes are commercial rather than civic ones—the tame, cool virtues of the 'middling' ranks. Indeed, as was shown in Chap. 3, those who act with a view to the wider public interest are likely to do more harm than good. Smith's preference was for everyone to withdraw into full *economic* citizenship. The good polity is the natural market economy of self-regarding, lawful and mutually forbearing agents. As far as is possible, government should become more distant, temperate, professional and disinterested. Notably, however, although the business of governing should be restrained, it should also be taken more seriously than it has in the past; that is to say, it should be a vocation rather than an avocation of corrupt and self-interested aristocrats, self-regarding factions, grasping, monopolising traders and intolerant ecclesiastics.

Smith on Conflict and Order

Smith's vision of the new politics partly has its source in his aversion to all forms of conflict and social disharmony; in fact '[t]he peace and order of society, is of more importance than even the relief of the miserable' (*TMS*, Vi.ii.1.20: 226; *TMS*, VI.ii.2.12: 231). He particularly abhorred political faction fighting. Political factions have a tendency to 'deceive and impose upon the Public' and to 'oppress' rather than serve government (*Corr.*, 1987: 286). Faction fighting 'distract[s] the nation' and is equal to the vice of 'fanaticism' in its capacity to corrupt morality and the 'moral sentiments' (*TMS*, III.3.43: 155–56).[14] In fact '[o]f all the corrupters of moral sentiment … faction and fanaticism have always been by far the greatest'. Factions corrupt the moral sentiments because where faction prevails, the impartial spectator is disarmed. In the midst of 'the violence and rage of contending parties' the impartial spectator ceases to exist altogether and so, therefore, does good 'judgement', candour and fair play (*TMS*, III.3.43: 155–56). The behaviour of factions is generally 'atrocious', violent and unjust (*TMS*, V.iiii.12: 242; *TMS*, III.3.2: 146) and they have an unerring tendency to fan the terrifying fires of sectarian conflict (*WN*, V.i.g.7: 791–92).

Once a sound constitution has been put in place, politics seems to have been reducible to the rational administration of populations and the management of the practical exigencies of security, both economic and military. There appears to be little for the average commercial agent to do in Smith's ideal, pared-back polity. This attitude contrasts with the classical approach to corruption, where active citizenship and other-regarding public spirit are promoted as the main guards of constitutions. For Smith, a directly opposite kind of character is the preserver of his natural, healthy polity.

Politics should be subdued, domesticated, defactionalised, secularised and professionalised. The first step to achieving this is to establish a sound constitution characterised by limited government, the separation of powers, properly remunerated officers and rules that effectively patrol the boundaries between public and private (see Chaps. 2 and 5). Once this constitution has been established governors can get on with the rational administration of populations and the management of the practical exigencies of security, both economic and military. The greatest 'public benevolence' that 'statesmen' can bestow on a people is to 'project and form alliances among neighbouring or not very distant nations, for the preservation ... of ... the balance of power, or of the general peace and tranquillity of the states within the circle of their negotiations' (*TMS*, VI.ii.2.6: 230; see also Chap. 6). The new era of commerce and development would be constituted by cosmopolitan, polite strangers busily absorbed in the pursuit of their own happiness and prosperity and largely indifferent to the violent machinations of religion, clan and politics.

Superiority and Desirability of the Commercial Age?

At this point it is worth pausing to defend more fully the assumption made throughout this book that Smith unreservedly welcomed the commercial age and that his politics was therefore designed to suit such a stage. As discussed in the previous chapters, it is sometimes suggested that he either was hostile to commercialism or saw it as doomed to self-destruct. However, neither of these hypotheses seems warranted, first, because the disadvantages of the commercial age are far outweighed by the advantages and, second, because Smithian historiography is clearly progressivist and linear.

The Commercial Age: Pros and Cons

As mentioned above, Smith recognised the problems of isolation and alienation that accompanied urbanisation (*WN*, V.i.g.12: 795–96); appreciated the 'alienating' effects of the division of labour; thought that commercialism undermined education (*LJ[B]*, 329–30: 539–40) and noted that commercial labour involved inequality and even exploitation (*WN*, I.viii.14: 85; early draft of *WN*, 6, in *LJ[B]*: 564; see also *LJ[A]*, 26: 340). He also regarded the state of 'savagery' as a state of relative equality and autonomy. Yet there is no nostalgia about this former state of equality; although we might 'expect … that the savage should be much better provided than the dependent poor man who labours both for himself and for others', in fact, 'the case is far otherwise' (*LJ[A]*, 26: 340; see also *WN*, I.viii.1–2: 82). Compare the forlorn poverty of the 'savage' age with the 'general security and happiness that prevails in the ages of civility and politeness' (*TMS*, V.2.8–9: 205), and observe that '[i]n the midst of so much oppressive inequality' even the 'lowest and most despised member of civilized society' enjoys a level of 'affluence and abundance' far superior to 'the most respected and active savage'(*LJ[B]*: 564).

The entire system of commercialism, with its ever more refined system of task specialisation, generates unprecedented levels of liberty and independence for all members of society, regardless of class location (*LJ[A]*, vi.46–49: 348–49). Specialisation is good because it delivers security and is the source of almost all of the growth, progress and prosperity of the commercial age (*TMS*, I.i.10–111: 22–24). This is significant because, for Smith, the happy society is the prosperous, materially abundant society. 'The happiness of mankind', he tells us, 'seems to have been the original purpose intended by the Author of nature when he brought [it] into existence' (*TMS*, III.5.7: 166). Prosperity is a necessary condition for the 'flourishing and happy' society (*WN*, I.viii.36: 96) and Smith refers to our natural, God-given tendency to 'sympathize with the joy of our companions when in prosperity' (*TMS*, II.2.4: 70). Indeed, we have been endowed with certain self-regarding drives with a divine purpose in mind: a tendency to produce the 'beneficent ends' of 'the great Director of nature', namely, the physical safety, security, prosperity and perpetuation of the species (*TMS*, II.i.5.10: 77–78; *LJ[A]*: 300–301; *LJ[B]*: 527).

Rather than atomising individual agents, specialisation actually enhances social cohesion. It transforms the quality and means of *inter*dependence while at the same time enhancing personal and private *in*dependence.[15] The division of labour enhances social life precisely because it is a key dissolver of those charitable, philanthropic, paternalistic and dependency relationships he persistently deprecated. The ability of humans to specialise and exchange the products of this specialisation with strangers is what holds mass commercial society together (*WN*, I.ii.1–3: 25–27). The almost complete self-sufficiency of 'savages' and 'barbarians' did not benefit them; rather, it gave them a world of meagre and somewhat one-dimensional social relations. From Smith's point of view, the main problem with the adverse effect of the division of labour is not 'alienation' or the imminent collapse of commercialism itself, but its entirely ameliorable consequences for public order and personal comportment. Smith regarded this problem as soluble within prevailing social relations via the establishment of a compulsory and publicly funded school system (*WN*, V.i.i.5–6: 815; *WN*, V.i.f.57: 786; see also Chap. 7).

On balance, then, and despite its ill effects, the division of labour yields more, rather than less, human happiness. In general, Smith's thought testifies to a sanguine belief that, generally speaking, the world is neatly and propitiously ordered despite any negative (but generally correctable) side effects of that order. In particular, the intellectually and morally debilitating effects of specialisation are naturally offset by the more general gains in knowledge and refinement brought about that same process. Smith's biographer Dugald Stewart captures Smith's reasoning neatly: 'The extensive propagation of light and refinement ... aided by the spirit of commerce, seems to be the *remedy provided by nature*, against the fatal effects which would otherwise be produced, by the subdivision of labour accompanying the progress of the mechanical arts' (Stewart 1980: 313).

Smith sees the negative aspects of commercialism as regrettable but tolerable (and in most cases ameliorable) by-products, and, most importantly, *symptoms*, of material prosperity. He ultimately rejects simple social forms in favour of large-scale, non-particularistic communities based on self-command, civilised strangership, 'calculation' and 'self-interest', and regulated by impartial justice (*LJ[B]*: 538–39, 528; *WN*, I.ii: 26; see also Berry 1992: 80–82). In a world moderated by the predictable and temperate rhythms of 'sympathy', the impartial spectator and a formal system of justice and defence, cool virtue, happiness, social harmony and prosperity will likely proliferate exponentially.

Good Governance, Social Capital and an Expanding Middle Class

Smith both approved of and was optimistic about the future of the commercial age, not only because it enhanced prosperity and freedom and brought order, but also because it naturally led to a superior political culture and better government. Commercial societies are more orderly and just than their 'rude and barbarous' predecessors, due to the diffusion of 'probity and punctuality' that 'always accompan[ies]' the development of commerce. Further, commercial societies are characterised by higher levels of social capital and trust (*LJ[B]*, 327: 538). 'A polished people', opines Smith, inevitably 'become frank, open and sincere' compared to '[b]arbarians' who 'necessarily acquire the habits of falsehood and dissimulation' (*TMS*, V.2.11: 208); the more commercial a nation, the more are its people 'faithfull to their word' (*LJ[B]*, 327: 538).[16] There is a direct connection between progress in 'commerce and manufactures' and the introduction of order, and 'good government' and the 'liberty and security of individuals' (*WN*, III.Iii.12: 405; *WN*, II.iii.36: 345). Hume agreed that 'progress in the arts' is 'favourable to liberty, and has a natural tendency to preserve, if not produce a free government'. This was partly because commerce drew 'authority and consideration to that middling rank of men, who are the best and firmest basis of public liberty' (Hume 1987: 277). Hume followed Aristotle in arguing that a large middle class of 'tradesmen and merchants' preserves liberty because, on the one hand, its members refuse to 'submit to slavery' but, on the other, have no desire to 'tyranniz[e] over others'. Rather, they only 'covet equal law' in order to 'secure their property and preserve them from monarchical, as well as aristocratical tyranny'. In fact, Hume attributes the gathering influence of the 'lower house' of Parliament to the 'encrease of commerce' (Hume 1987: 278).

In their attitude to luxury—and commerce in general—thinkers like Smith and Hume drew upon the *doux commerce* thesis promulgated by Montesquieu. On this view, economic development was not an inlet to degenerative corruption. Rather, it had a positive, softening effect on the manners of a people and was responsible for the pacification of conflict between states and conspecifics. Montesquieu wrote that 'it is an almost general rule that everywhere there are gentle mores, there is commerce; and everywhere there is commerce, there are gentle mores' (Montesquieu 1989: 338).

The commercial age is also politically superior because it has begun to deal with the problem of systemic corruption (as shown in Chap. 5). That Smith delighted in the age of commerce is also reflected in his advertised belief that commerce is synonymous with (or at least a necessary 'requisite' for) civilisation and refinement in the arts, sciences and manners of a people. Indeed, the 'desire of elegance and refinement' is innate and therefore an irresistible spur to industry (*LJ[A]*, 24: 340). The art of prose composition is especially improved because it is 'naturally the Language of Business; as Poetry is of pleasure and amusement' (*LRB*: 137). Hume also observed that the more opulent and refined a civilisation, the more industrious, knowledgeable and humane is the culture and the less 'excess[ive]', licentious and self-indulgent are its individual members (Hume 1987: 270–71). And, of course, as has already been discussed, the commercial age is the age of greater internal and external security (*WN*, III.iv.4: 412).

Conclusion

From the long view, Smith is a technology and development optimist: the world is basically benign, progressive and driven by natural laws. There is a 'natural progress of things towards improvement' despite human errors and perverse policy and institutions (*WN*, V.i.g.24: 802–803). The social changes that made thinkers like Rousseau and Ferguson so anxious give Smith cause for complacency and optimism. Market society transforms social interaction dramatically and for the better in a number of ways; it purges relationships of their intensity and makes possible less intense but more universal, ubiquitous, diffuse and pacific forms of instrumental association. The modern commercial state provides security from external threat and regulates conflict between conspecifics. Commerce domesticates competition, invidious comparison and avarice out of a general imperative to promote markets and cultivate clientage. Particularistic cleavages have been broken down and a more universalistic and moderately civil society established: the exchange culture is one of calm friendliness.

Smith's vision is a categorically modern one. He describes and endorses a community held together, not by total forms of rule and muscular states, but by spontaneous and voluntaristic mechanisms in which the obligatory and total aspects of monolithic institutions like the church, feudal estate, extended family and corporation have been broken down. Independent agents are now governed by constrained sympathy, the cool virtues and the amiable conventions of commercial strangership, while their interactions are regulated and sustained by the division of labour, exchange and a regular system of justice. Partly because the secure state is the more regular and tolerant state and partly because commercial agents are better self-governors, the people will also have more liberty than has been possible at any other stage of history.

Notes

1. Mechanical and organic solidarity refers to 'the distinction drawn by Emile Durkheim between two types of social solidarity; mechanical ... based on the similarity between individuals, the form ... predominant in simple ... societies, and organic ... based on the division of labour and complementarities between individuals ... ideally occurring in modern advanced societies' (Jary and Jary 1991: 389).
2. Further discussion of the relationship between self-interest and the other-regarding virtues in Smith's thought is found in Hill (1996).
3. As noted by Ernest Gellner in relation to the archetypal liberal agent generally (Gellner 1994: 99–100).
4. According to Ferguson: 'the citizen ... must submit to personal hardship for the benefit of his country' (1792, I: 412).
5. As reported by Dugald Stewart (1980) in a document no longer in existence (Winch 1978: 4, n.2).
6. 'The life of a savage, when we take a distant view of it, seems to be a life either of profound indolence, or of great and astonishing adventures' (Smith 1980: 251).
7. Note, however, that Smith's cosmopolitanism is neither moral nor political but mainly economic (see Chap. 6).
8. The *Oxford Latin Dictionary* defines 'necessitudo' as 'a bond or tie between persons, obligation, connection, affinity ... a bond or affinity between things'. Lewis and Short's *Latin Dictionary* defines it as 'a close connection ... relationship, friendship, intimacy, bond'. It is the source of the archaic English term 'necessitude'.
9. Clubs and societies were extremely important to the social and intellectual life of the milieu that Smith inhabited. Although some 'were little more than glorified drinking clubs others were highly formal, highly institutionalized organizations' (Phillipson 1981: 19, 27, 31–32).
10. 'Self-command is not only itself a great virtue, but from it all the other virtues seem to derive their principal lustre' (*TMS*, VI.iii.11: 241).
11. Smith opines that the passions of 'savages' are better concealed but fiercer than those of polished people (*TMS*, V.2.11: 208).

12. '[W]thout the disposition to truck, barter and exchange, every man must have procured to himself every necessary and conveniency of life which he wanted. All must have had the same duties to perform, and the same work to do, and there could have been no such difference of employment as could alone give occasion to any great difference of talents.' That same disposition to trade 'renders the difference' between people 'useful'; it brings the 'different geniuses and talents' of people into the 'common stock' thereby 'contribut[ing] to the better accommodation and conveniency of the species' (*WN*, I.ii.5–6: 29–30).
13. Smith notes that 'the hardiness demanded of savages diminishes their humanity; and perhaps, the delicate sensibility required in civilized nations sometimes destroys the masculine firmness of the character' (*TMS*, V.2.13: 209; see also *TMS*, V.2.8: 205).
14. Hume agreed. See Letter 141 from Hume to Smith, St. Andrews Square, 13 Feb. 1774 (*Corr.*:171).
15. This is very similar to the dynamic later identified by Emile Durkheim. As Robert Merton describes Durkheim's insight: 'the division of social labour ... while it enhances, nay compels, individuation, also occasions an "organic solidarity" based upon the interdependences of co-operatively functioning individuals and groups' (Merton 1934: 320).
16. Smith attributes this partially to more ordered security, justice and policing, but he also attributes some of these effects 'to self interest, that general principle which regulates the actions of every man ... A dealer is afraid of losing his character, and is scrupulous in observing every engagement' (*LJ[B]*, 327: 538).

References

Berg, M., & Eger, E. (2003). *Luxury in the Eighteenth Century*. New York and Basingstoke: Palgrave Macmillan.

Berry, C. J. (1992). Adam Smith and the Virtues of Commerce. *Nomos, XXXIV*, 69–88.

Berry, C. (1994). *The Idea of Luxury*. Cambridge: Cambridge University Press.

Eriksson, B. (1993). The First Formulation of Sociology: A Discursive Innovation of the Eighteenth Century. *Archives-Europeennes-de-Sociologie, 34*(2), 251–276.

Ferguson, A. (1792). *Principles of Moral and Political Science: Being Chiefly a Retrospect of Lectures Delivered in the College of Edinburgh, in Two Volumes*. Edinburgh: Printed for A. Strahan and T. Cadell, London, and W. Creech, Edinburgh.

Gellner, E. (1994). *Conditions of Liberty: Civil Society and Its Rivals*. London: Penguin Books.

Griswold, C. (1999). *Adam Smith and the Virtues of the Enlightenment.* Cambridge: Cambridge University Press.

Hill, L. (1996). 'Ferguson and Smith on 'Human Nature', 'Interest' and the Role of Beneficence in Market Society', *Journal of the History of Economic Ideas*, Adam Smith Special Edition, *IV* (1–2), 353–399.

Hill, L. (2006). Adam Smith and the Theme of Corruption. *Review of Politics, 68*(4), 636–662.

Hill, L. (2011). Adam Smith on *Thumos* and Irrational Economic Man. *European Journal of the History of Economic Thought, 17*(4), 1–22.

Hume, D. (1983). *The History of England, in Six Volumes*, William B. Todd (Ed.), Indianapolis: Liberty Classics.

Hume, D. (1987). Refinement in the Arts. In E. F. Millar (Ed.), *Essays Moral, Political and Literary* (pp. 272–278). Indianapolis: Liberty Classics.

Ignatieff, M. (1984). *The Needs of Strangers.* London: Chatto and Windus.

Jary, D., & Jary, J. (Eds.). (1991). *The Collins Dictionary of Sociology.* Glasgow: Harper Collins.

Merton, R. K. (1934). Durkheim's Division of Labor in Society. *American Journal of Sociology, 40*(3), 319–328.

Mizuta, H. (1976). Towards a Definition of the Scottish Enlightenment. *Studies in Voltaire, 154*, 1459–1464.

Montesquieu, C. L. (1989). *The Spirit of the Laws* (A. M. Cohler, Trans. and Ed.). Cambridge, B. C. Miller & H. M. Stone.

Perelman, M. (1989). Adam Smith and Dependent Social Relations. *History of Political Economy, 21*(3), 312–329.

Phillipson, N. (1981). The Scottish Enlightenment. In R. Porter & M. Teich (Eds.), *The Enlightenment in National Context* (pp. 19–40). Cambridge: Cambridge University Press.

Reesor, M. E. (1951). *The Political Theory of the Old and Middle Stoa.* New York: J.J. Augustin.

Rosanvallon, P. (2006). The Market, Liberalism and Anti-Liberalism. In S. Moyn (Ed.), *Democracy Past and Future* (pp. 252–282). New York: Columbia University Press.

Silver, A. (1989). Friendship and Trust as Moral Ideals: An Historical Approach. *European Journal of Sociology, 30*, 274–297.

Smith, A. (1976 [1759]). *The Theory of Moral Sentiments*, D. D. Raphael & A. L. MacFie (Eds.). Oxford: Clarendon Press.

Smith, A. (1978). *Lectures on Jurisprudence (A and B)*, R. L. Meek, D. D. Raphael & L. G. Stein (Eds.). Oxford: Oxford University Press.

Smith, A. (1979 [1776]). *An Inquiry into the Nature and Causes of the Wealth of Nations*, R. H. Campbell & A. S. Skinner (Eds.). Oxford: Clarendon Press.

Smith, A. (1980). Letter to the Edinburgh Review. In I. S. Ross (Ed.), *Essays on Philosophical Subjects.* Oxford: Clarendon Press.

Smith, A. (1987). The Correspondence of Adam Smith, E. C. Mossner & I. S. Ross (Eds.). Oxford: Oxford University Press.

Stewart, D. (1980 [1793]). Account of the Life and Writings of Adam Smith, LL.D, I.S. Ross (ed.). In W. P. D. Wightman & J. C. Bryce (Eds.), *Adam Smith: Essays on Philosophical Subjects*. Oxford: Oxford University Press.

Strasser, R. (1976). *The Normative Structure of Sociology: Conservative and Emancipatory Themes in Social Thought*. London: Routledge/Kegan Paul.

Winch, D. (1978). *Adam Smith's Politics*. Cambridge: Cambridge University Press.

Wootton, D. (1993). David Hume "The Historian". In D. F. Norton (Ed.), *The Cambridge Companion to David Hume* (pp. 447–479). Cambridge: Cambridge University Press.

CHAPTER 5

Adam Smith on Political Corruption

Introductory Comments

It is little appreciated that Smith was an important anti-corruption theorist who partially drove the emergence of the 'modern' conception of political corruption. Smith evidently wished to take the pessimistic moralising out of corruption debates in favour of confronting and ideologically accommodating the 'facts' of human nature and the material and economic realities of commercial life. His new framework for conceiving and addressing corruption rejected the endist eschatologies of classical and medieval corruption discourses and focused on the positive aspects of luxury, interest, commercial progress and worldly pride, phenomena hitherto condemned as symptoms of degenerative corruption. Corruption was no longer to be understood as an inevitable consequence of prosperity, a diffuse condition infecting the entire polity, or a problem of virtue to be remedied by a return to more primitive conditions and the cultivation of classical civic virtues. Rather, it was increasingly a matter of boundaries, good governance and rules instituted by a minimal, properly constituted and appropriately separated state that governed in the interests of *all* the people not just self-interested elites. Some attention is paid here to alleged proto-Marxist corruption tendencies in Smith's thought.

Smith's sustained defence of what are now standard liberal values—impartiality, universalism, neutrality, liberty, formal equality of opportunity, government restraint and rule of law—is at the bottom an attempt to address the problem of political corruption and its attendant maladaptivities; namely,

L. Hill, *Adam Smith's Pragmatic Liberalism*,
https://doi.org/10.1007/978-3-030-19337-9_5

a dysfunctional state, 'crony capitalism', relentless interstate conflict, high levels of public debt, suboptimal productivity levels, economic inefficiency, food insecurity and an ungovernable, resource-draining empire.

Smith has sometimes been portrayed as a thinker with either a classical approach to the decline of nations or else a proto-Marxist interest in the corrupting effects of early capitalism. Smith is certainly interested in the corruption theme, but he is better understood as a shaper of the modern, (proto-)liberal conception. Indeed, it might be more accurate to put this the other way around because, in his attack on corruption, he emerges as an important shaper of the liberal tradition itself which, by its nature, is at least partly a response to the endemic corruption that prevailed in Britain (and elsewhere) as that tradition was emerging and crystallising. Before continuing, the term 'corruption' as used in this discussion requires some clarification.

Defining Corruption

The term 'corruption' has been notoriously difficult to define (Philp 1987) but scholars have typically distinguished between the 'classical' ('degenerative') and 'modern' ('public office') senses of the term, dominating at different periods of history. The first, which Bruce Buchan and Lisa Hill (2014) have labelled 'degenerative corruption', dominated the classical period and persisted in prominence until well into the eighteenth century. 'Degenerative corruption' has a much broader meaning than 'public office' corruption and refers 'less to the actions of individuals' than to the general moral health of the body politic (Johnston 1996: 322). Within the classical tradition,[1] the typical candidate for corruption is the prosperous, over-extended empire and its usual triggers are *hubris*, aggressive militaristic expansion, irreligiousness, hedonism, civic withdrawal, systemic wealth inequality, over-reliance on mercenary armies and a consequent forfeiture of political virtue in both citizenry and political elites. Corruption was not so much an individualised breach of rules or duties as a condition that spread contagiously and diffusely throughout the polity affecting leaders and citizens alike. On this understanding, corruption was linked to fears of a general degeneracy caused by 'the idleness, luxury, or sinfulness of the young, of women, of the rich, of foreigners or of the entire populace' and was capable of undermining 'good laws and order, proper government, or even whole empires' (Buchan and Hill 2014, ch. 1, *passim*).

Britain's increasing prosperity and imperialistic tendencies inspired contemporaries of Smith like Edward Gibbon and Adam Ferguson to draw parallels between ancient Rome and contemporary Britain. The decline of Republican Rome was blamed on the triumph of Epicureanism over Stoicism; the former described a godless world governed by chance, reduced morality to hedonism and defined all good as private. Therefore, cures for the ills of the ailing nation were seen to lie in the recovery of virtue as conceived by Stoicism, the traditional adversary of Epicureanism (see, for example, Ferguson 1834: 169–70). This dichotomy was a popular one in seventeenth- and eighteenth-century moral and political discourse and it was commonly asserted that the British populace was succumbing to Epicureanism (Dickey 1986: 606).

For millennia the degenerative conception tended to dominate corruption debates. But the narrower, 'modern' conception—known as 'public office corruption', with which we are now familiar—began to eclipse it in the eighteenth century. 'Public office corruption' refers to the abuse of public office for private gain and denotes behaviour that deviates from the formal duties of a public role because of private-regarding (personal, close family, private clique) pecuniary or status gains; or that violates rules against the exercise of certain types of private-regarding influence. This includes such behaviour as bribery (use of reward to pervert the judgement of a person in a position of trust); nepotism (bestowal of patronage by reason of ascriptive relationship rather than merit); and misappropriation (illegal appropriation of public resources for private-regarding uses) (Nye 1989: 966).

A Modern Smith

Smith wrote at a time when the idea of corruption was being refined due to pressure from a number of broad historical trends. The first was the expansion of commercialism and British domestic and foreign markets. As Britain's empire and economy grew so did the opportunities and scope for corruption; this, in turn, hastened the emergence of new understandings of the relationship between private interests and public duties. Another set of pressures was brought about by the development of the modern state which was expanding rapidly in terms of the 'expansion of material infrastructure and social administration' (Langford 2002: 105; see also Innes 2002: 112).

English governance was becoming somewhat more sophisticated and organised during this period (Langford 2002: 105; see also Innes 2002: 112). With that complexity and increasing organisation came a sharpening of the line between private market and public state affairs that was accompanied by the emergence of proto-liberal sensibilities. Modern, liberal values like impartiality, merit, neutrality and egalitarianism were increasingly invoked to combat the absolutism, nepotism, particularism and patronage that attended feudal and aristocratic forms of governance and were still in play during Smith's heyday. Although many eighteenth-century thinkers continued to employ the term 'corruption' in its classical sense (Hirschman 1977: 40; Buchan and Hill 2014), scholars and reformers increasingly drew attention to practices and institutions that would now qualify as sins against modern sensibilities. Smith was on the latter side of the discussion in a period when the distinction between classical/degenerative and modern/public office conceptions of corruption was becoming unstable. Indeed, Smith was one of its key destabilisers. He was not only clear in his own mind about what corruption meant but he sought to bring the rest of the world around to his own way of thinking on the topic.

Smith's vision is a decidedly modern one, reflecting his determination to work towards three goals: first, to make a decisive break with the past and traditional aetiologies of social disorder; second, to develop the 'science' of political economy; and, third, to solve applied problems of public governance that affected the public welfare. Many British political thinkers of the eighteenth century saw their society as 'shot through with corruption and venality' (Prest 1991: 68). Politics was seen as 'a racket, run by particular groups within the ruling classes largely for their own benefit' (Corrigan and Sayer 1985: 89) and the general view was that government, in all its forms, was 'parasitical' and wasteful, existing mainly to serve and enrich elites (Pocock 1975: 119–20). Corruption took the form of such practices as the extension to political cronies of government sinecures, reversions,[2] 'pensions, government contracts ... church preferments' (Hellmuth 1999: 22–23), the dispensation of monopoly grants to favoured patrons, electoral bribery and rotten boroughs, patronage, (Phillips 1979: 76–100) and the control of state institutions by party factions (Innes 2002: 109). Public debt and government profligacy were also implicated in the corruption problem and were of special interest to Smith. However, Smith's critique of the British state was neither 'degenerative' nor even 'proto-Marxist', as some have claimed, because, not only does Smith welcome the advent of commercialism and prosperity, but his progressivist historiography—as canvassed in previous chapters—precludes the kind of pessimistic or endist attitudes to commercialism that underlie both degenerative and Marxist accounts.

A Pessimistic Smith?

A number of scholars have argued that Smith is pessimistic about the corrupting tendencies of the commercial age and even that he perceives in 'capitalism' the seeds of its own inevitable destruction.[3] I have already argued that, while Smith is by no means oblivious to the disadvantages of the commercial age, nevertheless, there are a number of reasons to cleave to the standard characterisation of Smith as optimistic about the future prospects of the commercial polity[4] and to see his approach as a decisive break with antique and neoclassical discourses of corruption. Within the latter account, it is assumed that corruption is triggered by the virtue-sapping consequences of imperial conquest, wealth inequality, standing armies and the dissipating effects of commercialism, prosperity, luxury and conspicuous consumption (Dickey 1986: 606). Except for empire-building, none of these things bothered Smith; indeed, he enthusiastically embraced them.

Smith as a Degenerative Corruption Theorist?

To begin with, in contrast to classical accounts, Smith sees the traditional threats to prosperous empires as either minimal or no longer imminent where Britain was concerned. For example, a common cause of decline in classical accounts is the professionalisation of armies. Smith denied that professional standing armies threatened either the virtue or the security of the polity as many theorists of the seventeenth and eighteenth century influenced by classical discourses had insisted (Schwoerer 1974; Robertson 1985). Not only do they provide better security than citizen militias but they also generate positive changes in the social fabric. By releasing the citizenry from public duties, standing armies allow citizens to carry on with their independent commercial pursuits. Further, in providing internal security, standing armies engender the high levels of trust, order, liberty and security necessary for such pursuits to flourish (*WN*, I.xi.i: 256; see also *WN*, I.xi.g: 213–14; *WN*, V.i.a.41: 706–707).

Another important source of corruption in classical accounts of empire decline—systemic inequality (see Buchan and Hill 2014: 25–27)—was not something Smith sought to eradicate, as has been shown in more detail in other chapters. Although he quite definitely sought to raise the living standards of both the poor and 'middling' classes, his main goal was to alleviate absolute rather than relative poverty. Rather than threatening the commercial state, Smith believed that rank distinctions and wealth inequalities were a natural product of modernity due to equally natural developments in the accumulation, maintenance and legal regulation of private property (*LJ[A]*, 26: 340). This is not the same as saying that Smith was unconcerned about the problem of poverty among the lower classes. It is clear Smith's concern for the poor—novel among his contemporaries—ran deep (see Chap. 1).

But Smith thought that the maintenance of social hierarchies (so long as they were accompanied by other structures and policies that permitted the poor to gain independence) was important for the achievement of the kind of economic growth and prosperity that was capable of benefiting everybody, especially the poor. The mechanism at work here is invidious comparison. In a class system that tolerates and protects the existence of models for emulation (the rich), the labouring poor will be incentivised to work and save in order to buy those items of 'ostentatious avidity' enjoyed by their social superiors (*TMS*, I.iii.2.1: 50–51).

Luxury

Neither is Smith the least bit worried about the potential effects of luxury upon commercial subjects; in fact, as shown in previous chapters, he considers it a major source of prosperity and growth. He notes that although basic human needs are limited, our 'desire of the conveniencies and ornaments of building, dress, equipage, and household furniture' is, naturally, without limit (*WN*, I.xi.c.7, 180–82). Smith defined happiness largely in terms of material abundance (*WN*, I.V.iii.36: 96) and explicitly rejected those 'popular ascetic doctrines' that denied the social and economic utility of 'luxury, sensuality, and ostentation' (*TMS*, VII.ii.4.12: 313). Note that 'luxury' was a more or less pejorative term during this period and Smith was careful to stipulate that his use of the term was not intended 'to throw the smallest degree of reproach upon the temperate use' of it (*WN*, V.ii.k.3: 870). Along with David Hume and James Stewart, Smith argued that luxuries were necessary for growth and full employment; their production and consumption encouraged innovation (*TMS*, VII.ii.4.12: 313), stimulated the circulation of money and commodities and even encouraged population growth (*WN*, I.xi.c.7, 180–82; see also Chap. 4).

For Smith, the whole luxury debate was built on unstable foundations since the idea of a luxury was relative, varying from place to place and dependent on local customs and norms (*WN*, V.II.k.3: 869–71). The consumption of luxuries was not corrupting—and was quite definitely economically productive—provided it was moderate (*WN*, V.ii.k.3: 869–70). In a nation where luxury consumption is ubiquitous it is more likely to be healthy and progressive than in imminent danger of decline (see, for example, *WN*, I.i.11: 23–24; *WN*, I.viii.35: 95–96).

Smith's rehabilitation of luxuries is closely bound up in his more general rehabilitation of the body and the self-regarding drives. There was much to gain in this rehabilitation: if so-called 'luxury' consumption were seen as natural and respectable, it would be taxed less, disapproved of less and be more ubiquitous, all of which stimulated the economy and unleashed growth. Further, if Smith could counteract the puritanical moralising of those who objected to the luxury consumption of the poor, he had a further justification for raising their wages and a demonstrable means for increasing their enjoyment and happiness, as was shown in previous chapters.

Smith sees himself as a realist who understands that an increasingly large-scale, market society cannot be sustained by other-regarding virtues and a denial of bodily needs. He sought to rehabilitate those basic urges of the body condemned by both classical and Christian teachings as sinful, dangerous and in need of repression. Our physical needs and urges were given to us by our Creator as a gesture of concern and affection and therefore are nothing to be ashamed of or denied (*LJ[B]*, 300: 527). Self-interest—and all the other drives associated with it—is not vicious but an adaptive, morally neutral survival mechanism that is both natural and benign.

Worldly Pride

Smith not only rehabilitates the concerns of the body in his political economy; he also rehabilitates the closely related urge of worldly pride. Prideful self-interest was a major source of corruption for medieval thinkers working within the degenerative tradition. Saint Augustine, Saint Paul and John of Salisbury were all disdainful of the chief sin of pride or self-love which, as Salisbury decreed, was the 'root of all the evils that feed mortality … infecting the vital organs' of the body politic (Buchan and Hill 2014: 65). On this account, those infected with pride have rejected God in favour of sensuality, money and earthly power.

But Smith takes the morality out of worldly pride, emphasising its naturalness and adaptiveness. Not only is prideful self-interest ('spirit' or 'ambition') natural; an absence of it should be looked upon as a constitutional and psychological defect. Anyone who fails to pursue worldly success and 'the objects of self-interest' demonstrates a cavalier regard for his or her own 'rank' and reputation; whether the 'prince' who is 'not anxious about conquering or defending a province' or the gentleman who disdains to 'exert himself to gain an estate', all are described contemptuously as 'mean-spirited' persons of 'dull regularity' whom Smith compares unfavourably with the spirited 'man of enterprise' (*TMS*, III.6.7: 173–74). He applauds the pragmatic virtues of the industrious, consumeristic and economically productive commercial agent (*WN*, V.i.e.29: 772) and argues that it is not the self-denying ascetic but rather he or she who exercises the 'passion' of ambition ('within the bounds of prudence') who is really and 'always admired in the world' (*TMS*, III.6.7: 173).

Proto-Marxist?

Not only is Smith not pessimistic in the manner of degenerative accounts of corruption; neither is he pessimistic about the future of commercial societies in the manner of a proto-Marxist, as has sometimes been claimed. For example, because of his extremely negative and apparently pessimistic observations about the 'alienation' effects of specialisation on workers it has been suggested that Smith's comments on the division of labour in Book V of the *Wealth of Nations* 'constitute a major source of inspiration for the socialist critique' of capitalism (Rosenberg 1965: 127) and that it was Smith 'who first broached the potentially explosive topic of the effects of the division of labour' (Forbes 1967: 47).[5] Along similar lines Robert Lamb has argued that Smith regarded factory workers as alienated in the fullest sense as Marx applied it (Lamb 1973: 273). It has even been suggested that Smith's comments should be interpreted as a sign that he anticipated the decline and eventual annihilation of the commercial age. For example, Robert Heilbroner suggests that, for Smith, laissez-faire capitalism contains the seeds of its own destruction (Heilbroner 1973) while Spencer Pack argues that Smith sees 'capitalism' as only one level or stage of human development that must eventually give way to something else because of its adverse effects on moral character (Pack 1991).

Such claims exaggerate the real extent of Smith's concerns.[6] It is true that Smith was well aware of the 'alienating' consequences of the division of labour, noting that the worker involved in factory labour is affected both intellectually and morally. This was no trivial concern but affected 'the great body of the people' in every commercial society (*WN*, V.i.f.49–50: 781–82). There is no doubt that Smith's outline of the dehumanising effects of specialisation on workers pre-empts Marx's discourse on the same subject to the extent that it hints at the effects of fragmentation, product alienation (Kettler 1965: 8–9) and even exploitation. In fact, Smith indirectly inspired Marx's critical polemic on the same subject[7] and Marx cited Smith repeatedly as an authority on this and other subjects (Marx 1969: 129, 131; 1977: 129).

But, in contrast to Marx, Smith conceives specialisation as a perfectly natural development originating in an innate urge to 'truck, barter and exchange' (*WN*, II.1: 25) and in our inventive, progressive faculties. Most importantly, as already discussed, the division of labour, even where it extends to martial functions, generates great levels of liberty and independence for all members of society, including the working poor. On balance, Smith sees the adverse effects of specialisation more as 'inconveniences' (*LJ[B]*, 328: 539) than anything else and they are far outweighed by the benefits. The division of labour is enormously beneficial, generating almost all of the progress and prosperity of the commercial age (*WN*, I.i.10–111: 22–24). Those most affected by those benefits are the poor since 'there is no order that suffers so cruelly from [economic] decline' as those who live by wages (*WN*, I.xi.9: 266).

Although Smith's analysis of the drawbacks of specialisation is extremely prescient and considerate of the working poor, it is not radical: he never advocates any reform of the system but merely says that its bad effects can be addressed within existing social and political arrangements. From Smith's point of view, the main problem with the adverse effect of the division of labour is not the loss of civic virtue or the imminent collapse of the whole commercial system but its largely ameliorable consequences for public order and personal comportment. Smith regarded the problem of worker 'alienation' as soluble through the establishment of a compulsory and publicly funded school system to inculcate patterns of orderliness and civility suitable for market society subjects (*WN*, V.i.f.61: 88; see Chap. 7). And contrary to Marx, Smith regards specialisation, and the social inequality it perpetuates and entrenches, as a natural, inevitable and socially adaptive process, as has already been argued.[8] From Smith's perspective, if things go as they are meant to, progress will happen and this is to be welcomed. At the same time some adjustments might be necessary to offset some of the inevitable externalities of commercial progress.

Pessimistic and endist interpretations of Smith therefore exaggerate Smith's apprehensions about the commercial age and Smith does not see the declining or stationary state as a likelihood in either the classical or Marxian sense. As a realist, he does not attempt to paper over the dark side of development; but at the same time, there is no portent of impending decline or tragedy lurking beneath the darker aspects of his analysis. Rather, his discourse on the likely causes of corruption is framed within a progressivist, open-ended and basically optimistic historiography (see Chaps. 4 and 7).

For Smith, the degenerative account of corruption had no explanatory power for mass, commercial societies of increasingly prosperous, distant and independent economic producers, and his work on this topic seeks to outline a more appropriate approach to guaranteeing the strength and security of modern orders, keeping it free from corruption. A return to the alleged halcyon age of small-scale, agrarian virtue called for by the classical approach was not an option; rather, institutional and economic solutions had to be found for managing large and fast-expanding economies and to secure them from the 'public office' corruption that he now considered more relevant and pressing.

Public Office Corruption

As both state and market activity expanded and gradually separated, Smith sought to clarify their relationship within his political economy. This largely involved cordoning off the private sphere of activity from the public so that the market—and the individual actors who operated it—could work properly. Smith does not show much interest in the typical anxieties of classical republicans or Christian moralisers. There is no defence of classical virtue because corruption does not arise from political apathy, hedonism, selfishness or an inattention to the public sphere (as per classical accounts) but is conceived in a new way as a product of maladaptive political and economic arrangements: an insufficiently unseparated state; sluggish, paternalistic, particularistic, dependency-generating forms of governance and control; heavy taxation; a debt-ridden economy and a state captured by religious and sectional interests at the expense of individual consumers and the system in general. This is quite definitely a 'public office' discourse on corruption.

Smith saw government profligacy as synonymous with corruption (*WN*, V.ii.k.64: 898) because it pointed to the fact that rulers were ruling in their own interests, rather than in those of the people. He also drew attention to practices that are now standard forms of public office corruption, criticising the practice of sinecure granting and the domination of Parliament by sectional interests (*WN*, IV.ii.43: 471; *WN*, IV.vii.b.49:

584; *WN*, IV.viii.17: 647; *WN*, V.i.e.4: 733). He remarked that '[i]n a Country where Clamour always intimidates and faction often oppresses the Government, the regulations of Commerce are commonly dictated by those who are most interested to deceive and impose upon the Public' (*Corr.*: 286). In a letter to William Eden in 1783 he frankly opined that the laws governing trade were 'in every case a complete piece of dupery, by which the interest of the State and the nation is constantly sacrificed to that of some particular class of traders' (*Corr.*: 272).

Smith also complained of the unrepresentative character of the Parliament (*LJ[A]*, v.134–35: 323–24), noting elsewhere that corruption always attends 'absolute government' where 'favours are bestowed and all publick offices conferred on the favourites of the king' (*LJ[A]* V.15: 275). He was also interested in the problem of judicial bribery,[9] specifically describing it as a form of 'corruption' (*LJ[A]*, v.23: 279; *LJ[B]*, 67: 423; *WN*, V.i.b: 719). He wrote pointedly that '[p]ublick services are never better performed than when their reward comes only in consequence of their being performed, and is proportioned to the diligence employed in performing them' (*WN*, V.i.b: 719).

Imperialism and Corruption

One of the most egregious violations of the system of natural liberty—and therefore an extremely productive source of corruption—was British imperialism and the Mercantilism that went hand in hand with it. I have mentioned above that imperial conquest, over-extension and national *hubris* are major sources of corruption within the degenerative account, hence it might be thought that Smith displays some antique tendencies here. However, Smith's interest is more proto-liberal than classical. In his critique of British imperialism he is concerned with violations of the market broadly understood: the system of natural liberty, not the luxury, prosperity and hedonism that imperial expansion generally brings with it. Indeed, as we have seen, he welcomed these things as natural. Further, he is no little-Englander and his antidote to the over-extended state is not a return to small-scale agrarian simplicity, as in the classical account; rather, it is a transnational market between sovereign states spanning the globe, as is shown in more detail in Chap. 6.

Smith agreed with Adam Ferguson that empire originated with, and was perpetuated by, *hubris* and that it was a sure path to national (i.e. British) ruin, but not because of its effect on virtue so much as its disastrous consequences for both the domestic and global economies, its impracticality and its implications for British sovereignty, good governance and the all-important distinctions between public and private, government and economy. Smith's critique of British imperialism was related to his dislike of Mercantilism and its monopolistic practices. He also railed against the never-ending interstate conflict that empire promised. This led to rising taxes and unsupportable levels of public debt (Kittrell 1965: 190), which, in turn, exacerbated the system of patronage,[10] all of which contributed to the corruption of the British state (Hellmuth 1999: 19–21; Brewer 1976: 249f).

Just as domestic constraints, like the poor laws, are an egregious violation of the natural laws of motion that govern interactions between economic agents, so too is imperial Mercantilism. As a consequence of the dispensation of monopoly grants and the arbitrary bestowal of 'extraordinary privileges' and 'restraints' upon different sectors of industry by government, certain individuals were able to enrich themselves at the expense of others yet without, at the same time, enriching the nation (*WN*, IV.iii.c.9: 493). Monopolies were both a cause and a symptom of corruption because they could only come into existence via corrupt, non-market means. Specifically, it was common practice that 'stockholders of the competing Old and New East India companies' bid 'for the votes of small and corrupt boroughs in order to secure the controlling interest in Parliament', thereby enabling them to eliminate any rivals for the lucrative East Indies trade (Curtis 1979: 244).

Corruption and the 'Natural' Solution: The System of Natural Liberty

Smith's picture of corruption is best understood in relation to his attempt to establish the science of political economy which, from his own perspective, was a purely social-scientific, morally neutral exercise divorced from standard moralistic virtue narratives or normative critiques of progress and commercialisation. Corruption consists in violations of the system of natural liberty, including violations that corrupt the naturally self-governing behaviour of individual actors. In other words, corruption is instigated by obstructions to the 'natural' course of progress rather than by progress itself; accordingly, *more* progress is generally his solution to any of the pathologies of modernity. The problem is not modernity, prosperity, hedonism, martial specialisation, civic withdrawal, commercialism or any of the other triggers of corruption found in classical accounts but rather a *lack* of commercial progress, a *lack* of modernity and a *lack* of withdrawal into private and individuated concerns.

Pre-commercial social and political arrangements generate corruption because of their tendency to discourage individual autonomy on the one hand and interfere with the natural laws of the market on the other. Enumerated among these (public office) corrupting remnants of pre-commercial stages are religious fanaticism and sectarianism; political faction; and monolithic, paternalistic and intrusive forms of governance, including any institutional and legal impediments to the free play of the market and the development of independent moral character. Among the latter variety Smith included monopolies (legally sanctioned or otherwise), poor laws, the laws of settlement, corporation privileges, apprenticeship laws, statutes of apprenticeship, restrictions on international trade and regulations governing the institutions of entail and primogeniture. These restrictions could not only corrupt individual agents but could also threaten the prosperity and security of entire nations.

Although all of these archaic phenomena persisted in commercial societies, Smith's point was that they did not *naturally* belong in them. In his view they needed to be purged in order to deliver society into its 'natural' state and thereby secure the commercial stage from stalling, in the long term, and to prevent consumers from being victimised by its effects, in the short (*WN*, IV.V.iii.49: 660). The first step towards restoring the market or system of natural liberty was therefore to reduce the interfering and distorting reach of the state into the lives of individuals.

Reforming and Restraining the State

Smith never tired of pointing out the English's state's profligacy, wastefulness and hypocrisy in seeking to control the personal spending 'of private people' (*WN*, II.iii.35–36: 344–46). As he saw it, most public institutions contained the potential for 'negligency and corruption' (*Corr.*: 173) and he was strongly averse to any 'profusion of government' (*WN*, II.iii.36: 345) (see Chap. 3 for a fuller discussion). Since public office corruption is a problem largely created by archaic social forms and an over-intrusive, clique-ridden state, Smith's market solution starts with the reform of bloated and over-wieldy government and its reduction to the small—or at least smaller—night-watchman state. Ideally, this would take place in the wider context of a universe dominated by private commerce, not public politics.

Smith was alert to the possibility that non-state actors could infringe on the freedoms of individuals just as the state could. He cautioned against the spirit of monopoly, admonishing the 'mean rapacity' and 'monopolising spirit of merchants and manufacturers' (*WN*, IV.iii.c.9: 493) who often enjoy the protection and collusion of the state. According to Smith, 'master's monopolistic conspiracies'—or 'combinations' as he referred to them—were regular events. He noted that '[p]eople of the same trade seldom meet together' without in the end contriving 'to raise prices'. While it is 'impossible ... to prevent such meetings, by any law which either could be executed, or would be consistent with liberty and justice' by the same token 'it ought to do nothing to facilitate such assemblies; much less to render them necessary'. The kind of laws Smith had in mind here included any 'regulation which obliges all those of the same trade in a particular town to enter their names and places of abode in a public register' and also, notably, any law that requires 'those of the same trade to tax themselves in order to provide for their poor, their sick, their widows, and orphans'. The latter would make meetings necessary while the former would 'connect individuals who might never otherwise have known to one another' (*WN*, I.x.c.27–29: 145).

A particularly egregious imposition was the state-sanctioned power asymmetry that normally characterised relations between employers and employees in negotiations about wages. Smith finds it outrageous that whenever workers petition for higher wages '[i]t is not difficult to foresee which of the two parties must, upon all ordinary occasions, have the advantage in the dispute, and force the other into a compliance with their terms'. This is because the 'masters, being fewer in numbers, can combine more easily', but more importantly because 'the law ... authorises, or at least does not prohibit, their combinations, while it prohibits those of the workmen' (*WN*, I.viii.12–13: 83–84). When '[m]asters' collude to keep wages low', they do so with legal impunity but when 'workmen ... enter into a contrary combination of the same kind, not to accept of a certain wage ... the law would punish them very severely'. If the law 'dealt impartially, it would treat the masters in the same manner' (*WN*, I.x.c:61: 158). Smith is clear that the state is in breach of its duty when it acts otherwise: 'justice' dictates that the sovereign owes '*equality of treatment ... to all the different orders of his subjects*' (*WN*, IV.viii.30: 654; emphasis added).

Smith laments that '[w]e have no acts of Parliament against combining to lower the price of work, but many against combining to raise it'. Yet, in 'all such disputes, the master can hold out much longer' because 'he' has the resources, even without the labour of workers, 'to live a year or two upon the stocks, which [he has] already acquired' whereas most 'workmen could not subsist' a month or even a week 'without employment' (*WN*, I.viii.12–13: 83–84). Therefore, the laws—as well as public opinion—favour the side that already has the advantage in the relationship. And yet Smith's sympathies are clearly with the wage labourer here, not just because he or she is in the weaker position but partly because the interests of those who live by wages usually coincide with those of the public, whereas the interests of those who live by profit—the masters—tend to be at odds with those of the public (*WN*, I.xi.10: 266).

Smith notes with irritation that there is always a public outcry when workers collude to protect their own interests but rarely so when 'masters' do the same. And yet, Smith insists that they routinely do conspire against workers, usually in sinister and surreptitious ways:

> We rarely hear ... of the combination of masters, though frequently of those of workmen. But whoever imagines, upon this account, that masters rarely combine, is as ignorant of the world as of the subject. Masters are always and everywhere in a sort of tacit, but constant and uniform combination, not to raise the wages of labour above their actual rate ... We seldom, indeed, hear of this combination, because it is the usual, and one may say, the natural state of things, which nobody ever hears of ... *These are always conducted with the utmost silence and secrecy*. (*WN*, I.viii.12–13: 83–84. Emphasis added)

When workers attempt to resist, often by admittedly 'tumultuous combinations', they are invariably overwhelmed, 'partly from the necessity' from which 'the greater part of [them] are under of submitting for the sake of present subsistence' but also because of 'the interposition of the civil magistrate' who never intervenes to break up the same sort of monopolistic combinations of 'masters'. Instead, workers usually end up being punished for their collective attempts to resist and the 'ringleaders' eventually 'ruin[ed]' by it (*WN*, I.viii.12–13: 83–84). Despite his evident sympathy for workers in these passages, at no point does Smith suggest that worker combinations should be permitted to offset those of masters.[11] Rather, he seems to be suggesting that both should desist from the practice and that the state should stop colluding with masters. Neither does he recommend that the power differential between masters and workers 'be counteracted ... through legislation', as has been suggested (see Boucoyannis 2013: 1055–56).[12]

In any case, all the above impositions and restrictions were viewed by Smith as both corruptions of natural social laws and violations of the personal rights of individuals. They are not only extremely 'hurt[ful] to the natural state of commerce' (*LJ[B]*, 306–307: 529) but they are usually obtained via corrupt (i.e. non-free market) means, namely, through patronage or electoral and related forms of bribery. For example, due to its enjoyment of a powerful, state-protected monopoly of British/Asian commerce, the East India Company was a regular target for Smith's unsparing condemnation (see, for example, *WN*, IV.vii.c.91: 631; *WN*, IV.vii.c.107: 641). The privileged position of the company led to a situation where consumers 'paid' for not only the company's 'extraordinary profits ... but for all the extraordinary waste which the fraud and abuse, inseparable from the management of the affairs of so great a company, must necessarily have occasioned' (*WN*, IV.vii.c.91: 631). On a more practical and prosaic note he also opined that '[m]onopolists very seldom make good work' (*Corr.*: 174).[13]

Smith complained about the English state as generally inefficient but noted with irritation that one aspect of its administration was extremely well managed. In order to finance its war efforts the eighteenth-century English state had developed a relatively efficient and professional system of tax gathering (Hellmuth 1999: 8; see also Brewer 1988).[14] It was not only Smith who objected to the brutal tax regime 'necessitated by decades of practically continuous warfare'; it had also become extremely unpopular with the public, prompting government reform efforts towards state minimalism, professionalism and efficiency (Harling and Mandler 1993: 52–53).

Throughout the 1780s, Pitt the Younger sought to centralise government and establish a more effective, professional and less wasteful public service. Practices such as the granting of sinecures that flourished in the war years were gradually phased out in favour of procedures that embodied norms of professionalism, rationality, impartiality, merit and disinterested public service. These norms were buttressed by the gradual introduction of practical measures such as proper salaries for public officials (Harling and Mandler 1993: 55–56) and administrative mechanisms that included prime ministerial and cabinet government, Commons select committees, royal commissions and the streamlining of affairs into individual departments. The English state was slowly moving away from 'patrimonialism'[15] towards a more modern, rational, bureaucratic structure (Cohen 1941) under pressure, not only from the public, but from vocal critics like Smith.

Smith rarely portrays 'modern' public office corruption as a breach of individual morality or even as an offence against the judgements of the impartial spectator, but rather as a function of either legally sanctioned market manipulation or an absence of regular, impartial justice. Monopolies do not just come into being because merchants are knaves; they exist because they are officially endorsed or at the very least tolerated. Similarly, 'negligency and corruption' within universities is rife because the sector is artificially oligopolised and lacks a system of regularly constituted inspections or '[v]isitations' by neutral government officers (*Corr.*: 173). Judicial corruption arises, not because judges are immoral but because the norms of behaviour pertaining to court fees and 'gifts' and payments are 'arbitrary and uncertain' (*WN*, V.i.b.16: 718). The fees paid to 'attorneys and clerks' are unregulated and therefore the latter naturally succumb to the 'temptation' of rent-seeking (*WN*, V.i.b.22: 721). The irregularity and 'uncertainty of taxation encourages the insolence' and 'corruption' of tax collectors (*WN*, V.ii.b.4: 825–26).

Accordingly, corruption could only be eradicated on the social-system level via appropriate corrections to the legal framework that either restored the system of 'natural liberty' or else legally prevented actors from introducing distortions into the market. This, in turn, was assumed to change norms but, once again, the bottom line is that the moral sentiments by themselves will not effectively address the problem of corruption as conceived by Smith. Some degree of state intervention would always be needed, provided, of course, that the state itself had been reformed, regularised and secured from corruption.

As discussed in Chap. 2, a key step to making things work better is to ensure that the different parts of the executive are properly separated so that the judiciary does not collude with a state often in thrall to private interests (*WN*, V.i.b.25: 722–23). The judiciary should also 'be separated from the executive power' and 'rendered as much as possible independent of that power'. This can be achieved via 'regular payment' of salaries and security of tenure independent of 'the caprice … good-will, or even … good economy of that power' (*WN*, V.i.b.25: 722–23; *LJ[A]*, V.5: 271). By the same token, to secure the public against the abuse of power by judges, the power of 'extending or correcting the meaning of the laws' should be kept out of their hands and in the hands of the Parliament exclusively (*LJ[A]*, v.8–9: 273).

A Large Middle Class as Natural Preventative

Smith points to another way of preventing corruption that is less institutional and more to do with the civil society in which he was so interested. It was one of his natural solutions, bound to emerge provided the system of natural liberty prevailed. This was the expansion of the 'middling' and aspirational classes. Smith recognised the norm and class-bound nature of corruption, noting that it was not a major problem among people in the 'middling and inferior stations of life' where the 'road to virtue and that to fortune' is generally one and the same. Such people are generally not above the law and are therefore less inclined to break it. Further, their success is usually dependent, not on birth or wealth, but on their own 'real and solid professional abilities' as well as the 'favour and good opinion of their neighbours and equals', something that cannot be obtained 'without a tolerably regular conduct' (*TMS*, I.iii.3.5: 63). The standards of impartial spectator surveillance that are exercised over (and by) these classes are much stricter and less forgiving than those that are supposed to constrain the vices of people in 'exalted stations' (*TMS*, I.iii.3.4: 63).

It is those who are either above the law or in a position to manipulate it in order to serve their own ends who are responsible for most of the corruption that Smith has in mind. His focus is on criticising the corrupt yet legal norms and behaviours of the elite classes, norms that enabled them to not only exploit and control those in the lower orders but, in the long run, undermine the prosperity of the nation. Therefore, the future lay in a large middle class as both the solution to and the ongoing preventative of public office corruption.

The expansion of the 'middling' commercial class is both an engine and an indicator of material progress, partly because it alone possesses the requisite, *modern* virtues for the uncorrupt modern economy. This industrious, 'bustling', self-governing and enterprising (*TMS*, I.iii.3.5: 63; *LJ[A]*, v.124: 320) class of people have developed and internalised the cool, instrumental, practical virtues of prudence, propriety, self-command, frugality, sobriety, vigilance, circumspection, temperance, constancy, firmness, punctuality, faithfulness, probity, enterprise, 'attention and application of thought' and industry (e.g. *TMS*, VII.ii.3.15–20: 304–305; *TMS*, IV.2.8: 189–90; *LJ[B]*: 528) that Smith ultimately favoured over classical, warm virtues like beneficence, martial valour and group loyalty. In the 'scheme which the Author of nature has established for the happiness and perfection of the world' the 'industrious, prudent and circumspect' invariably achieve their reward and 'proper recompense', namely, '[s]uccess in every sort of business' and '[w]ealth and external honours' (*TMS*, III.5.7–8: 166). A large commercial class is therefore a key means for keeping the commercial polity uncorrupted, solvent, free and expanding. Although I have mentioned that Smith believes that the system of rank distinctions is necessary, this does not mean that he precludes the possibility for class mobility; in fact, this is one of their main purposes, namely, to incentivise aspirational workers.

Conclusion

Within his political economy, Smith is reaching towards—and helping to shape—a broadly modern, 'public office' conception of corruption that is made necessary by the growth of the market, the emergence of the modern state and his desire to prevent the latter from stifling or unduly interfering with the former. As both state and market activity expanded, Smith's political economy was an attempt to clarify their relationship and to quarantine the private from the public realm in order to liberate the market and individual actors so that they could, at last, work properly or 'naturally'.

The eighteenth century was the scene of the most significant changes to the way political corruption was conceived insofar as it saw the virtual demise of the degenerative conception in favour of the public office approach. Smith was implicated in this shift by redefining and clarifying the proper sphere of state action and thereby helping to push both the public and state elites towards a more 'modern', public office conception of corruption. The degenerative ('civic humanist', classical republican and Christian) approach was increasingly unable to accommodate the realities of material progress and prosperity, the necessary rehabilitation of the self-regarding drives, expanding trade, demographic change, the emergence of mass society, the exigencies of security and the problems created by an increasingly bureaucratised and centralised state. Corruption was no longer to be understood as an inevitable consequence of prosperity, a diffuse condition infecting the entire polity, or a problem of classical or Christian virtue to be remedied by a return to more primitive conditions, asceticism or the cultivation of civic virtues. Rather, it was a matter of boundaries, good governance and rules instituted by a properly constituted and clearly separated state that governed in the interests of *all* the people not just self-interested elites. It was also about a new kind of civil society inhabited by industrious and just agents whose behaviour was regulated by the cool, modern virtues of commercial strangership.

Notes

1. As transmitted to the Enlightenment in the writings of such antique figures as Plato, Thucydides, Tacitus, Lucretius, Posidonius, Polybius, Seneca, Epictetus and Cicero.
2. A reversion denoted 'the right of succession to an office or place of emolument after the death or retirement of a holder'. This allowed office holders to pass on valuable positions to family members and was therefore a form of nepotism (Hellmuth 1999: 19–21).
3. For readings of Smith that see a general pessimism in his thought, see Winch (1997), Brown (1994), Rosenberg (1965), Alvey (1998), Alvey (2003).
4. As best exemplified by Joseph Cropsey when he argued that, despite Smith's acknowledgement of the many defects of commerce, he saw it as the best way to 'generat[e] freedom and civilisation' (Cropsey 1957: 95).
5. W.F. Campbell asserts that Smith regarded the division of labour as 'an important flaw in the very pillar of his economic scheme' (Campbell 1966).
6. As Edwin West also suggests in his exploration of the alienation theme in Smith and Ferguson (West 1969).
7. I say 'indirectly' because Smith and Ferguson probably worked together on the ideas, informally in conversation. Notably, Marx gives most of the credit to Ferguson (Marx 1977, vol. 1: 342).
8. Strictly speaking, however, Marx also saw the *early* stages of specialisation as a natural consequence of 'differences of sex and age' (Marx 1977, vol. 1: 82; 332; 343).
9. By this time William Blackstone had defined the problem in modern, 'public office' terms as occurring whenever 'a judge, or other person concerned in the administration of justice, takes any undue reward to influence his behaviour in office' (Prest 1991: 67–68).
10. A good deal of the national debt was offset by public credit that was perceived as enlarging the Crown's tendency towards patronage (Pocock 1972: 119–20; see also Peck 1979).
11. For a stronger reading of Smith's intent here see Riccardo Rosolino, who writes that 'Smith hinted (without stating it explicitly) that the only way to ensure that wages achieved a proper balance, at their 'natural' market level, was to allow salaried workers to resist capitalists' conspiratorial strategies by using their own weapons against them: by having the two monopolistic conspiracies neutralise one another (Rosolino 2018: 297).
12. This is not to say that Smith reserves no role for a strong state in constraining and regulating other power asymmetries, as Boucoyannis demonstrates (2013: 1057).
13. For a full exploration of Edmund Burke's equally critical attitude here, see Whelan (1996).

14. For a discussion of the birth of the modern state as a consequence of the need for a more efficient taxation system, see Ogborn (2002).
15. 'Patrimonialism' is a term that originates with Max Weber. It denotes the organisation of government 'as a directed extension of the royal household' (Bendix 1960: 119, n. 7).

References

Alvey, J. (1998). Adam Smith's Three Strikes Against Commercial Society. *International Journal of Social Economics, 25*(9), 1425–1444.

Alvey, J. (2003). Adam Smith's View of History: Consistent or Paradoxical. *History of the Human Sciences, 16*, 1–25.

Bendix, R. (1960). *Max Weber: An Intellectual Portrait.* London: Doubleday & Co.

Boucoyannis, D. (2013). The Equalizing Hand: Why Adam Smith Thought the Market Should Produce Wealth Without Steep Inequality. *Perspectives on Politics, 11*(4), 1051–1070.

Brewer, J. (1976). *Party, Ideology and Popular Politics at the Accession of George III.* Cambridge: Cambridge University Press.

Brewer, J. (1988). *The Sinews of Power: War, Money, and the English State, 1688–1783.* London: Century Hutchinson.

Brown, V. (1994). *Adam Smith's Discourse.* London: Routledge.

Buchan, B., & Hill, L. (2014). *An Intellectual History of Political Corruption.* Basingstoke: Palgrave Macmillan.

Campbell, W. F. (1966). Adam Smith's Theory of Justice, Prudence and Beneficence. *American Economic Review, LVII*(2), 571–577.

Cohen, E. W. (1941). *The Growth of the British Civil Service, 1780–1939.* London: George Allen & Unwin Ltd.

Corrigan, P., & Sayer, D. (1985). From Theatre to Machine: Old Corruption. In P. Corrigan & D. Sayer (Eds.), *The Great Arch: English State Formation as Cultural Revolution* (pp. 87–113). Oxford: Basil Blackwell.

Cropsey, J. (1957). *Polity and Economy: An Interpretation of the Principles of Adam Smith.* The Hague: Martinus Nijhoff.

Curtis, L. A. (1979). *The Versatile Defoe: An Anthology of Uncollected Writings*, edited and Introduced by L. A. Curtis. London: G. Prior.

Dickey, L. (1986). 'Historicising the 'Adam Smith Problem': Conceptual, Historiographic, and Textual Issues. *The Journal of Modern History, 58*, 579–609.

Ferguson, A. (1834). *The History of the Progress and Termination of the Roman Republic.* London: Jones & Company.

Forbes, D. (1967). Adam Ferguson and the Idea of Community. In D. Young, A. J. Youngson, G. E. Davie, D. Forbes, L. Cameron, & A. Frazer (Eds.), *Edinburgh in the Age of Reason: A Commemoration* (pp. 40–47). Edinburgh: Edinburgh University Press.

Harling, P., & Mandler, P. (1993). From 'Fiscal-Military' State to Laissez-Faire State, 1760–1850. *Journal of British Studies, 32*(1), 44–70.
Heilbroner, R. L. (1973). The Paradox of Progress: Decline and Decay in the Wealth of Nations. *Journal of the History of Ideas, 34*, 243–262.
Hellmuth, E. (1999). Why Does Corruption Matter? Reforms and Reform Movements in Britain and Germany in the Second Half of the Eighteenth Century. In T. C. W. Blanning & P. Wende (Eds.), *Reform in Great Britain and Germany 1750–1850*. Oxford: Oxford University Press.
Hirschman, A. O. (1977). *The Passions and the Interests*. Princeton: Princeton University Press.
Innes, J. (2002). Changing Perceptions of the State in the Late Eighteenth and Early Nineteenth Centuries. *Journal of Historical Sociology, 15*, 107–112.
Johnston, M. (1996). The Search for Definitions: The Vitality of Politics and the Issue of Corruption. *International Social Science Journal, 48*, 321–335.
Kettler, D. (1965). *The Social and Political Thought of Adam Ferguson*. Indiana: Ohio State University Press.
Kittrell, E. R. (1965). The Development of the Theory of Colonization in English Classical Political Thought. *Southern Economic Journal, 31*(3), 189–206.
Lamb, R. (1973). Adam Smith's Concept of Alienation. *Oxford Economic Papers, 25*(2), 275–285.
Langford, P. (2002). The Management of the Eighteenth Century State: Perceptions and Implications. *Journal of Historical Sociology, 15*(1), 102–106.
Marx, K. (1969). *The Poverty of Philosophy*, with and Introduction by F. Engels. New York: International Publishers.
Marx, K. (1977). *Capital*, 3 Vols. Moscow, Progress Publishers.
Nye, J. (1989). Political Corruption: A Cost Benefit Analysis. In A. J. Heidenheimer, M. Johnston, & V. Levine (Eds.), *Political Corruption: A Handbook*. New Brunswick: Transaction Books.
Ogborn, M. (2002). Wherein Lay the Late Seventeenth-Century State? Charles Davenant Meets Streynsham Master. *Journal of Historical Sociology, 15*, 96–101.
Pack, S. J. (1991). *Capitalism as a Moral System: Adam Smith's Critique of the Free Market Economy*. Aldershot: Edward Elgar.
Peck, L. L. (1979). *Court Patronage and Corruption in Early Stuart England*. Boston: Unwin Hyman.
Philp, M. (1987). Defining Corruption: An Analysis of the Republican Tradition. *International Political Science Association Research Roundtable on Political Finance and Political Corruption*, Bellagio.
Phillips, J. A. (1979). The Structure of Electoral Politics in Unreformed England. *The Journal of British Studies, 19*(1), 76–100.
Pocock, J. G. A. (1972). Virtue and Commerce in the Eighteenth Century. *Journal of Interdisciplinary History, 3*, 119–134.

Pocock, J. G. A. (1975). *The Machiavellian Moment.* Princeton: Princeton University Press.

Prest, W. (1991). Judicial Corruption in Early Modern England. *Past and Present, 133*, 67–95.

Robertson, J. (1985). *The Scottish Enlightenment and the Militia Issue*. Edinburgh: John Donald.

Rosenberg, N. (1965). Adam Smith on the Division of Labor: Two Views or One. *Economica, 33*, 127–139.

Rosolino, R. (2018). Resisting Economic Conspiracies: Adam Smith, the (Labour) Market, and the Moral Basis of Antimonopolistic Resistance. *History of Political Thought, 39*(2), 297–324.

Schwoerer, L. (1974). *'No Standing Armies!' The Anti-Army Ideology in Seventeenth Century England*. Baltimore: John Hopkins University Press.

Smith, A. (1976 [1759]). *The Theory of Moral Sentiments*, D. D. Raphael & A. L. MacFie (Eds.). Oxford: Clarendon Press.

Smith, A. (1978). *Lectures on Jurisprudence (A and B)*, R. L. Meek, D. D. Raphael & L. G. Stein (Eds.). Oxford: Oxford University Press.

Smith, A. (1979 [1776]). *An Inquiry into the Nature and Causes of the Wealth of Nations*, R. H. Campbell & A. S. Skinner (Eds.). Oxford: Clarendon Press.

Smith, A. (1987). *The Correspondence of Adam Smith*, E. C. Mossner & I. S. Ross (Eds.). Oxford: Oxford University Press.

West, E. G. (1969). The Political Economy of Alienation: Karl Marx and Adam Smith. *Oxford Economic Papers, 21*(1), 1–23.

Whelan, F. (1996). *Edmund Burke and India: Political Morality and Empire.* Pittsburgh: University of Pittsburgh.

Winch, D. (1997). Adam Smith's Problem and Ours. *Scottish Journal of Political Economy, 44*, 384–402.

CHAPTER 6

Adam Smith's International Thought

Introductory Comments

In this chapter I explore Adam Smith's international thought by examining his conception of the ideal global regime of commercial strangership and his attitudes to imperialism, global integration, American Independence, Stoic cosmopolitanism, war, Mercantilism, the changing character of international relations under commercialism, patriotism and his own alleged nationalism. There is a special focus on his attitude to British control over America because it offers insight, not only to his views on international affairs, but to his skill as a political strategist and navigator of public opinion. It shows that Smith was extremely well equipped to engage with the realities of political life.

Some scholars see Smith as basically cosmopolitan and anti-imperialist in his outlook while others read him as anti-cosmopolitan. I show that, although he was neither a moral nor a political cosmopolitan he was certainly an economic cosmopolitan. This is hardly surprising given his realism and pragmatism. He was also an early and insightful theorist of 'globalisation'. This, in turn, shaped his controversial and influential opinions on international relations. As per his domestic policy advice, Smith's approach to many international controversies is driven by his social science, his progressivist historiography, his pragmatism and his regard for the welfare of ordinary people.

L. Hill, *Adam Smith's Pragmatic Liberalism*,
https://doi.org/10.1007/978-3-030-19337-9_6

Competing Perceptions of Smith

Due to his well-known attitudes to Mercantilism, a common characterisation of Smith is that he is cosmopolitan and anti-imperialist in his outlook. For Peter Minowitz, Smith adopts the 'detached tone of the cosmopolitan scientist' and like Marx 'chronicles and welcomes the growth of a world economy and the interdependence it entails, in part because of its possible contribution to world peace' (Minowitz 1989: 306; see also Wight 1991; Fitzgibbons 1995; Gilpin 1971; Berdell 2002; Carr 1946; Waltz 2001; Pitts 2005). Yet, others see Smith as decidedly anti-cosmopolitan: according to Andrew Wyatt-Walter 'Smith firmly rejected the idea of a natural harmony of interests' and 'on international matters' he 'is often closer to the Realist and mercantilist traditions … than to liberal internationalism' (Wyatt-Walter 1996: 7). Much earlier, Joseph Shield Nicholson decreed that '[t]he popular idea that Adam Smith was cosmopolitan … is exactly the reverse of the truth. He was intensely nationalist' and protectionist (Nicholson 1909: 9–11). On this reading, because Smith dismisses the idea of universal benevolence, he cannot be seen as in any way cosmopolitan (Nicholson 1909: 9–11). Such a reading also assumes that local loyalties (such as Smith often evinced towards Britain) preclude cosmopolitan sympathies and especially espousal of a global free market. For Marc-William Palen, Smith 'left behind an ambiguous legacy on the subject of empire' that allowed his thought to be enlisted for imperialistic advocacy in the nineteenth century (Palen 2014: 179).

Due to his acceptance of the durability of national loyalties and rejection of the idea of universal benevolence, Smith was certainly no moral or classical cosmopolitan; but he was quite definitely a pioneer of economic cosmopolitanism, a commercial and instrumental cosmopolitanism based on 'amicable strangership' that happened to bring with it many desirable political and moral effects. Smith had a particular idea of what the ideal global regime should look like. In order to understand his ideal system, I begin by examining his negative assessment of the prevailing state of international affairs, specifically his attitude to empire, Mercantilism and global integration.

Commercial Cosmopolitanism: Empire, Mercantilism and 'Globalisation'

Smith's prescient and insightful exploration of the nature and future of international trade makes him an early theorist of globalisation. Smith did not, of course, use the term 'globalisation', which was not coined until the twentieth century. Yet, the Enlightenment was in fact—if not in name—'an age of globalisation' (Reinert 2011). The term 'globalisation' is generally taken to mean increasing global connectivity, integration and interdependence in the economic, social, technological and political senses. Smith's preferred term is 'commerce', which in the eighteenth century had a far broader meaning than it does today, denoting not only 'the market-oriented manufacture and trade of goods, but also … interaction, exchange, and communication more generally' (Muthu 2008). Therefore, as Sankar Muthu rightly points out, while using the term 'globalisation' in relation to Smith's thought is obviously anachronistic, it is, nevertheless, more conceptually apposite than 'commercial'. This is because it 'better captures the wide array of institutions, practices and sense of flux that many Enlightenment thinkers had in mind' when they referred to 'commerce' in its transcontinental sense. In this context it 'referred broadly to the frequent crossing of borders, to navigational and communications technologies that seem to draw the world closer together, and also to increased trade, capital flows and the development of transnational social, economic and political institutions and networks' (Muthu 2008). This is exactly how Smith thought of it.

Smith was especially interested in what we would now refer to as economic globalisation, namely, the process whereby prices, products, wages, rates of interest and profits converge towards the norms of developed countries (Shariff 2003: *passim*). What we now call 'globalisation' was an emerging fact of life in Smith's time.[1] Imperial expansion and the Dutch, English, French and Swedish East India Companies were forging the expansion and integration of domestic markets and Smith frequently adverted to the problems faced by nations 'who have attempted to tax the revenue arising from stock whose "proprietor" is a "citizen of the world"'(*WN*, ii.f.6: 848–49); capital could now 'wander about from place to place, according as it [could] either buy cheap or sell dear' (*WN*, II.5.14: 364).

Smith was strongly in favour of global integration but the passages in which he outlines its wrongheaded execution have been frequently misread as either indicative of resistance to it or ambivalence about it. Some have even seen it as reflecting his parochialism. Some early-twentieth-century scholars went so far as to describe Smith as pro-imperialist, partly because he did see some advantages in Britain's colonies (see Fay 1930: 34, Nicholson 1909: x). Smith's outlook is therefore open to interpretation. Indeed, Klaus Knorr has observed that 'up to the very present [Smith] has been cited with apparently equal assuredness and alacrity alternately by imperialists and anti-imperialists, colonial protectionists and free traders' (Knorr 1944: 185). Along similar lines, Donald Wagner suggests that Smith offered 'comfort' to those who both attacked and defended the British Empire in a manner 'somewhat like the man who, it is said, mounted his horse and rode off in opposite directions' (Wagner 1932: 74).

Yet, when we look closely at everything Smith had to say on the subject, it becomes clear that Smith welcomed the fact that the world was opening up and beginning to integrate. It should be noted, however, that when Smith refers to the 'world' he is not always thinking of the entire globe; for much of the time his focus seems to be limited to the Atlantic economy and Western Europe. But there are also times when he clearly has in mind the entire navigable world. He celebrated the 'discovery of America, and that of the passage to the East Indies by the Cape of Good Hope' as the 'two greatest and most important events recorded in the history of mankind', observing that the widening of global horizons opened 'a new and inexhaustible market to all the commodities of Europe', thereby permitting the division of labour room to expand outward in its natural tendency. The enlargement of the navigable world brought ever more novel 'divisions of labour and improvements of art, *which, in the narrow circle of the antient commerce, could never have taken place*' (*WN*, IV.i.32: 448; emphasis added). Further, throughout Europe the 'productive powers of labour were improved … and together with it the real revenue and wealth of the inhabitants'. Europe and the Americas had new and exciting 'commodities' to offer each other, a state of affairs 'which should naturally have proved as advantageous to the new, as it certainly did to the old continent' (*WN*, IV.i.32: 448). However pleased he was about the globally integrating world, Smith was extremely critical of the means by which it had so far been effected.

Imperialism

The way the imperial project was being managed was not only economically disastrous; it also brought untold hardship and suffering to those invaded and dispossessed by it. Whereas 'commerce' should naturally be a source of 'friendship' between nations, under the aggravating influence of Mercantilism it 'has become the most fertile source of discord and animosity' due to the way in which trading monopolies promoted national hostilities and even war (*WN*, iii.c.9: 493; *WN*, IV.ii.38: 467; *WN*, V.ii.g.2:

852). Due to imperialism—and especially Mercantilism—'the natives', particularly of 'the East and West Indies' have received no 'commercial benefits' but only 'dreadful misfortunes'. 'The savage injustice of the Europeans rendered an event, which ought to have been beneficial to all, ruinous and destructive' to many 'unfortunate countries' (*WN*, IV.vii.a.16: 561).[2] Smith admonished the people of Britain that, far from enriching 'the mother country', all their imperialistic ambitions had managed to achieve was to 'rais[e]' the destructive and corrupt 'mercantile system to a degree of splendour and glory which it could never otherwise have attained to' (*WN*, vii.c.81: 627). Smith complained of '[t]he real futility of all distant dominions' and considered the topic of empire to be one 'upon which the public prejudices of Europe require most to be set right' (*Corr.*, 221: 262).

Smith attacked as destructive the two great systems of monopoly governing the 'global connections of the mid-eighteenth century', namely, on the one hand, the colonial system whereby empires monopolised the markets of their colonies and, on the other, the system of exclusive companies like the East India Company (Rothschild 2004: 4). The 'invidious and malignant' (*WN*, IV.vii.c.18: 595) monopoly of colonial trade evinced many evils: it caused a 'malallocation of resources', discouraged investment, induced 'profligacy and prodigality among the favoured merchants' and provoked wars (Kittrell 1965: 190) and therefore unconscionable levels of public debt.[3] The monopoly of trade of the 'mother country' that went hand in hand with British imperialism operated as a 'clog' that 'cramp[ed]' and depressed the 'the enjoyments and industry of all ... nations', imposing a 'dead weight upon the action of one of the great springs which puts into motion a great part of the business of mankind' (*WN*, IV.vii.c.9: 592). Whereas under the system of natural liberty 'the private interests and passions of individuals naturally dispose them to turn their stock towards the employments which ... are most advantageous' and 'agreeable to the interest of the whole society', Mercantilism, whose 'sole engine' is monopoly, 'necessarily derange[s] more or less this natural and most advantageous distribution of stock' (*WN*, vii.c.88–89: 630). Restrictions on the right to choose how best to employ one's resources and labour are 'a manifest violation of the most sacred rights of mankind' (*WN*, I.x.c.12: 138; *WN*, IV.vii.b.44: 582) that are borne by the colonies as 'impertinent badges' of their 'slavery' (*WN*, IV.vii.b.44: 582).

The system of colonial monopoly represented an economic security threat due to its failure to spread risk. Whereas natural forces would have led Britain to accommodate its industry 'to a great number of small markets', monopoly trade has caused it to put all its eggs in one basket, to accommodate itself 'to one great market.' Trade between the colonies and the mother country is likened to a major artery, any 'rupture' of which would certainly occasion 'convulsions, apoplexy, or death' (*WN*, vii.c.43: 604–606). In order to reduce exploitation within international economic relations (*WN*, vii.c.16: 594–95) and ensure enduring productivity, progress and plenty for all, there should be no limitations on the nature and extent of the market because this limits the natural growth of the division of labour. But, since empire and Mercantilism went hand in hand, the mutually enabling benefits of free trade could not be brought about and specialisation could not develop outwards in its natural tendency.

Implicit in Smith's historical and economic analysis of the issue was his rejection of the Machiavellian precept of Mercantilism that war and 'external growth' were the primary sources of 'national survival and *grandezza*' (Hont 2005: 74). The fatal error of Mercantilism, as Smith saw it, was its perception and treatment of international trade as a competitive, zero-sum game whereby one nation's gain is another's loss (Minowitz 1993: 104). As Smith wrote: 'Nothing … can be more absurd than this whole doctrine of the balance of trade upon' upon which almost all 'regulations of commerce are founded'.

> When two places trade with one another, this doctrine supposes that, if the balance be even, neither of them loses or gains; but if it leans to any degree to one side, that one of them loses, and the other gains in proportion to its declensions from the exact equilibrium. Both suppositions are false. A trade which is forced by means of bounties and monopolies … is disadvantageous to the country in whose favour it is meant to be established … But that trade which, without force or constraint, is naturally and regularly carried on between any two places, is always advantageous, though not always equally so, to both. (*WN*, IV.iii.c.2: 488–89)

Mercantilism indoctrinated 'nations' with the most unhelpful and misguided notion 'that their interest consisted in beggaring all their neighbours' (*WN*, IV.iii.c.9: 493; *WN*, IV.viii.48: 660). Unlike the mutually enabling system of 'natural liberty', monopoly retards other countries' progress and yet, according to Smith, it does not even enhance that of the 'mother country'. In fact, it has the reverse effect: 'The unjust oppression of the industry of other countries falls back … upon the heads of the oppressors and crushes their industry, more than it does that of those other countries' (*WN*, IV.vii.c.83: 627–8). Therefore, the colonies yielded few benefits but at vast cost to everyone except the merchants (*WN*, IV.vii.c.65: 616).

Smith's attitude here is a function of his social science; the colonial system was objectionable because it was a violation of the natural laws of motion governing interactions between economic agents. As laid out in Chap. 3 he believed everyone has the 'natural right' to act in a way that is consistent with his or her self-regarding inclinations. People have a 'natural right' to 'free commerce' (*LJ[A]*, 12–13: 8), to do whatever they 'ha[ve] a mind' to do and to enjoy their 'liberty free from infringement' (*LJ[B]*, 11: 401; *LJ[A]*, i.24: 13). There can be no legitimate interference with exchange either by private persons or by public bodies and every person is entitled to the 'liberi commercii'; the 'right of trafficking with those who are willing to deal with him' (*LJ[A]*, i.12–13: 8).

Imperial Mercantilism with its restrictions, monopolies and aggressive militarism violated this right in every way possible. The East India Company (EIC), with its powerful, state-protected monopoly of British/Asian commerce, was a particular target for Smith, who repeatedly inveighed against its exclusive position and the inordinate degree of power it wielded both inside and outside Britain. Apart from the fact that the 'work' of 'monopolists' was 'seldom' any good (*Corr.*: 174), what bothered Smith even more was that the EIC's privileged position led to a situation whereby consumers not only 'paid' for the company's 'extraordinary profits' by their unjust exclusion from markets; they also paid for 'all the extraordinary waste … fraud and abuse' of the company (*WN*, IV.vii.c.91: 631). Perhaps the most serious consequence of this dynamic was its effect on food security, an issue very close to Smith's heart, as was shown in Chap. 1. He claimed that the company was powerful enough to impose such 'improper regulations' and 'injudicious restraints' as to induce even a 'famine' (*WN*, IV.v.b.6: 527).

Smith lays out two means by which trade restrictions and the activities of monopolies like the EIC can induce a famine: 'The first is when wage income declines rapidly.' This occurred in Bengal in 1770 due to the oppressions and mismanagement of the EIC. The second cause is bad government policies that restrict the free trade in corn and convert a dearth of food into a famine (Rothschild 2001: 73). Lamentably, the 'freedom of the corn trade is almost every where more or less restrained, and, in many countries, is confined by … absurd regulations' (*WN*, IV.v.b.39: 538–39). Restrictive trading regulations and monopolistic companies like the EIC, Smith concluded, 'are nuisances in every respect; always more or less inconvenient to the countries in which they are established, and destructive to those which have the misfortune to fall under their government' (*WN*, IV.vii.c.108: 641).

It is sometimes suggested that Smith's critique of imperialism was mainly economic and unconcerned with questions of justice or 'irrevocable rights' (e.g. Campbell and Ross 1981: 81). Although it is true that the bulk of his thoughts on the subject are devoted to the inefficiencies and indefensible costs of empire, Smith did not neglect the moral aspects and there are many references to the injustices of empire (e.g. *WN*, IV.vii.b.58–59: 258; *WN*, IV.i.32: 448; *WN*, IV.vii.c.80: 100; *WN*, IV.vii.c.80: 626; *WN*, IV.vii.c.100: 634). By no means a moral cosmopolitan (Forman-Barzilai 2006), nevertheless, like Zeno and the early Stoics (Erskine 1990: 181), he condemned empire for the injustice, exploitation and 'dreadful misfortune' it necessitated (*WN*, IV.vii.c.80: 626). The colonisation of 'the sugar colonies', for example, was a project of shameful 'injustice of coveting the possession of a country whose harmless natives, far from having ever injured the people of Europe, had received the first adventurers with every mark of kindness and hospitality' (*WN*, IV.vii.b.59: 588; see also *WN*, IV.i.32: 448). Yet, Britain clung to its colonies out of irrational national 'pride' and pressure from those able to exploit nationalistic sentiment for their own ends, namely, the merchants and government elites (*WN*, IV.vii.c.66: 616–17).

On the question of Britain's retention of the colonies he wrote with ill-disguised sarcasm that founding 'a great empire for the sole purpose of raising up a people of customers' was not only 'unfit for a nation of shopkeepers', it was also extremely unfit 'for a nation whose government is influenced by shopkeepers' (*WN*, IV.vii.c.63: 613). What Smith wanted was a *voluntaristic* and naturally unfolding global economic regime based on mutual enablement rather than conquest and exploitation, in which the regime of cosmopolitan commerce subdues war and interstate hostilities, engenders amicable strangership between all nations, enhances both independence and interdependence among nation-states and distributes opulence *equally* throughout the globe. Allowing the satellites to go their own way and prosper under their own steam would make them valuable trading partners; after all, '[p]lenty of good land, and liberty to manage their own affairs their own way' are 'the two great causes of the prosperity of all new colonies' (*WN*, IV.vii.16: 572).

Despite the irrational obstinacy of much of the British public, decolonisation, he noted in private correspondence, was historically inevitable, 'necessary' and 'natural' (*Corr*: 383). Such views, as well as his broader perspective on global issues, became crystallised in Smith's treatment of the American situation, which is dealt with in more detail below. Oddly, he simply ignores the slightly less vexed question of what should be done about India. Although Smith was 'deeply critical' of the 'abuses of the East India company' he, nevertheless, 'sidestepped the question of what Britain's relations with India ought to be, and indeed whether British rule of India could be justified' (Pitts 2005: 55).

Patriotism, Benevolence and Classical Cosmopolitanism

In assessing the character of Smith's cosmopolitanism it makes sense to start by looking at where he stood in relation to classical moral cosmopolitanism. His attitude towards particular attachments and patriotism is a good place to begin given how important to cosmopolites is our willingness and ability to transcend them. Although Smith occasionally refers to the nobility of acts of bravery inspired by nationalistic sentiment, he did not much like patriotism, arguing that it stood in the way of mutually beneficial relations between states (*LJ[A]*, vi.164–5: 391–92), provoked and prolonged war and isolated, segregated and de-sensitised us to the world outside our own narrow sphere (*WN*, V.iii.37: 920). But he does concede that 'national sentiment' is an extremely powerful and resilient passion that could not be ignored. He also says that patriotism is partially animated by the other-regarding passions and hence not all bad.

By the same token, such passions are in no way related to the universal variety of other-regarding passions posited by the ancient Stoics—the existence of which he denies—because they are restricted to conspecifics (*TMS*, VI.ii.2.4: 229–30). Smith says it is perfectly natural for us to put ourselves, family, friends and compatriots before the world at large; although he sometimes enjoins us to 'love ourselves only as we love our neighbour', on the whole he believes that our greater interest in ourselves first, our nearest and dearest afterwards and strangers little at all is both reasonable and inevitable (*TMS*, III.3.9–10: 139–40.). He is careful to point out, however, that it would be a mistake to see our more compelling ties as forged by common material origin (e.g. biology, ethnicity, consanguinity): 'the force of blood, I am afraid, exists no-where but in tragedies and romances'. It is really the 'centripetal pull of proximity and familiarity' or 'habitual sympathy' that generates intense 'affection' (*TMS*, I.ii.1.7: 220).

In the common-sense priority thesis adopted by Smith we generally imagine our primary, secondary and tertiary duties to others as ranked geographically: distance regulates the intensity of obligation and people will invariably give priority to intimates before strangers and compatriots before foreigners. For Smith, Stoic cosmopolitanism is untenable because its underlying moral psychology is implausible. According to the Stoics, our duties are arranged in concentric circles. The individual is at the centre, with family, friends, city, nation and the world (in that order) occupying the circles that fan outwards. Contrary to common-sense conceptions of emotional attachment and duty (such as Smith favoured), the degree of obligation is reversed according to distance. Our obligations to intimates are more binding than those to ourselves, obligations to the state more binding than those to our family or friends, while obligations to the world at large are more binding still (Xenakis 1969: 126).[4]

This anticipates the utilitarian doctrine that the wider the loyalty, the greater the moral claim it has on us, simply because the further out in the concentric image we go, the more people there are, and, therefore, the greater the quantity of happiness there is at stake (Oldenquist 1982). Social *oikeiosis*[5] is a developmental achievement that begins, naturally, in a state of self-regard and greater concern for intimates, from which we move, in an equally natural direction, towards impartial other-concern. For Stoic cosmopolites, judgements about the welfare of others are always impartial; 'persons' are equal units of concern regardless of their contingent status or relationship to us. Assuming that impartial, universal benevolence exists and is capable of being exercised, they aimed for a developmental trajectory beginning in youth and immaturity with variable quality of attachment towards others, proceeding to a state of invariable quality of attachment towards the world at large. Virtue is synonymous with impartiality; the cosmopolite seeks a *sameness* of feeling for all, regardless of social distance (Annas 1993: 265–66).

Ever the pragmatist and psychological realist, Smith is wholly unconvinced by the Stoic view, insisting that the 'plan' laid out for humankind is 'altogether different' from theirs (*TMS*, VII.ii.1.47: 292). The idea of universal benevolence is a myth (*TMS*, III.3.9: 139–40) and inciting concern for the interests of strangers 'can produce' no 'advantage to them' and only unnecessary 'anxiety to ourselves'. Strangers are certainly 'entitled to our good wishes' but little else. Consider the point of view of 'a man of humanity in Europe', muses Smith, on hearing that 'the great empire of China, with all its myriads of inhabitants, was suddenly swallowed up by an earthquake'. This distant stranger would no doubt express 'sorrow', 'make many melancholy reflections upon the precariousness of human life' and even contemplate the effects of 'this disaster' upon international commerce. Yet he would still go about his daily business 'with the same ease and tranquillity, as if no such accident had happened'. Although the thought of losing his own 'little finger' would doubtless keep him awake all night he would still 'snore with the most profound security over the ruin of a hundred millions of his brethren' (*TMS*, III.4: 136–37).

Smith's complacency about this state of affairs is very striking, albeit consistent with his moral psychology: our indifference to those 'very remote from us' is not only normal but even 'wisely ordered by Nature' (*TMS*, III.3.9: 39–41). The 'universal happiness of all rational and sensible beings is the business of God and not of man', to whom is 'allotted a much humbler department' that is far better suited 'to the weakness of his powers' and 'narrowness of his comprehension', namely, 'the care of his own happiness, of that of his family, his friends, his country' (*TMS*, VI.ii.3.6: 237). Nature has wisely determined that we limit our sense of responsibility to 'events' over which we have some control and 'management' (*TMS*, VII.ii.1.43: 292).

The Stoic insistence on the cultivation of universal benevolence invites only wasted emotional energy and anxiety. Although in a very abstract sense our 'good-will' is inexhaustible and 'may embrace the immensity of the universe', our 'effectual good offices can very seldom be extended to any wider society than that of our own country' (*TMS*, VI. Ii.3.1: 235). To feel benevolent responsibility towards those we have not means to actively assist is not only pointless and needlessly distressing but it may even cause us to neglect our more immediate and pressing responsibilities (*TMS*, VI.ii.3.5: 236; *TMS*, II.iii.3.3: 106). The furthest point to which the average person's aid, interest and sympathy can stretch is at the borders of 'countries' or 'sovereign' states and even within these borders it is severely strained. In the normal course of things, the sovereign state is '*the greatest society* upon whose happiness or misery, our good or bad conduct can have much influence'. This is because 'all the objects of our kindest affections, our children, our parents, our relations, our friends, our benefactors … are commonly comprehended within it; and their prosperity and safety depend in some measure upon its prosperity and safety' (*TMS*, VI.ii.2.2: 227–28. Emphasis added).

The Stoics were therefore mistaken in their expectation that people could and should be able to transcend local sympathies and attachments. Yet, this does not mean that Smith rejects the whole idea of a global community or is pessimistic about the chances of global peace and cooperation. The world-state or *cosmopolis* he imagined was not to be held together by such lofty bonds as *reason*, *philanthropia* or *sympatheia*—as per the Stoic account (Hill 2000)—but by the more spontaneous, self-interested motives animating international commerce.

International Trade and Natural Liberty

International trade operates very like domestic trade; just as national wealth is secured via the self-regarding activities of individuals, so 'the great society of mankind' is 'best promoted by directing' the attention of individuals 'to that particular portion of it, which was most within the sphere' of their 'abilities' and 'understanding' (*TMS*, ii.2.4: 229.). One constraint on the ability of agents to pursue this interest internationally is the existence and perseverance of 'countries' or 'sovereign states', which still had to be treated as the fundamental unit of political analysis. Smith says that it is understandably 'the great object of the political œconomy of every country … to encrease the riches and power of that country'. But if a state wants to achieve this, it ought not to let blind patriotism mislead it down the stultifying path of protectionism and therefore 'give no preference nor superior encouragement to the foreign trade of consumption above the home-trade, nor to the carrying trade above either of the other two'.

Sensible legislators will neither 'force nor … allure into either of those two channels, a greater share of the capital of the country than what would *naturally* flow into them of its own accord' (*WN*, II.v.31: 372; emphasis added). If allowed, the free market will deliver 'an equality of treatment to all nations' with infinite opportunities for 'commerce', whereas 'extraordinary' and artificial barriers and 'encouragement[s]' are demonstrably and 'in every case a complete piece of dupery' perpetrated against 'the interest of the State and the nation' in favour of 'some particular class of traders' (*Corr.*: 271–72). For Smith, China is the signal example of disastrous economic mismanagement; although rich in natural resources, it has 'been long stationary' because it 'despises foreign commerce' and therefore restricts 'the vessels of foreign nations into one or two of its ports only' (*WN*, I.ix.15: 111–12).

Smith was no doctrinaire free-trade advocate as is sometimes assumed, and he did make some notable exceptions to his rule; but, by and large, the standard characterisation of his attitude to the market is correct. At the same time, he was far from naïve and understood what were the practical impediments to his long-term goal of establishing the system of 'perfect liberty' throughout the globe. He cautioned that it was potentially destructive if not executed with a good deal of 'reserve and circumspection' (*WN*, IV.ii.40: 469) and clearly saw the 'manner' and order of opening the colonial trade (and thereby restoring 'natural, healthful, and proper proportion which perfect liberty necessarily establishes') as a process that would occur over time and under the careful supervision of successive generations (*WN*, vii.c.44: 606).

National boundaries can be broken down, not by benevolence borne of moral maturity, but by self-interest, a far more constant and dependable motive force (*TMS*, VII.ii.3.18: 305; *WN*, I.ii: 26–27). Self-interest is what will weaken self-defeating national loyalties and permit the spread of commercial strangership between states. Therefore, while Smith rejects much of classical cosmopolitanism, he certainly advocates and even pioneers the economic or commercial variety.

Smith's Alleged Nationalism

Given all this counter-evidence it is worth considering from whence comes the perception of Smith as a nationalist. There seem to be several sources. First, it is sometimes suggested that Smith was prejudiced towards British economic interests. Certainly—and understandably (given that he wrote to influence British policymakers and was a British national himself)—he was very often writing from the British perspective. But he was also attempting a universal political economy; what was good advice for Britain would also be good for the rest of the trading world, which he perceived as a (potentially) integrated system, hence the title *Wealth of Nations* rather than the more parochial *Wealth of the British Nation*. Smith's observation that capital naturally gravitated towards the home market (*WN*, IV.ii.6: 454) has also been taken as evidence that he was an economic nationalist. He wrote that 'every … merchant naturally prefers the home-trade to the foreign trade of consumption' (*WN*, IV.ii.6: 454) but this was just an observation intended to allay fears at home about opening up foreign markets. Second, as one remedy for the American situation Smith advocated an Imperial Parliament based at Westminster. But it was not his first preference (voluntary separation was); furthermore, were such a Parliament to eventuate, he predicted—without the slightest hint of regret—that the seat of power would eventually shift to America, which he complacently surmised would become a far superior economic and political power (*TMS*, IV.vii.c.79: 625–26).

Third, Smith exhibited some ambivalence about the 'virtue' of patriotism, noting that 'the mean principle of national prejudice is often founded upon the noble one of the love of our own country' (*TMS*, VI.ii.2.3: 228). Although he often adverted to the negative aspects of patriotism, Smith also insisted on the naturalness of strong nationalistic sentiments and even lauded certain acts of patriotism. Patriotism and love of the country that nurtures and protects us (and whose safety and prosperity coincides with our own) is powerful, real and sometimes useful (*TMS*, ii.2.2: 227–28). But, on balance, he conceives of patriotism as doing more harm than good.

The New Commercial Strangership: The Division of Labour and Smithian Historiography

Under conditions of free trade, the concentric circles of instrumental friendship will expand as markets are progressively enlarged and people become more and more habituated to intercourse with strangers and foreigners. Smith finds little romance in the necessitous and compelled relations of socially intimate societies; instead, he embraces the possibilities unleashed by interactions unanchored in place or time; impersonal, interchangeable, deracinated, cosmopolitan and mobile. Because impersonal and ubiquitous exchange is the paradigmatic social interaction in Smith's universe, amicable strangership displaces intense friendship and enmity as the archetypal affective orientation. The new global society will not be intense and exclusivistic in the way that pre-commercial forms of solidarity (e.g. kinship, clientage and compatriotism) were. Smith speaks to us of a world that has to be managed largely by and between strangers in which the intense passions attendant on local loyalties will be superseded by tamer, less ardent passions and virtues. He notes, for example, that '[t]oo violent a propensity to those detestable passions (hatred and resentment), renders a person the object of universal dread and abhorrence, who, like a wild beast, ought, we think, to be hunted out of all civil society' (*TMS*, I.ii.4.3: 40).

As was shown in Chap. 4, under commercial modernity, all strangers are no longer potential enemies but potential contractees; therefore, the exchange culture will be calm, open, rational, impersonal, instrumental, polite, flexible and voluntaristic. Although our 'ancestors' habitually 'considered strangers and enemies as one and the same thing', and had 'no knowledge' of 'other nations' except for 'what they have got when at war with them', under conditions of free interstate trade modern citizens learn to appreciate 'the benefit of having foreigners coming amongst them' who can 'carry out what is superfluous of the product of the country' and import 'the superfluities' of their home country for the 'convenience' and enjoyment of the recipients. Accordingly, and in order to 'encourage the settling of foreign merchants amongst them', states begin to offer diplomatic protection to foreigners (*LJ[A]*: 306–307) so that commerce between strangers becomes safer and more routine. Deracinated commercial agents will have more liberty and mobility than has been possible at any other stage of history: 'He' who possesses capital 'is properly a citizen of the world … not necessarily attached to any particular country', who can move himself and his stock freely from place to place (*WN*, V.ii.f.6: 48–49) and it is largely 'indifferent' to him 'from what place he carries on his trade'. Indeed, 'a very trifling disgust will make him remove his capital, and together with it all the industry which it supports, from one country to another' (*WN*, III.iv.24: 426).

There are three related forces that drive the weakening of sovereign states and the nationalistic sentiments that patrol their borders; the first two are self-interest and the powerful and natural urge to trade; the third is the equally natural division of labour. The effects of all three will be enhanced and entrenched by the force of habit and convention. The significance and effects of the division of labour bear special notice here given the central role of specialisation in Smith's historiography and in his conception of the future of international trade.

The Division of Labour and International Trade

According to Smith, the intense and exclusivistic loyalties attendant on sovereign states will be worn down by specialisation, just as it broke down our once fierce and seemingly indestructible loyalties to the extended family. We are not, as is commonly thought, tied to conspecifics by immutable ties of blood but simply by 'habitual sympathy' (*TMS*, I.ii.1.7: 220). Smith conceives the division of labour as an exponentially developing phenomenon that not only generates wealth and technical refinement; it also alters profoundly the social fabric. As discussed in more detail in previous chapters, it achieves this by working in two apparently contradictory directions: on the one hand, it allows a greater degree of social distance, while on the other, it also enhances and expands (impersonal) integration, thereby enlarging the ever-widening circles of amicable strangership. Smith's explanation of the breakdown of the extended family, the tribal community and the feudal estate, and the natural tendency towards larger and more impersonal social networks, suggests that global trade based on an international division of labour will, in similar fashion, weaken national ties and complete a long and natural historical process.

In an excursus comparing human and animal traits Smith explains that other species are destined to lead solitary lives because they are unable to divide their labour. Humans, by contrast, *do* know how to specialise and then to trade the results of their specialisation. This leads to increased interaction and impersonal inter-dependence (*WN*, I.ii: 30), creating mutual need and therefore social integration (*LJ[A]*, vi.46–49: 348–49; *WN*, I.ii.1–3: 25–28). But specialisation also, paradoxically, liberates individual agents from the intimate social structures upon which their survival once depended.

In order to obtain their wants and secure the cooperation of their fellows, specialising commercial agents no longer have to resort to the demeaning and unreliable method of cultivating the 'good will' of others but are increasingly independent—as well as *inter*dependent—because each 'stands at all times in need of the co-operation and assistance of great multitudes' (*LJ[A]*, vi.46–49: 348–49), thereby generating an impersonal but more extensive form of social cohesion among societies of distant strangers (*WN*, I.ii.1–3: 25–27). As markets expand outwards in their natural tendency, social and economic networks become increasingly less constrained by the maladaptive and irrational 'jealousy of strangers' (*WN*, I.x.c.22: 142).

The pursuit of self-interest within a complex division of labour promotes exchange relationships and, in turn, shifts the mechanisms of solidarity away from those generated by traditional associations towards increasingly wider and more impersonal spheres of contact. In fact, this process has been quietly building since the agricultural stage, whereby the 'silent and insensible operation of foreign commerce and manufactures gradually brought about' the end of feudalism, a particularly restrictive, dependency-generating and maladaptive form of social organisation (*WN*, III.iv.10: 418–19).

How Will the Division of Labour Exert the Same Effect in the International Realm?

The answer to this question lies in an appreciation of the division of labour's role in Smith's historiography, his theory of growth, his economics and his faculty psychology. The drive to specialise is universal and irresistible and has its source in the natural urge 'to truck, barter, and exchange one thing for another' (*WN*, I.ii.1: 25). Indeed, for Smith, it is so potent a force that it is the cause of almost all of the growth, progress and prosperity of the commercial age (*WN*, I.i: 13–24), capable of occasioning a 'universal opulence, which extends itself' even 'to the lowest ranks of the people' (*WN*, I.i.10: 22).

It is no exaggeration to say that specialisation is actually a key *cause* of commercialism because it leads everyone to 'live by exchanging, or becom[ing] in some measure a merchant, and the society itself grows to be what is properly a commercial society' (*WN*, I.iv.1: 37). Its energy is given further impetus by the fact that it has a necessary tendency to develop and expand perpetually, driven as it is, in turn, by two powerful, innate motive forces: the unlimited universal human desire for manufactured goods, luxuries and 'conveniencies' (*WN*, I.xi.c.7: 180–82) and the innate and irresistible drive to better our material conditions (*WN*, II.iii.36: 345; *WN*, II.iii.31: 343; and *WN*, IV.v.b.43: 540). But there is an irritating hitch to this natural process that Smith is keen to remove: the division of labour is limited by the extent of market (*LJ[B]*, 222–23: 494; *WN*, I.iii.31) and in Smith's time this was artificially constrained by mercantilist policies. Yet, he felt certain that the expansion of markets and relaxation of national borders were both inevitable, one way or another (*WN*, IV.i.32–3: 448–49; *WN*, IV.vii.c.5–6: 91).

Smith envisioned an international division of labour 'uniting … the most distant parts of the world' and 'enabling' separate nations to 'relieve one another's wants', 'increase one another's enjoyments' and encourage 'one another's industry' (*WN*, IV.vii.c.80: 626). Mercantilist policy unnaturally hindered this process and the policy urgently needed changing: 'Brittain should by all means be made a free port … and *liberty of exchange should be allowed with all nations and for all things*' (*LJ[A]*, 262–69: 511–14; emphasis added). Importantly, as discussed in Chap. 4, this process of opening markets should occur very gradually to avoid major disruption and financial loss.

According to the logic of Smith's historiography, commerce will—if allowed—expand indefinitely; in fact, the forces of history are so strong that this will happen even in spite of Mercantilism (*WN*, IV.v.b.43: 540. See also *WN*, IV.ix.28: 674; *WN*, II.iii.36: 345). In Smithian historiography, as has been shown, progress is driven by natural and irresistible laws. Smith posits a stadial sequence with four universal, developmental stages based on means of subsistence (hunting, pasturage, agriculture and commerce) through which all societies will pass (*LJ[A]*, i.27: 14; *LJ[B]*, 149–50: 459). The final stage is commercial society.

The history of the use of capital sits within these stages but, for obvious reasons, does not begin until the agricultural stage: it is an observable fact that 'the natural course of things' dictates that 'the greater part of the capital of every growing society is, first, directed to agriculture, afterwards to manufactures, and last of all to foreign commerce'. Smith insists that the sequence is both natural and universal, having been observed 'in some degree' in 'every society that had any territory'. Indeed, any digression from or inversion of this sequence is deemed 'unnatural and retrograde' (*WN*, III.i.8–9: 380). Each of these stages is characterised by increasingly larger, more complex and more impersonal social units, beginning with the family, later superseded by the tribal family or feudal estate, then the nation and finally the sovereign state (Berdell 2002: 40). For Smith, these stages are biologically and even divinely ordered since it is the result of the innate 'propensity to truck, barter, and exchange' (*WN*, I.ii.I: 25; Hill 2004).

But whether people will ever completely transcend the prejudices of the 'state or sovereignty in which [they] have been born and educated' (*WN*, VI.ii.2.2: 227) is debatable since Smith clearly regards patriotic sentiments as extremely resilient (*TMS*, VI.ii.2.2: 227–28). Nevertheless, he foresees that both the behaviour of individual states and relationships between states will alter significantly and permanently. Ultimately, he seems to believe that patriotic sentiments will be not so much transcended as demoted and de-intensified. With more and more free trade between disparate strangers, 'national friendship' will replace that '[m]ercantile jealousy' that 'both inflames, and is itself inflamed, by the violence of national animosity' (*WN*, IV.iii.c.13: 496). If allowed to take its natural course, global commerce will enrich all nations and, in the process, dispel the mercantilist myth that national greatness is a zero-sum game.

If it weren't for blind nationalism, it would be plain to everyone that freely practised commerce engenders infinite mutual enrichment. The 'national jealousies' that cause neighbours 'to spite and ill-will each other', and irrationally 'refuse to be supplied by them in any convenience of life', only 'lessen[s] the exchange of commodities, hurt[s] the division of labour, and diminish[es] the opulence of both' (*LJ[A]*, vi.164–65: 391–92). The patriot wrongly regards 'with the most malignant jealousy and envy, the prosperity and aggrandisement of any other neighbouring nation'. Accordingly, nations 'all live in continual dread and suspicion of one another' while every nation 'imagines it foresees its own subjugation in the increasing power and aggrandisement of any of its neighbours'. But an 'enlarged and enlightened mind', such as Smith hoped to engender among his readership, feels 'no aversion to the prosperity even of an old enemy' and will rejoice in 'the internal happiness and prosperity of the other, the cultivation of its lands, the advancement of its manufactures, the increase of its commerce, the security and number of its ports and harbours' and 'its proficiency in all the liberal arts and sciences' because these 'are all real improvements of the world we live in' and therefore available to everyone regardless of nationality (*TMS*, VI.ii.2.3: 228–29).

Here, Smith draws upon and endorses the *doux commerce* thesis popularised by Montesquieu who wrote that the 'natural effect of commerce is to lead to peace. Two nations that trade with each other become reciprocally dependent; if one has an interest in buying, the other has an interest in selling, and all unions are founded on mutual needs' (Montesquieu 1989, XX.2: 338). In the system of perfect liberty the patriotic prejudices that patrol a country's borders will not constrain the movement of goods, labour or capital (Berdell 2002: 39). Whereas the domain of politics is the sovereign state, the economy encompasses the entire globe.

A World-State?

Smith's failure to designate world government as the next stage of commercial governance does not disqualify him as a cosmopolite, as might be imagined. Contrary to the common perception, even classical cosmopolitanism does not demand the establishment of a world-state. The concept of the *oikoumenh*, 'the habitable world considered as a single unit' (Hadas 1943: 109), is more of a state of mind and way of life than a constitutional objective. It rests on a belief that community is derived from the fact of our common humanity and that the laws governing the conduct of daily life are the same for everyone else regardless of ethnicity, class or blood ties (Clarke 1987: 65, 70; Marcus 1964, 4.4: 65). Further, Smith's commercial cosmopolitanism, although in no way animated by benevolence, nevertheless, embodies and serves such other key Stoic values as universalism, pacifism, freedom from tyranny and exploitation and a corresponding demand for the respect of human dignity wherever it is found (Baldry 1965: 158; Edelstein 1966: 74–75). Once nations adopt what Smith calls 'the liberal system', they will operate as a single community of amicable but separate 'provinces of a great empire' (*WN*, IV.v.b.39: 538–39), held together by an international division of labour. In any case, Smith is definitely not a thinker likely to advocate any kind of monolithic government.[6]

It should not go unmentioned that Smith has moments of deep pessimism about the possibility of a system of natural liberty ever being allowed to assert itself. Even in his more optimistic moments he doubts whether such a system could 'ever be *entirely* restored' due to the 'prejudices of the publick' and the 'unconquerable ... private interests of many individuals' (*WN*, IV.ii.43: 471). Yet, such pessimism may have been used for rhetorical effect; he was, after all, attempting to steer government policy. In addition, if we quarantine Smith's personal reservations from his social theory, the logic of his historiography suggests that an imperfect or partial version of such a system would eventuate in the long run. Once his recommendations are adopted and free trade has become routine, Smith deems it highly likely that there will emerge a system of international deterrence and anarchy or equilibrium. 'Naturally' and 'necessarily' the 'extensive commerce from all countries to all countries' will bring equilibrium in international affairs. The 'natives' of subject colonies will grow 'stronger' and 'those of Europe ... weaker' and eventually the world's population will 'arrive at that equality of courage and force which, by inspiring mutual fear' can effectively 'overawe the injustice of independent nations into some sort of respect for the rights of one another' (*WN*, IV. vii.c. 80–1: 626–27).

Note that, unlike many contemporary *political* cosmopolitans, Smith did not believe that economic cosmopolitanism would create inequality. Although he was comfortable with rank distinctions in the domestic sphere, he considered inequality between nations an inlet for interstate conflict. The best means for achieving equity and balance is through free trade and the accompanying 'mutual communication of knowledge', 'improvements' and technology it 'necessarily' brings with it (*WN*, IV. vii.c. 80–1: 626–27). In the end, it appears that all states will become commercially developed and therefore able to defend themselves militarily, but the demand for defence capability will become less urgent as the pacific norms of global commerce take hold.

The End of War? Commerce as the Pacifying Medium for the New Cosmopolis

Evidently, Smith believed that commerce would become the universal alternative to war and therefore the medium for his imagined economic *cosmopolis*. A siblinghood of amiably disposed strangers would gradually displace a universe riven with suspicion, particularistic prejudice and conflict. Despite the commercial conflicts exacerbated by Mercantilism, Smith believed that when conducted according to the laws of natural liberty, commerce was 'naturally' a pacifying medium (*WN*, iii.c.9: 493).

Smith abhorred war partly because of its enormous cost, something he complained about bitterly and endlessly. The constant drain on the public purse occasioned by Britain's apparently unquenchable appetite for dispute exacerbated the public debt problem, and with it the equally egregious system of patronage. He also deplored war because it was a routine theatre of injustice; in conflicts with strangers, Smith's famous impartial spectator has no power of persuasion before the unusually partial audience of compatriots (*TMS*, III. 3.42: 154).

> When two nations are at variance, the citizen of each pays little regard to the sentiments which foreign nations may entertain concerning his conduct. His whole ambition is to obtain the approbation of his own fellow-citizens; and as they are all animated by the same hostile passions which animate himself, he can never please them so much as by enraging and offending their enemies. (*TMS*, III. 3.42: 154)

Under conditions of war, Smith observes despondently, 'the laws of justice' and 'nations' are 'very seldom observed' (*TMS*, III. 3.42: 154). Even in cases where war is waged according to the so-called 'laws of nations', the suffering visited on innocents is undiminished since such laws have been 'laid down with very little regard to the plainest and most obvious rules of justice' (*TMS*, III. 3.42: 154–55)[7]:

> Whenever it suits the conveniency of a public enemy ... the goods of the peaceable citizens are seized both at land and at sea; their lands are laid waste, their houses are burnt, and they themselves ... are murdered or led into captivity; and all this in the most perfect conformity to what are called the laws of nations. (*TMS*, III. 3.42: 155)

Obviously, war, interstate friction and all other forms of 'jealousies … between different nations' are also bad because they disrupt trade and are 'extremely hurtful' to commerce and 'public opulence'. For example, the long-standing conflict between Britain and France was particularly detrimental to trade: 'It were happy, therefore, both for this country and for France, that all national prejudices were rooted out, and a free and uninterrupted commerce established' (*LJ[B]*, 264–65: 512).

Smith was so outspoken on this issue that he is credited with inspiring the Parliament of 1784 'to establish profitable commercial relations between Britain and France'. Whereas previously there had existed 'between these countries … a war of prohibitions and high duties', which counter-productively encouraged smuggling, Smith's ideas had managed to shift public opinion towards an appreciation of the benefits of free trade, thereby assisting the peace settlement of 1783. An important component of this settlement was an article stipulating that France and England should resolve a commercial treaty. This treaty was effected in September 1786. Smith's influence on this relationship was to reverberate for decades after and in the trade policies of subsequent generations. 'Free trade … had been accepted by all parties as the settled policy of the nation, and the Anglo-French Commercial Treaty of 1860 was taken to herald it as the future policy of all nations.' Partly as a consequence of Smith's tireless proselytising on the question, '[p]rosperity, peace and progress' supplanted 'the unholy trinity of protectionism, militarism and imperialism' (Schuyler 1921: 538–39. See also Ross 1995: 352–53). Whereas once trade restrictions between the two countries had mirrored and exacerbated national hostilities, now commerce—via mutually enabling free trade—gave cause and sustenance to peace.

Smith welcomed the domestic deepening and expansion of commerce, partly because it brought with it an organised and stable state, thereby securing 'the liberty and security' of people who 'had before lived almost in a continual state of war with their neighbours' (*WN*, III.iv.4: 412). On the interstate level commerce also tended to have a pacifying effect because commercial states—with their particular interest in free trade—are more likely to seek alliances than to prosecute wars. Indeed, the 'state of peace' is synonymous with the state of 'commerce' (*WN*, IV.iii.c.11: 494). Commerce only gives rise to 'discord and animosity' under the aggravating influence of a 'monopolising spirit'.

Where there is 'peace and commerce', rich nations are better 'customer[s]' and sellers than poor ones. Common sense dictates that 'where little wealth circulates, there is little to be got' but 'where a great deal is in motion, some share of it may fall to' everyone. Prosperity is achieved, not by 'beggar[ing]' our neighbours via Mercantilism or achieving the same effect by invasion, but by allowing to proliferate myriad independent 'rich, industrious, and commercial nations' with whom one can trade for mutual benefit (*WN*, iii.c.11: 495). Accordingly, commerce is not only the route to global peace, prosperity and material enjoyment, but the circuit-breaker to a vicious 'spiral' whereby protectionism leads to poor economic performance, which exacerbates 'the political pressure for protection at home' and monopoly abroad, resulting, in turn, in 'heightened international animosity, resentment and warfare', with wartime debt completing the catastrophic spiral (Berdell 2002: 36).

Smith was aware that commerce could not put an immediate and decisive end to the threat of war. Although he thought that war was irrational where mutually enriching commerce was an alternative, he was also alert to human irrationality and the potential for nationalistic enmity to override good sense. Overall, however, Smith seemed to believe that, as global commerce radiates and becomes routine, war will become less common due to two forms of deterrence. In the short term, deterrence will be effected militarily via standing armies and technological advances in the arts of war are vital. Significantly, however, the main point of a militarily strong state is not to wage war but to provide deterrence; to preserve the peace, prosperity and liberty of states and to keep commerce in motion. In the longer term, Smith saw deterrence as effected, not by military strength, but by commerce, mutual enrichment and habituation to foreigners. Even our most intense and seemingly permanent loyalties are really only artefacts of habit (*TMS*, I.ii.1.7: 222). Over time, our passion for compatriots will be offset by our self-interested involvement in commerce with distant strangers.

Smith was not the only eighteenth-century figure to entertain these sorts of hopes. In contemplating the impending separation of Britain from its North American (and other) colonies, Anne Robert Jacques Turgot looked forward to trading as 'as a citizen of the world', while Francois Quesnay anticipated a system of universal commerce where all shared equally in the commodities and wealth of the globalising world.[8] But whether we can ever be *entirely* at ease with strangers from vastly different cultures is a matter for debate. Although some Smith scholars have seen the 'impartial spectator' (the internal surveillance mechanism or hypothetical observer that exists in the breast of every actor) as a potentially effective cosmopolitan device (e.g. Griswold 1999: 92, 96–99; Nussbaum 1995: 134, n.23), I am more inclined to Fonna Forman-Barzilai's view that 'the sort of impartiality achieved by Smith's impartial spectator ... is not the sort required to render unbiased cross-cultural judgments' (Forman-Barzilai 2006: 96). While the impartial spectator may be unable to *completely* transcend cultural differences and tolerate the seemingly bizarre practices of other cultures,[9] it can at least enable us to get along tolerably well with strangers. Moral cosmopolitanism might be beyond the reach of the impartial spectator but *commercial* cosmopolitanism, something far less morally and emotionally demanding, is probably something it can manage.

It is likely that Smith believed that the modes, rationalities and language of commerce would become a kind of lingua franca, a universal culture of civility and politeness that could both co-exist with and temper parochial cultures. 'Opulence and Commerce commonly precede the improvement of arts, and refinement of every Sort' (Smith *Corr.*: 137). For example, women 'in all polite and wealthy countries' are held in higher 'regard' and are better treated than those in 'poorer and more barbarous nation[s]' (*LJ[A]*, i.156: 66).

Smith on American Independence

The remainder of this chapter explores Adam Smith's attitude to America's War of Independence with Britain. Smith expended considerable effort attempting to resolve this problem and it makes for a very useful case study of how Smith operated as a political strategist, a theorist of government policy, a manager of public opinion and a cautious and creative agent for reform. I have mentioned that Smith had a particular idea of what the ideal global regime should look like but in the American case he was called on to devise second-best options. His approach to the problem has caused some confusion due to the apparent inconsistency of his advice and his own failure to be clearer on the matter. I attempt to throw light on these various confusions and inconsistencies, partly by locating what he has to say in the context of his broader social-science commitments and partly by arguing that he was first and foremost a pragmatist and political problem-solver rather than a political ideologue.

Both strains in his thought help to reconcile the exceptionalism of his attitude to America. Specifically, although he deplored Britain's retention of all its colonies, he proposed a number of strategies for solving the

American problem that accommodated that retention. Particular attention is devoted to his most surprising solution: the establishment of an Imperial Parliament, a supra-national assembly that gave the Americans representation in Parliament and made them equal economic and political partners with England. Some scholars have suggested that this is his favoured resolution above all others, something I challenge.

The American problem was an important test case for Smith's economic ideas and he believed that lessons drawn from this experience could not only relieve Britain from its crushing public debt but help to end 'the cycle of violence' that the perpetuation of the colonial system occasioned (Ross 1995: 250). It was an opportunity to deliver British leaders—and hopefully the highly prejudiced British public as well—a lecture in humility about Britain's real place in the world and, in the process, show the rest of the world where the future of colonialism really lay. He was, as Ian Ross has observed, 'coolheaded' about America and could see that it had 'come of age' (Ross 1995: 19).

Smith took his role as a public opinion-shaper very seriously, confessing that, although he was often at odds with 'the opinion of the public', he was well aware that he was obliged 'to have some regard' for it (*Corr.*, 9: 5). Accordingly, he worked assiduously to change attitudes about the American problem in order to reverse 'public prejudices' about it (*Corr.*, 221: 262). It was a difficult mission: the eventual loss of America was reportedly met by the British—and especially the Scottish—public with much 'silence and sorrow' (Skinner 1996: 117).

Smith fought the battle on two fronts, communicating his thoughts to the public as well as the political elites who sought his advice. Notably, the messages he sent to each audience were not always identical, as will be shown. Careful analysis and contextualisation of his public and private thoughts on the subject reveal a skilled political strategist highly attuned to the sensitivities of his audience and prepared, for the sake of Britain's economic and security interests, to use subterfuge where necessary.

Smith took a particular interest in American affairs. Hume observed in a letter to Smith in 1776 that his friend had been 'very zealous in American affairs' and even implied that he was delaying the publication of *Wealth of Nations* until 'the Fate of America be decided' (*Corr.*: 186). Smith deals with the American issue in *Wealth of Nations* and wrote letters on the issue of free trade with America to influential figures like Henry Dundas, Lord Carlisle, William Eden (one of the Lords of Trade) and Sinclair of Ulster (Campbell and Ross 1981: 84). Of particular interest is a document found among the papers of Alexander Wedderburn entitled 'Smith's Thoughts on the State of the Contest with America, February 1788'. The document was among the material acquired by the University of Michigan library in 1929 but was not identified as having been written by Smith until 1933 (see Guttridge 1933).

Wedderburn, a former student of Smith's and Solicitor-General in Lord North's administration probably asked Smith to draft this memorandum after Burgoyne's surrender at Saratoga in October 1777.[10] Smith also worked with Charles Townsend on the budget that affected the relationship between the 'mother country' and the American colonies, focusing on Britain's right to impose import duties, including the infamous tax on tea (Stevens in *Corr.*, App.B: 378; *Corr.*, 302: 332). It has been suggested that after Smith had published his thoughts on the matter it finally became 'possible to think of colonies in a new way' (though 'not impossible to treat them in the old'). His ideas 'bore their fruit in general opinion' and galvanised 'a generation of colonial reformers ... to bring forth a new and better colonial policy' (Benians 1925: 249). In particular, Smith's intellectual influence upon William Petty, Lord Shelburne (initially a leading member of Parliament and later Prime Minister), is reported to have caused the latter to abandon Mercantilism in favour of American Independence and trade liberalisation more generally (Morrison 2012).[11]

Although it has been claimed that 'Smith at no point denied that the relationship between Britain and America had brought great benefits to both parties' (Skinner 1977: 75),[12] in fact, Smith was highly critical. Amidst the 'confused scramble of politicks and war' and to the 'undiscerning eye of giddy ambition', a fertile and resource-rich country like America might seem 'a very dazzling object to fight for'. However, it was that very same 'splendour' and 'immense greatness' of trade that made its monopolisation all the more 'hurtful' to commerce in the long run (*WN*, IV.vii.c.85: 628). The colonial system retarded the progress of its satellites and exerted even worse effects on the 'mother country' (*WN*, IV.vii.c.83: 627–28). Monopolising the trade with America was also an affront to Smith's social science, specifically his theory of spontaneous order or 'system of natural liberty'. Any restrictions on the right to choose how best to employ one's resources and labour are 'a manifest violation of the most sacred rights of mankind' and so too is the restriction on 'a great people ... from making all that they can of every part of their own produce or from employing their stock and industry in the way that they judge most advantageous to themselves'(*WN*, IV.vii.b.44: 582; *WN*, IV.v.b.43: 540;

WN, I.x.c.12: 138); hence the monopoly of colonial trade is self-evidently 'contrary to the rights of mankind' (*Corr.*, 221: 262).[13]

The colonial system had brought nothing but trouble; for example, the American Revolution had caused a severe economic depression in Ireland, 'closing overseas markets for Irish linen and cutting of an extensive woollen trade between Ireland and the American colonies' (Teichgraeber 1987: 357). Maintaining the colonies was expensive, not only in times of war, but also in peace. The high day-to-day administrative costs of managing and holding on to the colonies (what Smith referred to as the 'peace-establishment') was due in large part to failure to extract sufficient tax revenue from them (e.g. *WN*, IV.vii.c.65–75: 616–24; *WN*, V.iii.92: 946). The whole point of getting and keeping colonies was to derive some material benefit, usually in the form of 'revenue' or a 'military force' in 'support of the empire'. America had contributed neither (*WN*, IV.vii.c.11–12: 593; *WN*, V.ii.92: 946). 'Under the present system of management', Smith concluded, 'Great Britain derives nothing but loss from the dominion which she assumes over her colonies' (*WN*, IV.vii.c.65: 616).

What to Do About America?

As Smith polished the final draft of *Wealth of Nations* in London from 1773 until 1776, the Parliament 'was increasingly preoccupied with tumult in the American colonies' and Smith is supposed to have attended debates on the subject. Indeed, Ian Ross suggests that 'the publication of *Wealth of Nations* was timed to seize Parliament's attention, and influence Members to support a peaceful resolution of the conflict' (Ross 1995: 250). In the private Memorandum he prepared for Wedderburn,[14] Smith outlined four possible courses of action for ending the 'unhappy' conflict with America.

The first (Option 1) would 'end in the complete submission of America' with 'all the different colonies ... acknowledging ... the supremacy of the mother country' as well as 'contributing their proper proportion towards defraying the expence of the general Government and defence of the Empire'. Smith wrote that this result could be achieved either by force or by 'treaty' (or a combination of both). By 'treaty' (Option 1b), Smith meant an imperial union which was far less oppressive than the 'by force' solution (Option 1a). On this scheme, America would be properly incorporated into the British state via representation in Parliament. America would 'assum[e] the burdens of defence and civil administration' and would also contribute tax revenue to the empire (Fagerstrom 1954: 259).

The second option (Option 2) would 'end in the complete emancipation of America', with 'not a single acre of land, from the enterance into Hudson's Straits to the mouth of the Mississippi, acknowledging the supremacy of Great Britain'. The third proposal (Option 3) would restore the 'old colonial system' of 1763, with the 'colonies acknowledging the supremacy of the mother country, allowing the Crown to appoint the Governors, the Lieutenant-Governors, the secretaries and a few other officers in the greater part of them, and submitting to certain regulations of trade; but contributing little or nothing towards defraying the expence of the general Government and defence of the empire'. The fourth and final proposal (Option 4) involved 'the submission of a part, but of a part only, of America: Great Britain, after a long, expensive and ruinous war being obliged to acknowledge the independency of the rest' (*Corr.*, App. B: 380). It has been repeatedly asserted that Smith personally preferred the imperial union or 'treaty' variant of Option 1 (1b) to all other options adverted to in his Memorandum. Given what we know about Smith's aversion to monolithic government, it warrants closer inspection.

Context, Rationale and Plan for an Imperial Parliament (Option 1b)

Smith did not much like the 'complete-submission-by-force' component of Option 1, concluding that to force submission would gain nothing but the 'disgrace' of oppressing 'a people whom we have long talked of, not only as of our fellow subjects, but as of our brethren and even as of our children'. It would necessitate 'military government', which is 'what of all others, the Americans hate and dread the most'. But Smith, and many of his contemporaries, also dreaded it most. Such a scheme was not only repugnant but 'impracticabl[e]' (*Corr.*, App.B: 381). Unfortunately, due to the irrational prejudices of the public and the stubborn pride of British leaders, Smith reckoned that, except for a 'few angry speeches in Parliament', this 'solution' would 'meet with scarce any opposition' in Britain (*Corr.*, App.B: 381). He castigated his fellow Britons that America would never 'voluntarily submit to us; and we ought to consider that the blood which must be shed in forcing them to do so, is, every drop of it, the blood either of those who are' or 'those whom we wish to have for our fellow citizens' (*WN*, IV.vii.c.75: 623).

Complete 'submission' by 'treaty'—by which Smith meant the institution of an Imperial Parliament (or what he also referred to as 'the States-General of the British Empire'), with America (and Ireland) enjoying representation in a London-based Parliament—struck Smith as far more attractive than 'submission by force'. The model Smith had in mind was along the lines of the Union of Scotland and England in 1707 (*Corr.*, App.B: 383) and would enable 'both parts of the empire' to enjoy 'the same freedom of trade' as well as a share in both 'the burden of taxation' and 'the benefit of representation'. It would also obviate the need for an 'expensive military force' to police the colony. Since the 'leading men' of America would be representatives in the Imperial Parliament, the allegiance of the Americans was, he believed, assured. Further, 'the necessary mildness of such a government, so exactly resembling that of the mother country, would secure the continuance of the prosperity of the colonies'. Of greatest advantage was the fact that the Americans would be 'taxed by their own representatives' and would therefore be 'disposed to contribute more willingly' (*Corr.*, App.B: 381).

Aside from the boon of peace and the many material benefits of the union, Smith believed (wrongly) that the idea would be attractive to the ambitions of American leaders who could now enjoy a much grander stage on which to strut politically (*WN*, IV.vii.c.75: 622–23). He also imagined that the Americans would be glad of an opportunity to free themselves 'from those rancorous and virulent factions which are inseparable from small democracies ... [and] which have so frequently divided the affections of their people, and disturbed the tranquillity of their governments' (*WN*, V.iii: 945). The benefits to Ireland would be similar. Greater freedom of trade would bring prosperity, but Ireland would also welcome the secondary benefit of 'freedom from an oppressive aristocracy' in the manner of Scotland (Benians 1925: 258). Smith further surmised that the Imperial Parliament would improve the quality of governance throughout the empire because it would now be constituted by better-informed decision-makers (*WN*, IV.vii.c77: 624).

It is interesting that Smith should even frame this option as a form of 'submission' since, in reality, it was highly concessional from the British point of view. What it meant was, not 'submission', but *acquiescence* through a new constitution that ensured 'the most perfect equality' between the 'mother country' and 'her colonies' (*Corr.*, App.B: 381). Smith's choice of words was doubtless strategic, designed to assuage British vanity and wear down public resistance.

A Radical Plan?

Smith's proposal might seem radical in hindsight but from his own perspective, it was merely a pragmatist's compromise. At the time Smith wrote about the imperial union he was well aware of the activities of a British radical movement led by figures like Major John Cartwright and Richard Price who disputed Britain's right to exercise political authority over other nations (Schuyler 1945). Yet, Smith was not part of this movement and neither were the majority of the Scottish Parliamentarians who supported the government against the Americans. There were lone voices like George Dempster, a member from 1761 to 1790 (Fagerstrom 1954: 256), who regarded Britain's efforts at conciliation as risible and American Independence as the only viable solution. As he wrote dismally: 'The limb is gangrened and amputation is better than death.'[15] Closer to Smith, David Hume also condemned Britain's colonial policy. In 1768 he wrote to Sir Gilbert Elliot on the topic: 'Let us … lay aside all Anger; shake hands, and part Friends' (Hume 1932: 184–85). Smith's view, omitted from the Memorandum, was identical.

Although Smith saw himself as isolated in advocating the idea of submission by treaty (*Corr.* App.B: 382), a few other prominent figures had proposed similar plans. Henry Home, Lord Kames, proposed a 'consolidating union' in his *Sketches of the History of Man* (1774), while the former governor of the Province of Massachusetts Bay, Thomas Pownell, recommended a federal union in successive editions of his *Administration of the Colonies* (1764–1767).[16] Even Benjamin Franklin wrote in 1754 that union would be 'very acceptable to the colonies', albeit with certain provisos.[17] In general, the Scots who knew about it and who did not prefer a continuation of the war were more receptive to the idea than the English, but not much more (Fagerstrom 1954: 260).

Although Smith often invoked the rhetoric of justice in his discussion of colonial management, his interest in de-colonisation was mainly economic and practical. Above all, should there be no option but to retain the colonies, he wanted, at least, to be able to tax them. This is why, on the one hand, he pushed for de-colonisation but, on the other, argued that, so long as they remained part of the empire, the Americans should pay their 'fair' share of taxes. Either way, the costs to Britain had to be managed better.

How to Solve the Public Debt Problem

Britain had a public debt problem directly related to the burden of the colonies and the States-General seemed a fair and reasonable solution for two reasons: first, it 'is not contrary to justice that both Ireland and America should contribute towards the discharge of the publick debt of Great Britain' since that 'debt has been contracted' in supporting and defending both colonies (*WN*, V.iii.88: 944). Second, the Imperial Parliament would embody the constitutional principle of 'no taxation without representation' (*WN*, V.iii.68: 933–34). This was a matter of 'justice': taxing the Americans could not be done 'consistently with the principles of the British constitution, without admitting into the British Parliament' equal representation of the provinces proportionate to the level of contributed taxes (*WN*, V.iii.68: 933). While Britain would maintain control of the assessment of taxation levels, nevertheless, the colonies would now be incorporated into a single state with Great Britain as equal partners.

Note that membership of the scheme was limited to Ireland and America, that is, subjects of 'British or European extraction', possibly as a means by which to contain resistance to the idea among a xenophobic public. Smith imagined an incorporating union similar to that introduced by the Act of 1707 and later extended to Ireland (Campbell & Skinner in *WN*, n.56: 617). By this method the 'British Empire' could become 'within itself an immense internal market for every part of the produce of its different provinces'. Extending free trade in this fashion 'would soon compensate both to Ireland and all the plantations, all that they could suffer from the increase of the duties of customs' (*WN*, V.iii.72: 935). This expansion in freedom to trade, while not as free or global as Smith would have preferred, was, nevertheless, preferable to the other alternatives, except of course, 'complete emancipation', which Smith ruefully regarded as the least likely to be adopted. The problems of empire, public debt and congested trade could be, at least partly, resolved by the adoption of an Atlantic economic community where trade would become 'as free as the coasting trade of Great Britain is at present' (*WN*, V.iii.72: 935). Smith had no illusions that the Union 'could be easily effectuated' but was adamant that none of the potential 'difficulties' were 'insurmountable' (*WN*, IV.vii.c.77: 624).

Smith the Pragmatist

Smith's pragmatism where international affairs were concerned clearly ran deeper than is commonly appreciated. Indeed, there are times when it approaches ruthlessness. As I show below, he was not averse to invoking the 'noble lie' in colonial matters. Another example is found in his attitude to Canada. As Smith was revising *Wealth of Nations*, the British Government was settling the government of Quebec. He does not say what he thought of the Quebec Act of 1774 but it has been suggested that he would have included Canada in the scheme 'had he thought of it', given that it was restricted to people of 'British or European extraction' (Benians 1925: 268; *WN*, V.iii.68: 397). However, it seems unlikely that Smith never 'thought of it' since he generally thought of everything; it is more likely that he deliberately left Canada out of the picture for a reason. The first might have been that Canada should be kept out to keep the States-General strictly Anglophone. Noisy voices demanding their equal rights in French (or at least French accents) would have been too much for the British public; further, he might have reasoned that the divided loyalties of Francophone Canadians would always be a problem in an assembly that was supposed to unify and pacify.

The other, and much more probable, reason is that Smith found a better use for Canada. This he reveals in the Memorandum and, significantly, in none of his published works. Here, he proposes a surprising piece of brutal Realpolitik. Were Option 2 to eventuate (i.e. 'the complete emancipation of America'), Smith advises the British to 'restore Canada to France and the two Floridas to Spain' in order to render 'our colonies the natural enemies of those two monarchies and consequently the natural allies of Great Britain' (*Corr.*, App.B: 383).

Smith's cool-headedness about America is displayed in another curious feature of his proposal; he predicted with (prescient) complacency the eventual transfer of power from Westminster to the former colonies. Confirming his well-deserved credentials as an economic cosmopolitan and not an economic nationalist (as has sometimes been suggested), he observed that America's rapid progress 'in wealth, population and improvement' meant that 'in the course of little more than a century, perhaps, the produce of America might exceed that of British taxation'. Since the proportion of representation was calculated according to tax, inevitably 'the seat of empire would … naturally remove itself to that part of the empire which contributed most to the general defence and support of the whole' (*WN*, IV.vii.79: 625–26).[18] Notably, this prediction appears in the earlier *Wealth of Nations* but is never mentioned in the Memorandum to Wedderburn, with Smith betting, perhaps, that the latter had not read the former very carefully. In any case, the States-General would turn out to be just a different pathway for American Independence, albeit one that led to Britain's eventual eclipse.

Was the States-General Smith's Preferred Solution?

Some scholars have claimed that imperial union was Smith's preferred pathway out of the American problem partly because of the extra space he devoted to sketching how it might work (Hewins 1903: 14). According to Ernest Benians, Smith's 'dream', 'his "courageous Utopia", was a "united empire"' (Benians 1925: 249; see also Nicholson 1909: x). Charles Ryle Fay claims that Smith 'pleaded with passion' for the imperial union because he was an imperialist and a nationalist (Fay 1930: 34). Andrew Skinner argues that Smith's personal 'preference' was for union (Skinner 1977: 76) and that, because he 'clearly believed that the project of Empire could have been successfully completed', he 'viewed the final outcome with dispassionate regret' (Skinner 1996: 130). Samuel Fleischacker sees Smith as 'unsympathetic to the American revolution' preferring 'a union under the British Crown to American independence' (Fleischacker 2004: 247). Even the editor of Smith's Memorandum—David Stevens—concludes that in Smith's 'opinion' the 'scheme offering most advantages to the British empire was that of a constitutional union with American representation' (*Corr.*, App.B: 379; see also Stevens 1975: 206).

At first sight, such interpretations seem plausible. After all, Smith does devote far more attention to the imperial union or 'States-General' solution than to any other option canvassed and he paid particular attention to the possible tax arrangements should it be effected. In fact, he mentions the idea of an Imperial Parliament twelve times in *Wealth of Nations* and again, at length, in the Memorandum. Smith did state that, should this plan 'be executed', it 'would certainly tend most to the prosperity, to the splendour, and to the duration of the empire' (*Corr.*, App.B: 382). However, this is not the same as agreeing that an Imperial Parliament is the best course of action overall; only that it is the best way of preserving the empire, assuming that this was what was wanted, which in Smith's case, it wasn't. The imperial union would simply enable Britain to make the best of a bad situation.

The States-General would have struck Smith as the only option remotely acceptable to Wedderburn, given the latter's obdurate resentment towards the Americans, hence the greater level of detail about how it might work. In laying out the proposal Smith devoted less space to rhetoric and more to the intricacies of how America could be taxed and incorporated (*WN*, V.iii.68: 934). This gives the impression that he thought it had some chance, particularly as it might at least forestall what otherwise looked inevitable. As Smith puts it in the *Wealth of Nations*: 'total separation from Great Britain', forced by the Americans themselves, seemed 'very likely to take place … unless prevented by a union of this kind' (*WN*, V.iii.90: 945).

The fact that Smith even entertained the idea of an Imperial Parliament is perhaps best explained in terms of his gradualism. Despite his progressivism and persistent urging of reform, as a spontaneous order theorist Smith could only ever advocate cautious reform. The parliamentary union seems to have been a perfect example of establishing not so much the 'best system of laws' as 'the best that the people can bear'. Even when urging his preferred solution—voluntary separation—Smith still took a conservative approach, insisting that the colonial trade should only be opened very 'gradually' (*WN*, vii.c.44: 606) and with extreme 'reserve and circumspection' (*WN*, IV.ii.40: 469).

Social-Science Reasons for 'Complete Emancipation' as Smith's Preferred Option

Any advocacy of 'supra-national governance' and transposition of government activity to a higher than national level runs counter to Smith's profound laissez-faire tendencies (Berdell 2002: 30) and well-deserved reputation as an advocate of the minimalist state. Smith tended to equate a large state with corrupt, profligate, parasitical and obstructive government (*WN*, II.iii.36: 345). For Smith, the larger the government, the more likely it is to be wasteful and incompetent in the management of public affairs (*WN*, II.iii.35–6: 344–46). Smith famously disapproved of any 'profusion of government' (*WN*, II.iii.36: 345), preferring instead a small, lean state so that 'the obvious and simple system of natural liberty' could 'establis[h] itself of its own accord' (*WN*, IV.ix.51: 687). His policy advice generally went in the direction of *reducing* the size and reach of government, not in enlarging it in the extravagant manner of a States-General.

In devising the States-General scheme, Smith was well aware that he was also violating other key principles of his social science, namely, any kind of rationalistic constructivism or utopianism (*WN*, IV.ix.50–51: 687; *TMS*, VI.ii.2.17: 233–34). Apparently self-conscious of the awkwardness here, he defensively reassured his reader that at least his 'new Utopia' was no 'more useless and chimerical than the old one', though admittedly less 'amusing'. Conceding that it was unlikely ever to be adopted, he reasoned that it was surely not improper for him to speculate about its character and likely effects (*WN*, V.iii.68: 934) since, in reality, none of the practical objections were 'insurmountable'. Further, he figured that this scheme had a better chance of acceptance than voluntary separation—which, on his estimation, had none at all.

The fact that Smith had positive things to say about—and devoted more attention to—the States-General solution does not mean that he preferred it to all others. The relative lack of detail given to his favoured solution—complete separation—is simply related to the fact that it needed no further explanation. Convinced that his first preference—voluntary separation—was an unlikely prospect, he devoted his energies to framing the most acceptable (to him) alternative. Separation was separation and did not need much elaboration; but the Imperial Parliament did (Knorr 1944: 187–88). At best, the States-General solution was his second-favourite option, partly because it conceded some ground to the Americans, partly because it would at least allow the 'mother country' to tax America in a fashion that did not invite further conflict, partly because it would mean free-er trade between the different parts of the empire and partly because it represented gradual, rather than violent, change.

Smith may have preferred complete and voluntary separation (Option 2) but he considered it even less likely to be adopted than the Imperial Parliament. As he wrote in the *Wealth of Nations:*

> To propose that Great Britain should voluntarily give up all authority over her colonies, and leave them to elect their own magistrates, to enact their own laws, and to make peace and war as they might think proper, would be to propose such a measure as never was, and never will be adopted, by any nation in the world. (*WN*, IV.vii.c.66: 616–17)

Further, the British government would not have the courage to carry out the scheme because doing so would bring 'discredit ... in the eyes of our own people', who would doubtless see it as a case of 'mal-administration'

(*Corr.*, App.B: 383). The idea was out of the question, more terrifying to the British public than the thought of an approaching 'Spanish armada, or a French invasion' (*WN*, IV.vii.c: 605). Yet, Smith persisted in promulgating the view that separation was really the best way forward, declaring that 'the complete emancipation of America' would immediately deliver Britain from 'extraordinary expence' (*Corr.*, App. B: 382) and guarantee prosperity-generating freedom of trade for all (*WN*, IV.vii.c: 617). Furthermore, '[b]y thus parting good friends, the natural affection of the colonies to the mother country', which had lately been badly damaged, 'would quickly revive' and might lead America to embrace a special relationship with Britain: to more or less permanently 'favour us in war as well as in trade'. Now, instead of being 'turbulent and factious subjects' they would 'become our most faithful, affectionate, and generous allies' in much the same manner as had ancient Greece and her effectively independent colonies (*WN*, IV.vii.c: 617).

That voluntary separation was favoured is further supported by the fact that Option 3 of the Memorandum—the ostensible resumption of the old colonial relationship of 1763—is really voluntary separation disguised as a variation on business as usual. Since the Memorandum was a private document for Wedderburn's eyes only, we can be reasonably sure that Smith was sincere in proposing that it be executed in the following covert—almost Machiavellian—manner: the 'English ministry and the American leaders should agree to restore the old colonial relationship of 1763, with the understanding, *not communicated to the English people*, that gradually the link should be severed' (Guttridge 1933: 715; emphasis added).

This scheme of deception, 'so contrived as to lead necessarily, but insensibly to the total dismemberment of America' (*Corr.*, App.B: 384), which Smith doubtless rationalised as a noble lie necessitated by the intractable 'national jealousy' of the British public (*LJ[A]*, vi.164–5: 391–92), would satisfy both sides since the British public would 'mistak[e]' and the American leadership fully 'understan[d] the meaning of the scheme'. Hopefully, in the long term, the scheme would 'bring about an event which, in the present distressful situation of our affairs, *is, perhaps, of all those which are likely to happen, the most advantageous to the state*' (*Corr.*, App.B: 384; emphasis added). But as with all the others, Smith holds out little hope for this option due to the fact that, on the one hand, 'the policy, the secrecy, the prudence necessary for conducting a scheme of this kind' are lacking in the 'British Government' while, on the other, the Americans would be unable to fake it and play dead for the time required (*Corr.*, App. B: 384).

Finishing the 'Project'

Although Smith disliked empires in principle, he knew that the British had no intention of voluntarily relinquishing theirs. His practical advice, therefore, was that Britain should either practise empire properly or not attempt it at all. In the final passage of the *Wealth of Nations* Smith states his position bluntly: 'The rulers of Great Britain' had for the past century 'amused the people' with the delusion 'that they possessed a great empire on the west side of the Atlantic'. But such an empire 'existed in imagination only'. It was not a proper empire so much as a costly, unprofitable and speculative '*project of an empire*; not a gold mine, but the *project of a gold mine*' (*WN*, V.iii.92: 946–47; emphasis added). He enjoined the government leaders to 'either realise this golden dream' in which they had been 'indulging' both themselves and the public or else 'awake from it … If the project cannot be compleated, it ought to be given up' (*WN*, V.iii.92: 947; emphasis added).[19]

By exhorting British leaders to complete the project, Smith meant the adoption of an imperial union in which the colonies are an integral part of the State and could be taxed. But if organising this was beyond the British leadership (and public) then complete emancipation was the only rational option. It is significant that Smith chooses to make America the topic of the very last lines of the eagerly awaited *Wealth of Nations*. Here he concludes on a sombre, admonitory note, his impatience with Britain's wilful delusions of grandeur and failure to see the writing on the wall ill-concealed: Britain should 'endeavour to accommodate her future views and designs to the *real mediocrity of her circumstances*' (*WN*, V.iii.92: 94; emphasis added) and part on friendly terms for the sake of peace, prosperity and security (*WN*, IV.vii.c.66: 617).

In terms of the long term, bigger picture, what Smith desired was freedom of trade throughout the globe; a naturally unfolding global economic regime based on mutual enablement rather than conquest and exploitation. Since even his ideal of 'restoring' the system of natural liberty had to occur slowly and by degrees, it is quite possible that he saw the States-General plan as a step or stage towards eventual and complete emancipation of America and, eventually, of all colonies everywhere. For Smith, withholding independence from America was costly, disruptive and had no discernible benefits. In resolving the American crisis it seems that American Independence (Option 2) is preferred by Smith to all other solutions given, not only from what he says on the matter, but in light of the strength and persistence of his broader commitments to liberty, economic cosmopolitanism, anti-colonialism, anti-utopianism and minimal government. This reading finds support in the fact that Options 1a, 2 and 3 all either amount to or are long-term pathways to complete emancipation. Since the only remaining option (Option 4) was a disastrous war that led to the retention of only a small part of America, Smith did his best to ensure that most roads led, one way or another, to his ultimate goal of free global trade.

The Imperial Parliament was his second-best plan: it would not offer perfect free trade but trade would at least be 'free-er' under this arrangement than was presently allowed. The idea had justice on its side but it also had a number of practical benefits, including the power to tax and an end to the war, both of which would go far to relieve the public debt crisis 'at home'. In attending to the intricacies of how Smith worked through this problem, we are able to appreciate his skill as a public opinion-maker and handler of political leaders. He was no ideologue or radical, but rather a strategic and pragmatic solver of extremely complicated political problems.

Conclusion

Smith's cosmopolitanism is obscured by the fact that it is only distantly related to classical or moral cosmopolitanism. It is hardly surprising that someone as practical as Smith should reject both moral and political cosmopolitanism in favour of the most pragmatic variant of liberal internationalism: economic cosmopolitanism. The fact that he rejected the Stoic doctrine of social *oikeiosis* and seriously doubted that universal benevolence had any role to play in the future of global relations did not, however, rule out the idea of a world community of like-minded, amiably disposed, commercial strangers; nor did it prevent him from evincing temperate concern for the welfare of other 'countries'. The best vehicle for the distribution of material enrichment as well as the realisation of such cosmopolitan values as pacifism, anti-imperialism, universalism and egalitarianism is the voluntaristic community of free trade. Such a community precludes conflict and territorial rivalry between nations who have much more to gain from amicable relations. Smith thus advocates an end to aggressive imperialism, needless war and the monopoly of colonial trade and promotes instead freedom of international trade and pacific 'global' relations.

The self-regarding, innate and insatiable drives for specialisation and exchange will spur the progressive enlargement of markets and therefore the widening circles of instrumental friendship upon which commercial cosmopolitanism rests, while economic 'interest' will displace suspicion and aggressive nationalism as the energising forces of interstate relations. Patriotism will not disappear, but it *will* be domesticated by habituation to dealing with foreigners and the benign effects of trade and development, while empire will be superseded by a self-equilibrating system of mutual enabling, non-interfering and favourably disposed trading partners. Fierce particularistic sentiments and intense alliances between security allies will become increasingly less important than the steadily proliferating forms of amicable *strangership* characteristic of commercial cosmopolitanism.

As with his domestic policy advice, Smith's approach to many international controversies is driven by his social science, his pragmatism and his deep-seated concern for ordinary people. His aversion to war stems largely from its disastrous effects on civilian populations, the tax-paying public and the lower orders of the military while his dislike of Mercantilism is largely related to its effect on economic and food security for everyone, but especially the poor.

Notes

1. The time of globalisation's birth has been contested. Flynn and Giraldez 'propose that globalisation began when the Old World became directly connected with the Americas in 1571 via Manila' (2004). Smith also dates the beginnings of globalisation from the discoveries of America and 'a passage to the East Indies, by the Cape of Good Hope' (*WN*, II.V.i.32–3: 448–49).
2. Smith does note, however, that imperial conquest can hasten development and stimulate population growth among the indigenous population (*WN*, IV.vii.b: 568–69). David Williams has argued, however, that 'Smith's opposition to colonial rule derived largely from its impact on the metropole, rather than on its impact on the conquered and colonised' (Williams 2014: 285).
3. For an excellent and detailed discussion of arguments made in this vein prior to Smith see Hont (2005).

4. The same image of concentric circles, or 'gradations of duty', appears in Cicero (trans. 1990, 1.160: 165), and in a fragment attributed to the later period Stoic Hierocles (reproduced in Annas 1993: 267–68).
5. *Oikeiosis* roughly translates as 'belonging' and implies a natural orientation towards one's own good; *social oikeiosis* is the social process of 'making akin to'.
6. Notwithstanding the Imperial Parliament he proposed as a last-ditch measure to resolve the American conflict and whose membership was limited to the British Isles and America (see below).
7. In spite of all this rhetoric of 'justice' in international relations, as Pitts notes, Smith nowhere specifies 'what rights nations should be understood to have: whether rights not to be interfered with, or perhaps simply not to be robbed and destroyed' (Pitts 2005: 57).
8. Condorcet dreamed, meanwhile, of a kind of international court to preside impartially over 'the execution of laws of commerce, seizures of foreign vessels, violations of territory, the interpretation of treaties, successions, etc.' (Rothschild 2004: 12).
9. Smith gives as his example the 'horrible, and therefore intolerable, practice of infanticide' (*TMS*, V.ii.13–16: 209–11).
10. According to Ian Ross, the ideas expressed in the Memorandum 'are similar to those of the *WN*' (Ross 1975: 14–15). However, there are some differences and omissions, as I show below.
11. Morrison contests late readings of Smith's influence here by refuting the 'materialist' thesis that the latter's ideas were only 'embraced' retrospectively 'because they fit Britain's new circumstances, namely, the loss of the American colonies'. Morrison instead 'defends the 'ideographic' counterfactual that if Shelburne had not engaged Smith's ideas, the American Revolutionary War would have ended on vastly different terms (Morrison 2012: 401–402).
12. Skinner notes that, objectively, there had been considerable mutual benefit in the arrangement since 'the colonists [were] confined to the production of primary products and the British to manufactures, thus creating a system of complementary markets' (Skinner 1977: 75; see also Skinner 1996 and Stevens 1975: 212).
13. According to Andrew Skinner, the acts of trade and navigation that Smith saw as 'unjust violations of natural liberty, were not at the same time seen in this light by the colonists themselves' and 'neither the Declaration of Colonial Rights and Grievances not the Declaration of Independence (which included a comprehensive indictment of British Policy) contained any critical reference to them' (Skinner 1996: 127).
14. The document is dated February 1778 and 'was first published by G.H. Guttridge in the *American Historical Review*, 38, 1932–33' (Skinner 1976: 68).

15. See Fergusson (1934) for Dempster's letters to Sir Adam Fergusson of 26 January 1775 and 4 February 1778.
16. However, by 1778 Pownell is reported to have told the House of Commons: 'Until you shall be convinced that you are no longer sovereigns over America, but that the United States are an independent sovereign people … it is of no consequence at all, what schemes or plans of conciliation this side the House or that may adopt' (see Stephens in *Corr.* App.B: 379–80).
17. He still evinced some sympathy for the idea as late as 1775 but soon after determined that only complete emancipation could be accepted (see Crane 1950: 72, n.28). Franklin was consulted by Smith on numerous occasions during the preparation of *Wealth of Nations* (Benians 1925: 252).
18. Others agreed that under a Union, America would eventually be dominant, among them, Thomas Pownell, as well as Benjamin Franklin, the latter of whom wrote to Lord Kames: 'Scotland and Ireland are differently circumstanced. Confined by the sea, they can scarcely increase in numbers, wealth and strength, so as to overbalance England. But America, an immense territory, favoured by Nature with all advantages of climate, soil, great navigable rivers, and lakes, etc. must become a great country, populous and mighty; and will, in less time than is generally conceived, be able to shake off any shackles that may be imposed on her, and perhaps place them on the imposers' (cited in Ross 1972: 340–41). John Adams thought the scheme practicable only if eventually 'Crown and legislature' 'migrate[d] to America' (Adams 1856: 119; Benians 1925: 263).
19. Smith's use of the term 'project' requires some explanation here. Going by his use of the term in comparable contexts, 'projectors' are mere speculators who get behind projects that they are ill-equipped to manage and conclude (e.g. *WN*, I.x.b.42:131; *WN*, II.ii.69: 310–12). Hence, when Smith refers to the Empire as a mere 'project' he means it pejoratively as a speculative scheme ill-executed and unrealised.

References

Adams, J. (1856). *The Works*, Vol. IV, C. F. Adams (Ed.). Boston: Little Brown and Company.

Annas, J. (1993). *The Morality of Happiness*. New York: Oxford University Press.

Baldry, H. C. (1965). *The Unity of Mankind in Greek Thought*. Cambridge: Cambridge University Press.

Benians, E. A. (1925). Adam Smith's Project of an Empire. *Cambridge Historical Journal, 1*(3), 249–283.

Berdell, J. (2002). *International Trade and Economic Growth in Open Economies*. Cheltenham: Edward Elgar.

Campbell, T. D., & Ross, I. S. (1981). The Utilitarianism of Adam Smith's Policy Advice. *Journal of the History of Ideas, 42*(1), 73–92.
Carr, E. H. (1946). *The Twenty Years' Crisis 1919–1939.* London: Palgrave.
Cicero. (1990). *On Friendship and the Dream of Scipio* (*Laelius de Amicitia* & *Somnium Scipionis*) (J. G. F. Powell, Trans. and Ed.). Warminster: Aris & Phillips.
Clarke, S. R. L. (1987). The City of the Wise. *Apeiron, 20*(1), 63–80.
Crane, V. W. (1950). *Benjamin Franklin's Letters to the Press.* Chapel Hill: University of North Carolina Press.
Edelstein, L. (1966). *The Meaning of Stoicism.* Cambridge, MA: Harvard University Press.
Erskine, A. (1990). *The Hellenistic Stoa.* London: Duckworth.
Fagerstrom, D. I. (1954). Scottish Opinion and the American Revolution. *The William and Mary Quarterly, 11*(2), 252–275.
Fay, C. R. (1930). Adam Smith and the Dynamic State. *The Economic Journal, 40*(157), 25–34.
Fergusson, J. (1934). *Letters of George Dempster to Sir Adam Fergusson, 1756–1813.* London: Macmillan & Co.
Fitzgibbons, A. (1995). *Adam Smith's System of Liberty, Wealth and Virtue.* Oxford: Clarendon Press.
Fleischacker, S. (2004). *On Adam Smith's Wealth of Nations: A philosophical Companion.* Princeton: Princeton University Press.
Flynn, D. O., & Giraldez, A. (2004). Path Dependence, Time Lags and the Birth of Globalisation: A Critique of O'Rourke and Williamson. *European Review of Economic History, 8*(1), 81–108.
Forman-Barzilai, F. (2006). Smith on 'Connexion', Culture and Judgment. In L. Montes & E. Schliesser (Eds.), *New Voices on Adam Smith.* Abingdon: Routledge.
Gilpin, R. (1971). The Politics of Transnational Economic Relations. *International Organisation, 25*(3), 398–419.
Griswold, C. (1999). *Adam Smith and the Virtues of Enlightenment.* Cambridge: Cambridge University Press.
Guttridge, G. H. (1933). Adam Smith and the American Revolution. *The American Historical Review, 38*(4), 714–720.
Hadas, M. (1943). From Nationalism to Cosmopolitanism in the Greco-Roman World. *Journal of the History of Ideas, 4*(1), 105–111.
Hewins, W. A. S. (1903, June 5). The fiscal policy of the Empire. *The Times.*
Hill, L. (2000). The Two Republicae of the Roman Stoics. *Citizenship Studies, 4*(1), 65–79.
Hill, L. (2004). Further Reflections on the 'Hidden Theology' of Adam Smith. *European Journal of the History of Economic Thought, 11*(4), 629–635.

Hont, I. (2005). Free Trade and the Economic Limits to National Politics: Neo-Machiavellian Political Economy Revisited. In I. Hont (Ed.), *Jealousy of Trade: International Competition and the Nation-State in Historical Perspective* (pp. 185–266). Cambridge, MA: Harvard University Press.
Hume, D. (1932). *Letters of David Hume*, J. Y. T. Greig (Ed.). Oxford: Oxford University Press.
Kittrell, E. R. (1965). The Development of the Theory of Colonization in English Classical Political Thought. *Southern Economic Journal, 31*(3), 189–206.
Knorr, K. E. (1944). *British Colonial Theories, 1570–1850.* Toronto: Toronto University Press.
Marcus Aurelius. (1964). *Meditations*, translated and with an Introduction by M. Staniforth. London: Penguin.
Minowitz, P. (1989). Invisible Hand, Invisible Death: Adam Smith on War and Socio-Economic Development. *Journal of Political and Military Sociology, 17*(Winter), 305–315.
Minowitz, P. (1993). *Profits, Priests, and Princes.* Cambridge: Cambridge University Press.
Montesquieu, C. L. (1989). *The Spirit of the Laws* (A. M. Cohler, Trans. and Ed.). Cambridge, B. C. Miller & H. M. Stone.
Morrison, J. A. (2012). Before Hegemony: Adam Smith, American Independence and the Origins of the First Era of Globalization. *International Organisation, 66*(3), 395–428.
Muthu, S. (2008). Adam Smith's Critique of International Trading Companies: Theorizing 'Globalization' in the Age of Enlightenment. *Political Theory, 36*(2), 105–139.
Nicholson, J. S. (1909). *A Project of Empire, a Critical Study of the Economics of Imperialism, With Special Reference to the Ideas of Adam Smith.* London: Macmillan.
Nussbaum, M. (1995). *Poetic Justice: The Literary Imagination and Public Life.* Boston: Beacon Press.
Oldenquist, A. (1982). Loyalties. *The Journal of Philosophy, 79*(4), 173–193.
Palen, M. W. (2014). Adam Smith as Advocate of Empire, c. 1870–1932. *The Historical Journal, 57*(1), 179–198.
Pitts, J. (2005). *A Turn to Empire.* Princeton: Princeton University Press.
Reinert, S. A. (2011). *Translating Empire: Emulation and the Origins of Political Economy.* Cambridge, MA: Harvard University Press.
Ross, I. S. (1972). *Lord Kames and the Scotland of His Day.* Oxford: Clarendon Press.
Ross, I. S. (1975). Political Themes in the Correspondence of Adam Smith. *The Scottish Tradition, 5*, 5–22.
Ross, I. S. (1995). *Life of Adam Smith.* Oxford: Oxford University Press.
Rothschild, E. (2001). *Economic Sentiments: Adam Smith, Condorcet and the Enlightenment.* Cambridge, MA: Harvard University Press.
Rothschild, E. (2004). Global Commerce and the Question of Sovereignty in the Eighteenth-Century Provinces. *Modern Intellectual History, 1*(1), 3–25.

Schuyler, R. L. (1921). The Climax of Anti-imperialism in England. *Political Science Quarterly, 36*(4), 537–560.

Schuyler, R. L. (1945). *The Fall of the Old Colonial System: A Study of British Free Trade, 1770–1870*. Oxford: Oxford University Press.

Shariff, I. (2003). Global Economic Integration: Prospects and Problems. *Economic Development Review, 1*(2), 1–25.

Skinner, A. (1976). Adam Smith and the American Economic Community: An Essay in Applied Economics. *Journal of the History of Ideas, 37*(1), 59–78.

Skinner, A. S. (1977). Adam Smith and the American Revolution. *Presidential Studies Quarterly, 7*(2/3), 75–87.

Skinner, A. S. (1996). Adam Smith: The Demise of the Colonial Relationship with America. *Cahiers d'Economie Politique, 27*(8), 113–130.

Smith, A. (1976 [1759]). *The Theory of Moral Sentiments*, D. D. Raphael & A. L. MacFie (Eds.). Oxford: Clarendon Press.

Smith, A. (1978). *Lectures on Jurisprudence (A and B)*, R. L. Meek, D. D. Raphael, & L. G. Stein (Eds.). Oxford: Oxford University Press.

Smith, A. (1979 [1776]). *An Inquiry into the Nature and Causes of the Wealth of Nations*, R. H. Campbell & A. S. Skinner (Eds.). Oxford: Clarendon Press.

Smith, A. (1987 [1778]). Smith's Thoughts on the State of the Contest with America, February 1778. In E. C. Campbell & I. S. Ross (Eds.), *The Correspondence of Adam Smith* (Appendix B). Oxford: Oxford University Press.

Stevens, D. (1975). Adam Smith and the colonial disturbances. In A. S. Skinner & T. Wilson (Eds.), *Essays on Adam Smith*. Oxford: Clarendon Press.

Teichgraeber, R. F. (1987). 'Less Abused than I had Reason to Expect': The Reception of the *Wealth of Nations* in Britain, 1776–90. *The Historical Journal, 30*(2), 337–366.

Wagner, D. O. (1932). British Economists and the Empire I. *Political Science Quarterly, 46*(2), 248–276.

Waltz, K. N. (2001 [1959]). *Man, the State and War*. New York: Columbia University Press.

Wight, M. (1991). *International Theory: The Three Traditions*. London: Leicester University Press.

Williams, D. (2014). Adam Smith and Colonialism. *Journal of International Political Theory, 10*(3), 283–301.

Wyatt-Walter, A. (1996). Adam Smith and the Liberal Tradition in International Relations. *Review of International Studies, 22*(1), 5–28.

Xenakis, I. (1969). *Epictetus: Philosopher-Therapist*. The Hague: Martinus Nijhoff.

CHAPTER 7

A Three-Stage Decision Tool for a Pragmatic Liberal

Introductory Comments

The aim of this chapter is to provide a guide as to how Smith worked through complex political and economic problems while balancing his various normative commitments. Smith's political method has been obscured by the fact that he sought to improve the art of governing in two distinct ways. On the one hand, he wanted it to be less ideological and therefore more social-scientific and, on the other, he hoped he could make it more productive of good effects. In other words, he was far less ideological and a lot more pragmatic and flexible than is generally thought. The fact that he evinced both progressivist and conservative tendencies has also caused confusion: while Smith was a progressivist, he also had a conservative streak borne, not of his allegiance to the Tory side, but of his social science. This, in turn, helps us to appreciate Smith's generally underestimated and sometimes dominating regard for social stability and order. Because he is ultimately a pragmatist, it sometimes seems as though his approach is rather ad hoc; however, he seems to have devised and used a discernible, if rather complicated, system whereby his position on any particular issue was arrived at by filtering the problem, policy or practice in question through three tests that I outline in this chapter. As a rather conservative (proto)-liberal this method allowed him to be experimental but in a cautious fashion.

Cases that exemplify this hierarchy are explored in the following sets of policy advice: Smith's attitude to improving the lives of the working poor;

L. Hill, *Adam Smith's Pragmatic Liberalism*,
https://doi.org/10.1007/978-3-030-19337-9_7

his advice about the British Empire; his stance on the abolition of slavery; his recommendations for compulsory public education and a range of other substantial market interventions (defence, justice, infrastructure and certain fiscal controls), all of which constitute exceptions to his 'system of natural liberty' and general policy of minimal state intervention. In unpacking this decision method, I also explore the hitherto undefined character and extent of rights in Smith's system, with a focus on their standing in relation to the system of natural liberty and Smith's understanding of liberty.

A Three-Stage Test

The main question that seems to have been uppermost in Smith's mind when writing about politics and governing was this: what values should leaders prioritise when making policy decisions? Or to be more precise, what values should leaders prioritise when forming each *particular* policy? Because he was wary about working from a priori commitments the answer to this question was never given or easy for Smith and the normative always had to withstand empirical challenges. In order to arrive at answers Smith tended to take each problem case by case. He applied three tests to each problem, the authoritativeness of which were apparently arranged in roughly ascending order. The first two of these were key elements of his theory of spontaneous order ('natural liberty' or 'invisible hand').

The first test is Smith's commitment to negative liberty, which he sees as both a condition and a motor of social and economic equilibration. Although it is Smith's first port of call (hence the popular conception that it is his primary and trumping commitment), liberty turns out to be the least compelling of his tests. Second is his judgement on whether the policy or behaviour accords with the gradualist dimension of his social-science commitments, specifically his theory of spontaneous order. The third and most authoritative test of all is whether the policy or behaviour has good outcomes and is conducive to 'positive liberty'. If it does, then Smith readily abandons his social-scientific commitments to liberty and gradualism, even if it has already passed the first two tests, which he generally expects it to; hence the third is really his test of last resort when all else fails.[1] Smith was more consequentialist than is normally allowed; further, and more controversially, where conflicts between 'positive' and 'negative' liberty occurred, he routinely favoured the former.

In bringing out the argument that he was a 'pragmatic' rather than doctrinaire or ideological 'proto-liberal', I explore where Smith's commitment to negative liberty begins and ends. So, this is really a story about the fate of liberty in its clashes with other Smithian values. Exploring the limits, scope and real character of liberty within Smith's system is also a useful way of drawing out Smith's *style* or approach to politics. I want to show that his ideological commitment to liberty is weaker than might be thought, highly contingent and easily unseated by his more strongly held conservative tendencies and even more powerful commitment to good social-systems outcomes; to order, utility, welfare and other practical considerations. Smith's model state is continually revising itself and its laws must be thought of as always under, or potentially under, construction. Laws that no long fulfil a social, political or economic need must revised or substituted for those that do (Samuels & Medema 2005: 225). In what appears to be a caution to himself about cleaving too tightly to the elegant *idea* of the system of natural liberty—and the policies and constitution it recommended—Smith insisted that 'constitutions of government' should only be honoured to the extent that 'they tend to promote the happiness of those who live under them' (*TMS*, IV.i.11: 185).

Because Smith is often inconsistent in his loyalty to liberty, his politics sometimes seems confused. But his approach makes more sense when we conceive him as a thinker who tries not to be doctrinaire, who takes everything case by case and who prefers to flexibly prioritise his commitments depending on the problem or issue at hand. The characterisation of Smith as a pragmatic—rather than doctrinaire—liberal is also related to the fact that he based his programme, not on abstract foundations (of which he was suspicious), but on principles derived from practical observation and experience. For example, in his discussion of the foundation of political obligation (canvassed in Chap. 2) he indicates that, unlike both Whigs and Tories, he is not interested in discovering the moral 'foundation' of obligation; instead, he wants to determine what factors have the 'effect' of bringing obligation about (*LJ[A]*, 120: 318). Dennis Rasmussen has made a similar observation in relation to Hume, Smith, Montesquieu and Voltaire generally, noting that they 'all adopted what today would be called an anti-foundationalist [or non-foundationalist] approach to politics':

> They rejected the leading foundationalist political theories of the seventeenth and early eighteenth centuries, social contract theory and the rationalist natural law tradition, and instead turned once again to empirical observation. These thinkers concluded that liberal practices and institutions are preferable not because they are in accord with Reason or Nature – as Locke, for example, had done – but because historical and comparative analysis revealed them to be relative improvements on the alternatives. That is why their political theories tended to blend empirical and normative concerns … [T]hey all concur that there are a number of important political ends or goods, that there is no simple or fool-proof means by which to rank them or adjudicate among them, and that liberal regimes generally provide a greater degree of a greater number of these goods than illiberal regimes. (Rasmussen 2013: 82; see also Hill 2009)

None of this means that Smith was politically neutral, even though he seems to have seen himself that way. In this chapter I also argue that Smith is no high theorist of 'liberalism' and that his account of rights and liberties is rather unresolved, from a theoretical point of view, because it is significantly constrained by practical and consequentialist considerations.

The following discussion shows how Smith's hierarchy of commitments plays out, that is to say, it explores the extent to which negative liberty (Level 1) is defended when it conflicts with Level 2 (gradualism) and when he is prepared to abandon both Levels 1 and 2 when desired consequences and pragmatism (Level 3) demand it. Smith admits that the system of natural liberty sometimes fails, making it necessary to violate some personal liberties for the sake of human flourishing. He defends liberal values only to the extent that they serve substantive ends and abandons them when the ends require it. Arguably, then, he frequently violates negative liberty for the sake of *positive* liberty. Showing how and why necessarily entails a close study of Smith's conservative tendencies.

I begin by laying out Smith's political and intellectual commitments, first, by discussing his attitude to liberty. Next, I sketch out his social-science commitments and identify cases where the protection or expansion of liberty as solutions to certain policy problems conflicts with his gradualist social science. I then examine cases that fail both the liberty and social-science tests; in these cases, Smith's main guide for policy is utility and pragmatism. How far did Smith's commitment to liberty go? What form did personal rights take and how secure were they within his system of natural liberty? To partially answer these questions, I identify cases where the expansion of liberty fails to ensure good public policy.

Rights and the System of Natural Liberty (Level 1)

We have seen that Smith is well-known as a defender of personal liberty, famously arguing that underlying the complex of conventional institutional constraints on human behaviour there was a system of natural and spontaneous economic—and indeed social—relations which, when given free rein, would function harmoniously. There exists a natural equilibrium with which both legislators and private individuals should, for the most part, avoid interfering; every individual is naturally the best judge of his or her own interest and should therefore be left unhindered to pursue it in their own way. In so doing, he or she will achieve not only their own best advantage, but that of society as well (*WN*, IV.ix.51: 687). In such an order, only a restrained government is appropriate (see Chap. 3).

Corresponding to this natural order (and contrary to the perception of many that he avoided the language of rights), Smith refers to the 'natural rights' of individuals to act in a way that is consistent with their self-regarding inclinations. People have a 'natural right' to 'free commerce' (including 'the right to freedom in marriage') (*LJ[A]*, 13: 8) and to enjoy their 'liberty free from infringement' (*LJ[B]*, 11: 401). He also tells us that '[t]he property which every man has in his own labour' is 'the original foundation of all other property' and therefore 'the most sacred and inviolable' (*WN*, I.x.c.12: 138). For Smith, '[j]ustice is violated whenever one is deprived of what he had a right to and could justly demand from others, or rather, when we do him any injury or hurt without a cause' (*LJ[A]*, i.9: 7). A person may be 'injured in his person' by either direct injury to his body or else by some restraint on 'his liberty' and he has a general 'right' to 'do what he has a mind when it does not prove detrimentall to any other person' (*LJ[A]*, i.13: 138). Smith also tells us that 'a man who by forcible confinement or other violence done to his liberty, or any threatenings' is compelled by another to do something he is injured in 'his liberty'; therefore, 'all such contracts or obligations which are forced from' him under 'duresse … are void' (*LJ[A]*, ii.131: 120).

All these rights, save for property rights, are, Smith says, natural. It is self-evident—according to the judgements of the 'impartial spectator' (*TMS*, II.ii.2.3: 84–85; *TMS*, II.ii.3.4: 86)—that we have a right to life, limb and reputation, but property rights 'require some more explanation' due to the fact that '[p]roperty and civil government very much depend on one another. The preservation of property and the inequality of possession first formed it, and the state of property must always vary with the form of government' (*LJ[B]*, 11: 401). (At this point the discussion becomes confusing given that Smith has already asserted that property in labour is a natural, 'sacred and inviolable' right.)

In any case, in a system of 'just liberty', agents should not be impeded in the use of '[t]he property which every man has in his own labour' (*WN*, I.x.c.12: 138). Labour for Smith is the primary source of value (*WN*, I.vi.9: 67–68) and since humans are naturally inclined to specialise their economic effort, it is their 'natural' right to exchange with others and not to be interfered with in that exchange (*WN*, I.x.c.12: 138). Smith's system of spontaneous order—the system of natural liberty—therefore depends upon agents' enjoyment of a high degree of freedom and mobility. As people work subrationally to secure social order, their capacity to do so depends upon their access to a minimum level of negative liberty, or, as Frederick von Hayek was later to put it, a large 'protected domain'. The 'ill-contrived law of settlements', for example, which restricts the free movement of labour, is an 'evident violation of natural liberty and justice' (*WN*, I.X.c.59: 157; see also *WN*, II.ii.94: 324 and *WN*, IV.ix.51: 687).

It should be noted here that the relationship between the natural laws governing human life and the rights that correspond to them is not explicitly laid out by Smith. But he seems to take it as given that rights—and our entitlement to them—are a function of natural laws, by which he means innate human tendencies. Smith does not defend our rights to certain liberties as ends in themselves but because such rights are consistent with people's natural drives and tendencies which, he believes, generally tend to good or adaptive effects.

This melding of rights and utility is not so implausible or incoherent as might be thought; after all, Russell Hardin has argued that liberal rights talk is based on a generally unadmitted utilitarian logic, namely, that rights are ultimately justified by their good effects. On this account rights can be thought of as 'institutional devices for achieving good outcomes' (Hardin 1986: 47). Smith evidently thought along the same lines with the effect that he allows the suspension of rights should honouring them lead to worse outcomes (see below).

Smith regrets that 'the natural effort of every individual to better his own condition' is frustrated by hundreds of 'impertinent obstructions with which the folly of human laws too often incumbers [sic] its operations' the effect of which is 'always more or less either to encroach upon its freedom, or to diminish its security' (*WN*, IV.v.b.43: 540; see also *WN*, IV.ix.28: 674). Any interference with the self-interested activities of agents is a result of either a presumptuous claim to knowing the individual's good better than he or she knows their own, a hubristic defiance of the equilibrating laws of nature or else a conspiracy by interested parties against the public.

Liberty (Level 1) Versus Gradualism (Level 2) in Smith's Social Science

Liberty clearly plays a (if not *the*) central role in Smith's theory of spontaneous order; further, his theory (like all such models) is basically progressivist. And yet 'gradualism' is also one of the five essential features of spontaneous order theories: the others are their undirected character, inevitability, progressivism and universality (Lehmann 1974: 176). Smith's theory was typical in exhibiting all these elements and all of them have been established in preceding chapters except for his gradualism. His ideal of liberty was always tempered with considerations of what 'the people can bear', what the people will accept and what, in fact, works best. As he admits, 'nothing is more difficult than perfectly to secure liberty' (*LJ[B]*, 191: 480). So, while on one level he has a typically Whiggish commitment to liberty, personal enterprise and economic freedom, any defence of these values needs to sit well with other values in his social science.

Despite his progressivism and constant urging of reform, as a spontaneous order theorist, Smith could only ever advocate cautious change.[2] The wise legislator respects the subtle interplay of social and historical forces that have brought existing arrangements into being insensibly and by degrees. 'He' will 'accommodate, as well as he can, his public arrangements to the confirmed habits and prejudices of the people; and will remedy as well as he can, the inconveniencies which may flow from the want of those regulations which the people are averse to submit to'. And 'when he cannot establish the best system of laws, he will endeavour to establish' laws that the 'interests, prejudices, and temper of the times would admit of' (*TMS*, VI.ii.2.16: 233). In other words, rulers will be patient, circumspect and judicious in their reform of maladaptive policies and practices in order to avoid the still greater evil of social upheaval.

Smith's goal was to advise leaders on when action was needed and when history and the mechanisms of the system of natural liberty should be permitted to spontaneously equilibrate the social and economic system. The wise legislator understands where the limits of state action begin and end; he or she will appreciate the importance of proceeding 'by trial and error' and strive to 'retain what experience shows to be valuable' (West 1976: 523). It is not only intelligence but 'real patriot[ism]'—by which Smith means a genuine love of the public welfare—that is called forth when such a leader is compelled to determine whether the 'authority of the old system' ought to be 'support[ed]' and 're-establish[ed]' or to 'give way to the more daring, but often dangerous spirit of innovation' (*TMS*, VI.ii.2.12: 231–32). Dugald Stewart rightly noted that Smith sought to improve society 'not by delineating plans of new constitutions, but by enlightening the policy of actual legislators.' Such plans, Stewart observed, had 'no tendency to unhinge established institutions, or to inflame the passions of the multitude'. Smith's proposed 'improvements' were to be 'effected by means too gradual and slow in their operation, to warm the imaginations of any but of the speculative few' (Stewart 1980: 309; 311).

Smith's attempt to balance his proto-liberal progressivism with his cautious, order-seeking streak is indicated in his policy on social classes and recommended improvements to the lives of the working poor. It is also reflected in his approach to the dismantling of the British Empire. Here, the tensions are shown to be a function of his determination to solve practical political problems associated with the scope of liberty and their compatibility with his other social-scientific commitments as well as the brute facts of life.

Case 1: Social Stratification and the Working Poor

Smith conceived modernity as the age of independence and improved mobility for individual agents. In general, he disliked traditional institutions and any social and political structures that had a tendency to immobilise agents and prevent them from unleashing their full mental, social and productive powers. The institutions of which he was most critical were monolithic, interfering governments, the established church, the extended family, the feudal estate, moribund laws and cultural traditions and unreflective prejudice, all of which immobilised people in various psychic and physical ways. Smith welcomed the fact that the stifling power of these institutions and practices was waning in the commercial stage. His new, modular archetype is not trapped in tradition, caste or ritual and has developed better and more sophisticated patterns of social *distance* and habits of independence. One of the reasons Smith has such faith in the expanding commercial classes (the 'middling ranks') is that they are busy 'spirited …

folk' who 'can't brook oppression' (*LJ[B]*, v.124: 320). In Smith's mind, they were always in forward motion, his preferred state.

Personal mobility was an extremely important concern for Smith and is central to his conception of individual liberty. Indeed, he seems to conceive the history of Western liberalism as, in large part, a history of dissolving impediments to personal mobility. Everyone should enjoy as much freedom in their bodies, minds and properties as is possible (*LJ[A]*, i.12–13: 8; *LJ[B]*, 11: 401). Furthermore, to 'hurt in any degree the interest of any one order of citizens for no other purpose but to promote that of some other' is a violation of the equality principle that should apply to all people and classes of people' (*WN*, IV.viii.30: 654).

It is not surprising, then, that Smith advocated reforms to improve the lives of the working poor, many of whom laboured under conditions of exploitation that often amounted to serfdom. During Smith's time, the low wages of the poor was not a function of market forces but of deliberate policy based on what Smith considered to be the deeply flawed premises of the 'utility-of-poverty' doctrine. The general idea was to pay wages so low that misery and desperation would incentivise labourers to work harder; doing so would also prevent them from consuming any luxury goods that might lead to their corruption and dissipation. As was shown in Chap. 3, Smith saw the deliberate suppression of wages as an egregious affront to natural liberty (*WN*, I.viii.15: 85) and he campaigned for higher wages for workers.

And yet, despite Smith's concern for the poor and his demand for a fairer wage system, he was not a progressive equalitarian in the standard liberal mould. He seems at first sight to be all for reform of the class system, but his position actually evinces an odd combination of conservative and libertarian values. Specifically, although Smith welcomed the demise of feudalism, the breakdown of the extended family and an expanding middle class (all of which enhanced social, economic and personal mobility), he did not want to eradicate the system of rank distinctions altogether. To begin with, increasing social stratification and wealth 'inequality' is a natural effect of highly desirable material progress, for 'wherever there is great property, there is great inequality' (*WN*, V.i.b.2: 709).

Further, in increasingly impersonal commercial societies, classes served as both a significant source of stability and a vital engine of productive effort. Class inequalities—especially in mass societies—were natural, inevitable and socially adaptive, an indispensable part of the architecture of a self-equilibrating society. The class hierarchy is generated and maintained by the 'natural' and instinctive deference of the poor towards the rich and this is highly desirable because in mass societies 'peace and order' depends on the maintenance of a well-structured system of rank distinctions (*TMS*, VI.ii.1.21: 226; *TMS*, I.iii.3.1: 61).

Although Smith denied that social inequalities were rooted in natural differences, he did believe that they were rooted in human faculty psychology, specifically, in an original human need for social recognition and dominance. The flip side of this need is a tendency to recognise and submit to the dominance of others. We have a natural 'obsequiousness' to our 'superiors' so strong that neither 'fear', 'hatred' nor class resentment can overcome it (*TMS*, I.iii.2.3: 52–53). This disposition performs a valuable and spontaneous law and order function in Smith's civil society because classes play a significant role in regulating behaviour.

Rank distinctions are a natural function of wealth and power and 'Nature has wisely judged that the distinction of ranks', and the order it brings with it, rests 'more securely upon the plain and palpable difference of birth and fortune, than upon the invisible and often uncertain difference of wisdom and virtue'. Notably, Smith concedes that this seems like a rather unfair arrangement, but since 'the *peace and order of society is of more importance than even the relief of the miserable*' it is all for the best. In fact, it is a clear sign of nature's 'benevolent wisdom' (*TMS*, VI.ii.1.21: 226; emphasis added).

Apart from their role in enhancing stability and order, rank distinctions are structurally indispensable because they incentivise labour (*TMS*, IV.i.9–10: 183–84). The wealthy enjoy an esteem to which all aspire while their ostentatious consumption spurs the lower ranks to engage in 'unrelenting industry' so as to acquire that sense of tranquillity and satisfaction in which they imagine the rich delight (*TMS*, IV.1.8: 182). We must tolerate class privilege, the conspicuous consumption of the rich and the exaggerated esteem in which they are held so that the poor can be incentivised to productive activity. Smith's critique of certain aspects of the class system was therefore far from radical; rather, the system of rank distinctions was a natural and integral part of civil society, a spontaneous product of natural human dispositions and therefore something to be preserved. It was one thing to demand higher wages so that workers did not starve and were incentivised to productive effort; quite another to undermine the very basis of an orderly society and to rebel against arrangements deeply embedded in human psychology.

Smith's attitude to the poor suggests that personal negative liberty was not necessarily the bottom line for Smith, who tended to be far more interested in the social-systems effects of any particular policy or behaviour and the way it related to his social science and faculty psychology. He reminded social reformers that sometimes 'the prosperity and preservation of the state' requires some 'diminution of the powers, privileges and immunities of [a] particular order' which, though seemingly 'unjust', is by no means 'useless' because 'it contributes in reality to the stability and permanency of the whole system' (*TMS*, VI.ii.2.10: 231). In other words, negative liberty might have to be compromised to secure something that looks like positive liberty. In Smith's mind, it was not a question of favouring one class at the expense of another but serving *all* classes in the long view. His treatment of this topic underlines that his politics was always subservient to either his practical goals or his social science, which, in any case, usually coincided. His ultimate goal in this case is an orderly, flourishing economy. This is partly achieved by rewarding workers, which requires reform in one area (wages) and conservatism in another (the class system).

While Smith certainly sympathises with the poor, radical reforms are strongly cautioned against. When well-meaning legislators are gripped at the same time by a 'spirit of system' and 'real fellow feeling and love of humanity' this inspires them to act hastily and radically in order to relieve the unfortunate of their 'inconveniences and distresses'. But their efforts generally 'obtai[n] nothing' but disruption whereas 'palliatives' and 'reasonable accommodations' would have had better and more long-lasting effects (*TMS*, VI.ii.2.15: 232–33).

Case 2: Dismantling Empire

Smith's recommendation for how best to approach decolonisation is another example of his desire to balance the gradualist dimensions of his spontaneous order theory with his progressivism and commitment to liberty. On the one hand, he was extremely desirous of reform of the 'invidious and malignant' colonial system of empire because he saw it as synonymous with Mercantilism. It represented a major corruption of the system of natural liberty and allowed certain nations to monopolise the markets of their colonies (*WN*, IV.vii.c.18: 595), thereby threatening food security and exacerbating interstate conflict. This, in turn, led to intolerable levels of public debt, high taxes and patronage and political corruption problems, as was shown in Chap. 6.

Yet, on the other hand, Smith cautioned against radical reform of this maladaptive system. Aware that his long-term goal of relaxing markets and establishing the system of 'perfect liberty' throughout the globe was a potentially destructive project he advised that it be executed with 'reserve and circumspection' (*WN*, IV.ii.40: 468–69). Were 'duties and prohibitions taken away all at once' home markets would be abruptly saturated with 'cheaper foreign goods' that would deprive 'many thousands of our people of their ordinary employment and means of subsistence' (*WN*, IV.ii.40: 469). It would also occasion 'great permanent loss' to investors. The market should be opened 'only by slow gradations', and a 'moderate and gradual relaxation' of the relevant laws (*WN*, IV.vii.c.44: 606). Changes should 'never be introduced suddenly, but slowly' and after a lot of 'warning' (*WN* IV.ii.44: 471). Smith's attitude here is consistent with the gradualist aspect of his theory of spontaneous order, the latter of which, as I have noted, combines *both* progressivist and conservative elements.

Respecting this aspect of his spontaneous order theory—even where it violated personal liberty—would, Smith believed, deliver benefits to everyone in the long run. Again, he does not, as might be expected, privilege liberal concerns with formal equality, freedom and merit over the conservative need for order or a utilitarian urge for material prosperity. Rather, he attempts to balance them within his social science, which is, he thinks, a much better way to secure welfare than by slavish adherence to abstract principles. Further, he is a thinker who looks at problems not only from a social-systems view but from the *long view* as well.

The Limits of Liberty: Violations of Natural Liberty on Pragmatic Grounds

For Smith, the third—and arguably most authoritative—test of any policy or practice is consequentialist. Despite his insistence that interference with the system of natural liberty is often a form of corruption and invariably a violation of natural rights and laws that would otherwise deliver prosperity, peace and progress, he is prepared to recommend such violations when utility required it. Personal rights become defeasible and natural laws violable when the exigencies of governing, security and public order demand it. I now examine a not insignificant set of cases where Smith felt this was justified.

Defence, Justice, Infrastructure

It makes sense to begin with Smith's three better-known exceptions to his insistence on government restraint in the market. As mentioned in Chap. 3, due to market failure resulting in a number of collective action problems, Smith allows 'three proper duties of government'. These are, first, to protect society from the invasion of other societies. Apart from the provision of standing armies, to this end, he also recommended the imposition of bounties upon the exportation of British sail-cloth and gun-powder (*WN*, IV.v.a.36: 522–23) and approved of the controversial Navigation Acts that controlled trade yet served defence interests (*WN*, VI.ii.30: 464–65). The second duty is to establish and administer a system of police and justice; and, third, to provide certain public works, such as roads, bridges, harbours, which, though essential for the proper functioning of a 'great society' can 'never be for the interest of any individual, or small number of individuals to erect and maintain' (*WN*, IV.ix.51: 687–88). Beyond these, the system of 'natural liberty' should be left to operate (*WN*, IV.ix.51: 687). All these recommendations are designed to either directly or indirectly facilitate commerce and enhance the mobility of economic agents. Smith never explains why the system of natural liberty leaves such large and inconvenient gaps in what he posits as an otherwise self-ordering human universe; he seems only to be interested in filling these gaps.

As was shown in more detail in Chap. 3, Smith argues that the problem of military defence poses a collective action problem that can only ever be resolved by the rationalistic intervention and 'wisdom of the state'. The natural process of specialisation brings the 'art of war' to a tolerable degree of sophistication where the 'mechanical aspects are concerned because so much of military technology is "necessarily connected" to other technological refinements that accompany the "progress of improvement"'. But the process hits a brick wall due to the natural self-interest of market actors for whom there is no economic incentive to specialise as soldiers without some concerted encouragement from the state: therefore, it falls to the state to establish and maintain professional standing armies (*WN*, V.i.a: 697).

It could be argued that these interventions in the system of natural liberty are less a betrayal of liberty than a realist's indirect defence of it. After all, Smith repeatedly acknowledged that without security, justice and police, liberty could not be enjoyed and the pursuit of national wealth would be pointless, even impossible. As Smith himself concedes in classic Realist tones, the restrictive Act of Navigation is neither 'favourable to foreign commerce [nor] to the growth of that opulence which can arise from it'. However, it is justified as 'perhaps, the wisest of all the commercial regulations of England' because 'defence … is of much more importance than opulence' (*WN*, VI.ii.30: 464–65). Only when '[t]he natural effort of every individual to better his own condition' is unleashed under conditions of 'freedom and security' will the society be prosperous and happy.

Similarly, an organised system of justice supported by regular armies is the only reliable means to secure rule of law and afford 'to industry' the 'encouragement which it requires', namely, 'some tolerable security that it shall enjoy the fruits of its own labour' (*WN*, I.xi.i: 256; *WN*, V.i.a.39–40: 705–706). Without the elements of a basic infrastructure, economic freedom and the right to personal mobility are significantly impeded. Therefore, Smith is prepared to sacrifice some negative liberties in order to secure other negative liberties as well as many positive liberties. The case of education is a good example of the latter.

Education

Beyond these exceptions to the system of natural liberty there is the less well-known example of Smith's advocacy of a publicly funded *compulsory* education system to offset the problems generated by economic development. Paradoxically, although the commercial age is a period of unprecedented development, it is also the age of declining literacy.[3] For Smith, task specialisation was a major cause of this problem. The division of labour 'affords an opportunity of employing children very young' which means they miss out on schooling and the civilising supervision of their own parents. In Scotland, for example, 'where the division of labour is not far advanced, even the meanest porter can read and write', whereas in England's 'commercial parts' such is not the case.

Smith posits the 'general' rule that 'in town they are not so intelligent as in the country, nor in a rich country as in a poor one'. Among England's 'lower' metropolitan orders, the education of children is 'greatly neglected'. This exposes them to no ideas of 'amusement … but riot and debauchery' (*LJ[B]*, 329–30: 539–40). The new independence of working children undermines the traditional 'authority' of fathers with the effect that the young, when at leisure, fall into bad habits of 'drunkenness and riot'. Further, the 'spirit' of commercialism—as well as its characteristic mode of production (specialisation)—'sinks the courage of mankind and tends to extinguish martial spirit', causing them to become 'effeminate and dastardly' (*LJ[B]*, 1766, 331: 540). Despite the fact that Smith regarded commercialisation as natural, inevitable and generally positive he was acutely aware of 'the disadvantages of a commercial spirit.' As he summarised them: '[t]he minds of men are contracted and rendered incapable of elevation, education is despised or at least neglected, and heroic spirit is almost utterly extinguished' (*LJ[B]*, 333: 541).

Smith also expresses his concern that the children of the poor miss out on a basic education because they are put to work too early (*WN*, V.i.f.53: 784–85). This is bad, because as Smith explains elsewhere, it is preferable that 'children are dependent on their parents' for as long as possible. It is during this period of early dependence that children learn the moral sentiments; to curb their own passions, to develop sociability and civility and 'to become usefull members of society' which is 'a chief and most essentiall part of education', the lack of which prevents 'the instilling of any others' (*LJ[A]*, iii.5:142; *LJ[B]*, 102: 438). Further, the trades that poor children engage in are 'generally so simple and uniform as to give little exercise to the understanding' and 'their labour is both so constant and so severe' that they have neither time nor 'inclination' to study (*WN*, V.i.f.53: 784–85). Smith makes clear that his scheme is strictly compulsory by stipulating that, in order to ensure public compliance everyone should be required to pass an 'examination' on the school curriculum before she or he is allowed to 'to obtain the freedom in any corporation, or be allowed to set up any trade either in a village or town corporate' (*WN*, V.i.f.57: 786).

So, for the sake of all-important public order, the well-being and moral development of children as well what we might now call 'positive liberty', Smith advocated the establishment of a compulsory and publicly funded[4] school system (*WN*, V.i.i.5–6: 815; *WN*, V.i.f.57: 786). He suggests that at a 'very small expense the public can facilitate … encourage, and … even impose upon almost the whole body of the people, the necessity of acquiring those most essential [i.e. vocational] parts of education', namely, reading, writing and accounting (*WN*, V.i.f.54: 785).[5]

The 'state derives no inconsiderable advantage' from the 'instruction' of the working poor (the rich were expected to fund their own education) due to its projected positive effect on political and social civility and its amelioration of the loss of 'martial spirit' occasioned by commercial development and the specialisation of labour. In fact, Smith suggests that even if the public were to derive no such advantage his suggestion would still be worth acting upon simply to 'preven[t]so great a publick evil' (*WN*, V.i.f.61: 787–88). Presumably Smith means that it would be worth doing for the sake of human flourishing and general happiness.

In any case, Smith insists that the state *does* gain a '[c]onsiderable advantage' from educating the poor. First, they are less likely to be subject 'to the delusions of enthusiasm and superstition, which among ignorant nations frequently occasion the most dreadful disorders'. Second, 'an instructed and intelligent people ... are always more decent and orderly than and ignorant and stupid one'. This is partly because they are 'more likely to obtain the respect of their lawful superiors' and, in turn, more likely 'to respect those superiors', something that was especially important in mass commercial societies. Finally, compulsory schooling will act as a safeguard of political stability because an educated populace is more politically sophisticated and quiescent:

> They are most disposed to examine, and more capable of seeing through, the interested complaints of faction and sedition, and they are, upon that account, less apt to be misled into any wanton or unnecessary opposition to the measures of government. In free countries, where the safety of government depends very much upon the favourable judgement which the people may form of its conduct, it must surely be of the highest importance that they should not be disposed to judge rashly or capriciously concerning it. (*WN*, V.i.f.61: 788)

Edward Cohen has plausibly suggested that Smith takes this issue so seriously because the impartial spectator mechanism and the ability of the poor to 'sympathize' is significantly impaired by commercial progress. This would have dire effects on order and progress: the poor would 'no longer sympathize with and attempt to emulate the rich' (a major impetus for productive effort) and 'respect for the magistrate and legal system would be damaged', as would 'the mechanism upon which the basic respect for justice depends'. As a result, 'the legislator would be almost helpless in his main task'. Without some remedy for public ignorance '[c]ommerce, usually a firm support for justice' becomes its 'deadliest enemy' (Cohen 1989: 68).

Significantly, there are three illiberal aspects to be noted about the education example: first, it is an admission that commercial progress is not always positive; second, that markets and negative liberty sometimes fail to get the job done; and, third, that there are collective action problems that can only be solved via a coordinating and coercive state. In other words, there are times when paternalism is warranted because liberty and the mechanisms of spontaneous order fail. There is a fourth point to be taken from this example and this is that human flourishing should be understood broadly, in which case there is room for a state to provide the conditions of positive as well as negative liberty.

Fiscal/Market Interventions

Other violations of the system of natural liberty in the name of economic and political expediency are suggested by Smith. Regulations governing the production and issuing of paper money is a good example, one that Smith readily admits is 'a manifest violation of the natural liberty of a few individuals'; and yet it is certainly justified because the free exercise of that liberty 'might endanger the security of the whole society'. All governments, whether 'despotical' or 'the most free' would be justified in doing so in the same way that they have a duty to oblige people to build 'party walls, in order to prevent the communication of fire' (*WN*, II.ii. 94: 324).

Similarly, in contradiction of his famously held view that the state should neither 'force nor … allure' the flow of trade beyond which it would 'naturally flow … of its own accord' (*WN*, II.v.31: 372), Smith identified two general 'cases in which it will generally be advantageous to lay some burden upon foreign, for the encouragement of domestick industry [i.e. protectionism]. The first is when some particular sort of industry is necessary for the defence of the country … The second … is when some tax is imposed at home upon the produce of the latter', in which case 'it seems reasonable that an equal tax should be imposed upon the like produce of the former' (*WN*, IV.ii.23–31: 463–65). Elsewhere he suggests that it might also be proper to impose a legal rate of interest intended to favour 'a more extensive access to credit particularly by such groups as small firms and sober investors which would otherwise be discriminated by the actions of speculative projectors'. Further, 'speculative projectors' might 'have to be legally restrained in order to reduce the occurrence of moral hazard and adverse selection' (Asso 2002: 27; *WN*, II.iv.15: 357). Finally, while admitting that 'few' monopolies are 'harmless', Smith defends the utility of allowing temporary monopolies in the case of inventions and new books 'as an encouragement to the labours of learned men' (*LJ[A]*, ii.30–3: 82–83; see also Winch 1983: 509).

Although Smith objected to the imperialist project as a systematic violation of the system of natural liberty (see Chap. 7) he made a number of what were, to his mind, judicious exceptions to his general position in cases where they enhanced the global mobility of labour and goods. First of all, some infant industries established in existing colonies could be justifiably granted monopoly privileges for an initial period so as to secure their success. The example he had in mind was the establishment of any experimental, 'dangerous and expensive' trade in 'some remote and barbarous nation', which he likened to 'temporary monopoly' laws that protected patent and copyright. Therefore, he countenanced a degree of 'commercial mercantilism' if the circumstances seemed to require it, going so far as to describe the above strategy as 'the easiest and most natural way' to compensate private citizens for hazardous ventures 'of which the publick is afterwards to reap the benefit' (*WN*, V.i.e.30: 754). He also suggested that Britain would be wise to retain its armed forts and settlements along the coast of West Africa in order to ensure the free flow of trade: he explained that there were '[s]ome particular branches of commerce' that were 'carried on with barbarous and uncivilised nations' that required 'extraordinary protection'. In order to defend the 'the goods of the merchants who trade to the western coast of Africa … from the barbarous natives, it is necessary that the place where they are deposited, should be, in some measure, fortified' (*WN*, V.i.e.1: 731).

In admitting that it is sometimes necessary for the state to 'violat[e]' natural liberty Smith signals that social systems do not always naturally self-equilibrate and that collective action problems are inevitable, especially in mass societies which are very complicated to govern (*WN*, II.ii.94: 324). He justifies all these measures by adverting to their good effects; their utility, their necessity and their tendency 'to facilitate commerce in general' (*WN*, V.i.e.1: 731). But he offers no plausible justification for them and does not seem to know why the economic system does not fully equilibrate in order to meet the necessary ends that these extraordinary measures are introduced to achieve. Neither does he seem particularly embarrassed about that. He just provides the remedy that seems appropriate to him.

Slavery

Smith's treatment and apparent complacency about the slave trade is a particularly telling example of the extent to which he was prepared to surrender liberal principle to the exigencies of political and economic life, a tendency one might expect to find in a spontaneous order theorist but not in a thinker often [mis]taken to be an archetypal and progressive liberal. We have seen in Chap. 3 with the cases of smuggling and dirty degrees that the laws of natural liberty are so respected by Smith that they should be allowed to trump positive law; yet in this example he indicates that there are times when it is permissible to violate the system of natural liberty for the sake of utility and in order to honour the gradualist dimension of his spontaneous order theory. This rather disappointing example underlines Smith's status as a highly pragmatic and cautious, rather than hardline liberal.

Thomas Clarkson in his *History of the Abolition of the Slave Trade* (1808) lauded Smith for denouncing slavery by holding up slave traders 'in a degrading light' and 'the injured Africans' in an 'honourable' one. He went on to congratulate the University of Glasgow for producing professors (Hutcheson and Millar are also mentioned) willing to offer 'public testimony against the continuance of the cruel trade' (Clarkson 1808: 1, 86–87). More recently Charles Griswold has suggested that 'Smith was well known as a critic of slavery and esteemed by abolitionists of his time' (Griswold 1999: 198). But if we read Smith's text carefully, his attitude to slavery is rather pragmatic and, at times, even complacent.[6]

Smith says that '[i]t is almost needless to prove that slavery is a bad institution' (*LJ[B]*, 138: 453) and concedes that almost every personal and natural right due to a person is violated by the institution of slavery; the slave has no right to 'the fruits' of his own labour; to property; to dignity; to freedom from arbitrary imprisonment and punishment and to marry whom he wishes, if at all. In fact, 'properly speaking' 'he' has no 'liberty at all' (*LJ[A]*, iii.90–99: 176–80). At the same time, Smith seems loath to admit how much of Britain's wealth was built on the institution of slavery, which is odd given his lifelong absorption with understanding and explaining how nations may gain and keep wealth.[7] Further, there is never any sustained or explicit condemnation of the institution on the grounds that it is a violation of those basic rights he enumerates. Nor does Smith at any point recommend abolition. He finds it far easier (and perhaps more interesting as a political economist) to argue that slavery is an extremely inefficient institution from an economic point of view and therefore not in the interests of slave owners. It is also possible that this appeal to utility was a strategic move on Smith's part.

In any case, he criticised the practice of slavery, not so much because it was inhumane (a fact that he readily acknowledged, though not, significantly, in the context of advocating abolition),[8] or a denial of a person's self-ownership—especially in the most 'sacred' form of property, namely labour—but because of its inefficient and maladaptive aspects. For a start, 'the experience of all ages and nations ... demonstrates that the work done by slaves ... is in the end the dearest of any' because it fails to harness the enormous productive power of self-interest. As he wrote:

> A person who can acquire no property, can have no other interest but to eat as much, and to labour as little as possible. Whatever work he does beyond what is sufficient to purchase his own maintenance, can be squeezed out of him by violence only and not by any interest of his own. (*WN*, III.ii.9: 387–88; *WN*, I.viii.41: 98–99)

Slavery is also an impediment to productivity and innovation (*WN*, IV.ix.47: 684; and *LJ[B]*, 299: 526) and an inhibitor of population growth (*LJ[A]*, iii.131–32: 192–93; *LJ[B]*, 138–40: 453–54; *LJ[B]*, 290: 523; *LJ[B]*, 299: 526). Nevertheless, slave owners would always resist abolition on the belief that slaves were the 'most valuable part of their substance'. Further, if such a policy were imposed, 'a generall insurrection would ensue' (*LJ[A]*, 116: 187). Due to these factors, and because of humankind's natural 'love of domination' over others, Smith resigns himself to the fact that slavery will never be abolished (*LJ[A]*, 114: 186). He surmises that wherever reform has already taken place, it could not have much affected the economic interests of the emancipators in question: 'The late resolution of the Quakers in Pennsylvania to set at liberty all their negro slaves, may satisfy us that their number cannot be very great. Had they made any considerable part of their property, such a resolution could never have been agreed to' (*WN*, III.ii.10: 388).

Therefore, despite the fact that slavery is the most egregious possible violation of liberties—and especially of self-ownership—Smith resists advocacy of reform and pays it scarce attention considering its key role in maintaining Britain's wealth. Or perhaps it is really *because* of its key role in maintaining Britain's wealth at the time that Smith avoided the subject. Smith was, after all, the author of the statement that 'the peace and order of society is of more importance than even the relief of the miserable' (*TMS*, VI.ii.1.21: 226) and here was an issue capable of causing great disruption.

Smith's reticence did not go unnoticed by at least one of his contemporaries. Arthur Lee, a Virginian who had taken his MD at Edinburgh in 1764, criticised Smith for failing to explicitly denounce the institution (Ross 1995: 171) and exert 'his [considerable] abilities in dissuading the Europeans from such a barbarous trade' (Lee 1764: 10, 46). Having decided that the cause of emancipation was a hopeless one, Smith probably thought it would be pointless to press for reform. Yet, his silence on the question of emancipation and the relationship of slavery to principles of natural justice and the system of natural liberty is at odds with his reputation as a champion of liberty and especially of economic liberty.

Smith's concern for slaves—as well as the poor—was evidently constrained by his desire for order and prosperity and by his prior spontaneous order commitments. Smith was likely intending to honour here (however misguidedly or unjustly) the gradualist dimension of his spontaneous order theory. As emphasised above, the wise legislator will, like 'Solon', act to 'accommodate, as well as he can, his public arrangements to the confirmed habits and prejudices of the people' and 'remedy as well as he can, the inconveniencies which may flow from the want of those regulations which the people are averse to submit to' (*TMS*, VI.ii.2.16: 233).

Legislators should seek also to 'respect the established powers and privileges' of individuals as well as 'the great societies, into which the state is divided'. Even if such powers and privileges are 'in some measure abusive' (which Smith obviously believed they could be), a ruler 'will have the wisdom to content himself with moderating, what he often cannot annihilate without great violence' (*TMS*, VI.ii.2.16: 233). After all, the 'principal security of every government arises always from the support of those whose dignity, authority and interest, depend upon its being supported' (*Memorandum*, in *Corr.*: 381). Accordingly, the dangerous and deep-seated 'prejudices of the people' should be treated, not with force, but with 'reason and persuasion'. Slavery seems to be another case where Smith took a pragmatic, social-systems view; where he could justify the 'unjust … diminution of the powers, privileges and immunities' of a particular 'order' for the sake of the 'the whole system' (*TMS*, VI.ii.2.10: 231).

An alternative and less benign interpretation is that perhaps what he is really siding here with is wealth, not only because of how much Britain depended on the work done by slaves (mainly in the Caribbean and North America) but also because he may well have anticipated the enormous costs of reparations to wealthy slave-owning Britons who would be forced to free their slaves.[9] His complacency here may also have been because he saw the slavery problem as a lost cause and Smith had a tendency to leave off pushing and proselytising in cases where he felt there was no chance of winning, as was shown in the case of American Independence (Chap. 6).

Conclusion

I have argued in this chapter that Smith's approach to the art of governing is shaped by three sets of commitments or tests, the strength of which seem to be ranked in ascending order and the first two of which are key to his social science (i.e. his theory of self-equilibration). At the least demanding level Smith is ideologically disposed to promote anything that expands liberty (Level 1) but he readily gives way when his gradualist tendencies and related desire for order and stability dictate otherwise (Level 2). Yet, without ever offering a justification, Smith believes that even liberty and social science sometimes have to give way to practical considerations about what, in the end, is simply feasible or tolerable (Level 3).

Smith is best described as a 'pragmatic proto-liberal'. The good life and how to achieve it for the greatest number of people seems to have been his primary preoccupation and ultimate commitment; broadly speaking, a more liberal society was the best way to achieve it. But Smith's liberal agenda is not unwavering because he is ends- not means-focused on economic prosperity, stability, public order, innovation and entrepreneurship, human happiness and food and military security. These are the issues around which his politics is made to fit, hence his inconsistent commitment to (negative) liberty. While at times his defence of liberty seems obstinate, even perverse, going so far as to defend illegal practices such as smuggling and the selling of university degrees in its name, there are other times when liberty is sacrificed to the demands of social science. There still are other times when liberty and social science can be violated for the sake of economic—and even human—flourishing. There seem to be no hard and fast rules in Smith for predicting when this should be done. But what he does make clear is that, although the system of natural liberty is basically reliable, it is not perfect and there would always be times when it failed and a constructivist remedy called for.

In sum, despite his persisting reputation as a stalwart defender of liberty, Smith could not properly be described in these terms; neither is he a high theorist of liberty, not only because he is sceptical about high political theory, but because he makes so many exceptions and qualifications to its practice. Liberty of the negative variety has limits to how much it can deliver and Smith does not seem very interested in explaining why this is the case. He defends liberty not as an end in itself, but for its effects; therefore, he abandons the principle when he believes it is failing to achieve desired outcomes. He is also disinclined to defend principles of liberty in cases where he thinks the cause is already lost. But he seems most disinclined to do so when, on balance, the enjoyment of liberty threatens stability and public order. This is seen most vividly in his urge for caution in rolling back the empire and apparent complacency about the slave trade and class inequality. Individual liberty was not the whole story for Smith. Rather, he tended to look to the big picture and the long view, to judge from the perspective of the welfare and stability of the society in general and in terms of what we might now label 'positive liberty'.

Notes

1. Note, however, that a lot of the time gradualism and utility turn out to coincide for Smith.
2. For a fuller discussion of the gradualism and conservatism of spontaneous order models in the Scottish Enlightenment see Hill (1998).
3. Smith's claim seems to have been historically accurate. By 1780 the national literacy rate in England 'was scarcely higher than it had been during the Elizabethan period'. Due to changed economic conditions 'the opportunity for children of the poor to learn to read was sharply curtailed' (Altick 1983: 30–31).
4. The salaries of masters should, however, be supplemented at a rate affordable to 'even a common labourer' in order to ensure that the master does not 'neglect his business' (*WN*, Vi.i.f.55: 785).
5. For a fuller discussion of Smith's views here see Alvey (2001).
6. Haakonssen (1981: 140) has also noticed this omission.
7. Slavery, upon which the sugar and cotton trades in the West Indies and North America thrived, was a key source of the wealth of the British Empire. From 1710 to 1810, approximately 3 million people were transported by British ships to a life of forced labour.
8. He notes that '[i]t is evident that the state of slavery must be very unhappy to the slave himself' (*LJ[A]*, iii.111–12: 185) and that 'domestic slavery' is 'the vilest of all states' (*TMS:* 282), and compiles an inventory of the ill treatment of slaves throughout history (*LJ[A]*, iii.90–99, 176–80; *LJ[B]*, 136: 452).
9. When slavery was legally abolished in the first part of the nineteenth century, the compensation paid to British slaver owners was estimated at 10 million pounds (Hall et al. 2014).

References

Altick, R. (1983). *The English Common Reader: A Social History of the Mass Reading Public 1800–1900*. Chicago: University of Chicago Press.

Alvey, J. E. (2001). Moral Education as a Means to Human Perfection and Social Order: Adam Smith's View of Education in Commercial Society. *History of the Human Sciences, 14*(2), 1–18.

Asso, F. (2002). The Home Bias Approach in the History of Economic Thought: Issues on Financial Globalisation from Adam Smith to John Maynard Keynes. In J. Lorentzen & M. De Cecco (Eds.), *Markets and Authorities: Global Finance and Human Choice* (pp. 20–40). Cheltenham: Edward Elgar.

Clarkson, T. (1808). *The History of the Rise, Progress and Accomplishment of the Abolition of the Slave Trade by the British Parliament in 2 Volumes*. London: Longman, Hurst, Rees and Orme.

Cohen, E. S. (1989). Justice and Political Economy in Commercial Society: Adam Smith's "Science of the Legislator". *The Journal of Politics, 51*(1), 50–72.

Griswold, C. (1999). *Adam Smith and the Virtues of Enlightenment*. Cambridge: Cambridge University Press.

Haakonssen, K. (1981). *The Science of the Legislator*. Cambridge: Cambridge University Press.

Hall, C., McClelland, K., & Lang, R. (2014). *Legacies of British Slave-Ownership: Colonial Slavery and the Formation of Victorian Britain*. Cambridge: Cambridge University Press.

Hardin, R. (1986). The Utilitarian Logic of Liberalism. *Ethics, 97*(3), 47–74.

Hill, L. (1998). The Invisible Hand of Adam Ferguson. *The European Legacy, 3*(6), 42–65.

Hill, L. (2009). Adam Smith's Pragmatic Liberalism. *Proceedings of the Santiago 2009 World Congress of Political Science*, IPSA Online, pp. 1–34, https://www.ipsa.org/system/files/node/conferenceproceeding/109858-adam-smiths-liberalism.pdf

Lee, A. (1764). *An Essay in Vindication of the Continental Colonies of America from a Censure of Mr. Adam Smith in his Theory of Moral Sentiments*. London: Printed for the Author.

Lehmann, W. C. (1974). Review of P. Salvucci's Adam Ferguson: Sociologica e Filosofia Politica. *History and Society, 13*(2), 163–181.

Rasmussen, D. C. (2013). *The Pragmatic Enlightenment: Recovering the Liberalism of Hume, Smith, Montesquieu, and Voltaire*. Cambridge: Cambridge University Press.

Ross, I. S. (1995). *Life of Adam Smith*. Oxford: Oxford University Press.

Samuels, W. J., & Medema, S. G. (2005). Freeing Smith from the "Free Market": On the Misperception of Adam Smith on the Economic Role of Government. *History of Political Economy, 37*(2), 219–226.

Smith, A. (1976 [1759]). *The Theory of Moral Sentiments*, D. D. Raphael & A. L. MacFie (Eds.). Oxford: Clarendon Press.
Smith, A. (1978). *Lectures on Jurisprudence (A and B)*, R. L. Meek, D. D. Raphael, & L. G. Stein (Eds.). Oxford: Oxford University Press.
Smith, A. (1979 [1776]). *An Inquiry into the Nature and Causes of the Wealth of Nations*, R. H. Campbell & A. S. Skinner (Eds.). Oxford: Clarendon Press.
Smith, A. (1987). *The Correspondence of Adam Smith*, E. C. Mossner & I. S. Ross (Eds.). Oxford: Oxford University Press.
Stewart, D. (1980 [1793]). Account of the Life and Writings of Adam Smith, LL.D, I.S. Ross (ed.). In W. P. D. Wightman & J. C. Bryce (Eds.), *Adam Smith: Essays on Philosophical Subjects*. Oxford: Oxford University Press.
West, E. G. (1976). Adam Smith's Economics of Politics. *History of Political Economy, 8*(4), 515–539.
Winch, D. (1983). Science and the Legislator. *The Economic Journal, 93*, 501–520.

CHAPTER 8

Conclusion

Adam Smith's reinvention of the 'science' of governing was an invitation to think about public management using new values and better methods. He also wanted to radically shift the focus from that of the best-off to that of the worst-off. Governing populations was not about the seemingly endless appetite of elites for power and glory, but about the people and their welfare. Further, when proposing to enhance the 'wealth of nations' legislators should forget about things like gold reserves, favourable balances of trade or the extent of territory. Instead, they should reconceive wealth in terms of human flourishing and as reflected in wage levels, food supply and affordability, mortality rates, population levels and general standards of living and well-being.

The picture, for Smith, was always a big, complex and global one because the political world could not be abstracted from the psychological, sociological, economic and historical context. Importantly, many, if not most, of the factors within these spheres are beyond our control. That, thinks Smith, is not necessarily a bad thing because humans do not always know what they are doing. The best they can do is to consult the laws of nature for guidance and to make limited decisions within its wise prescriptions.

Smith wanted to show how—and in what ways—the organised state and the positive laws it created related to the spontaneous civil society of self-regarding actors; getting that relationship right was key to making government and society work better. That project started with understanding the

L. Hill, *Adam Smith's Pragmatic Liberalism*,
https://doi.org/10.1007/978-3-030-19337-9_8

natural laws governing the human universe. Once this knowledge is attained we will know how to detect when the social, political and economic system should be left alone and when it should be adjusted. Although his advice usually tended towards relaxation, de-regularisation and the expansion of negative liberty, it could also entail a degree of state intervention to correct any market failures that obstructed liberty or else delivered unwanted outcomes. Often Smith is really advocating what we would today call 'positive liberty'.

Smith can be confusing and sometimes he seems to be sending mixed messages. This is because he is attempting to solve multiple problems within systems that are far more complex, subtle and problematic than most give them credit for. To complicate matters, he cherished a multitude of *desiderata* for the commercial world he lived in and wrote about. First, he hoped to see what I have called 'commercial strangership' diffuse throughout his own society—and the world in general—believing that his economic cosmopolitanism and the system of 'natural liberty' could resolve many of the issues he considered urgent. In the long term, he expected it to deliver a more prosperous, peaceful, secure, stable and happy world.

It should be recognised that market solutions were not, for Smith, a cure-all for everything; but they could ameliorate most of the things that were wrong with the way nations—and his nation in particular—were managed. Among other things, understanding the principles of natural liberty could help to reform a partial, wasteful and dysfunctional state that failed to rule equally in the interests of all the people. It could address the problems of food insecurity, low wages, high mortality rates and slow population growth. It could discourage government interference in realms within which it should not be meddling; it could repel corruption, Mercantilism, cronyism, relentless interstate conflict and high levels of public debt. If its precepts were only followed, there would be relief from suboptimal productivity levels, political faction-fighting and religious enthusiasm and interference. It could inspire the repeal of archaic laws controlling inheritance and workers' rights as well as those that obstructed competition, freedom of exchange, the free movement of labour and capital and equality of opportunity. It could also show that Britain's ungovernable and resource-draining empire should be given up.

In Smith's ideal world everyone enjoyed the highest possible levels of freedom, peace, security, prosperity, and, most of all, 'happiness'. All would live with dignity and Smith would never again have to see anyone begging or starving. Nor would there by anyone trapped in an unhealthy, restrictive, oppressive or unproductive dependency relationship. No one would be held in captive thrall to religious enthusiasm or sectarian rage and nor would they find themselves embroiled in destructive and unnecessary war.

For Smith, none of these gains had to come at anyone else's loss. Under conditions of freely circulating people, products and money, political and economic life was not a zero-sum game but rather, a scene of exponential and outwardly expanding mutual enablement. Everyone would have the means and freedom to pursue their interests in the way they saw fit, just as long as that freedom did not conflict with the freedom of others.

Of course, Smith was well aware that wanting all this was not the same as getting it; he lived in the real world of politics and understood that one had to be pragmatic, strategic, flexible and even wily. Sometimes the second-best option was the only option; sometimes the conservative approach was the more prudent one even if it meant a regrettable or unjust postponement of what needed changing. The human element was a perennial consideration and public opinion a major obstacle to much of what he sought to achieve. He worked tirelessly and patiently on managing and getting around both these things.

All of this—the complexity of the social world, the breadth of the problems that absorbed him and the irrationality of human beings—brought many tensions into Smith's thought. For example, he was a progressivist and yet an extremely cautious and conservative one. He welcomed the commercial world as natural and inevitable but took care to enumerate all its troublesome externalities. He urged government to let the system of natural liberty solve the problems of political and economic life and then pointed to all the cases where there was no chance of this happening. He disliked immobilising and deadening tradition yet feared sweeping change and defended the authority of kings and lords. He was a key (albeit eccentric) shaper of modern liberalism but also a tacit utilitarian. He cared most of all for 'the people' but was not a very enthusiastic democrat. He considered slavery to be the most egregious and unjust institution imaginable yet was silent on the question of abolition. He sympathised deeply with the poor and expected class mobility to occur on a regular basis; yet, he also supported the system of rank distinctions. He was enamoured of innovation, movement and bustle but of order and tranquillity even more so. He was intensely averse to monolithic government but suggested that a trans-Atlantic Imperial Parliament might solve the American problem.

That government should be properly constituted and more professional, more efficient and with better boundaries was as clear as day, but how quickly that should happen he could not say. He energetically championed liberty but abandoned it without looking backwards when it seemed unable to deliver results.

To manage his complicated outlook and the complexity and sheer breadth of the problems he sought to deal with, Smith took each issue case by case and applied a three-stage decision tool to arrive at decisions about the best way forward. The first of these tests was his commitment to negative liberty. Although this was his first port of call and seemingly his primary and trumping commitment, liberty turned out to be the least compelling of his tests. The second was his judgement on whether the policy or behaviour accorded with the gradualist dimension of his social science: Was the solution apt to cause more disruption than it was worth? Was eradicating the cause a threat to order and stability? Were the public even ready for this badly needed change? The third and most authoritative test of all was whether the policy or behaviour yielded a desirable result. Was it conducive to welfare or even *positive* liberty? If the answer was 'yes', then Smith readily abandons his commitments to liberty and gradualism.

As I have argued throughout this book, Smith was less libertarian and more consequentialist than is normally thought; further, where conflicts between 'positive' and 'negative' liberty occurred, he often favoured the former. He defended liberty not as an end in itself, but for its good effects. For Smith, the point of life, ultimately, was to be 'happy' and it was the state's duty to ensure that the conditions were in place so that happiness could be pursued and maximised. Therefore, Smith ultimately advocates whatever, in the end, will achieve this, not just for the few, but for everyone. As he insisted, the 'sole use and end' of any 'constitutio[n] of government' is 'to promote the happiness of those who live under' it (*TMS*, IV.i.11: 185).

Reference

Smith, A. (1976 [1759]). *The Theory of Moral Sentiments*, D. D. Raphael & A. L. MacFie (Eds.). Oxford: Clarendon Press.

Bibliography

Adams, J. (1856). *The Works*, Vol. IV, C. F. Adams (Ed.). Boston: Little Brown and Company.

Altick, R. (1983). *The English Common Reader: A Social History of the Mass Reading Public 1800–1900*. Chicago: University of Chicago Press.

Alvey, J. (1998). Adam Smith's Three Strikes Against Commercial Society. *International Journal of Social Economics, 25*(9), 1425–1444.

Alvey, J. E. (2001). Moral Education as a Means to Human Perfection and Social Order: Adam Smith's View of Education in Commercial Society. *History of the Human Sciences, 14*(2), 1–18.

Alvey, J. (2003). Adam Smith's View of History: Consistent or Paradoxical. *History of the Human Sciences, 16*, 1–25.

Anderson, G. M., Shughart, W. F., & Tollison, D. (1985). Adam Smith in the Customhouse. *Journal of Political Economy, 93*(4), 740–759.

Annas, J. (1993). *The Morality of Happiness*. New York: Oxford University Press.

Asso, F. (2002). The Home Bias Approach in the History of Economic Thought: Issues on Financial Globalisation from Adam Smith to John Maynard Keynes. In J. Lorentzen & M. De Cecco (Eds.), *Markets and Authorities: Global Finance and Human Choice* (pp. 20–40). Cheltenham: Edward Elgar.

Baldry, H. C. (1965). *The Unity of Mankind in Greek Thought*. Cambridge: Cambridge University Press.

Bendix, R. (1960). *Max Weber: An Intellectual Portrait*. London: Doubleday & Co.

Benians, E. A. (1925). Adam Smith's Project of an Empire. *Cambridge Historical Journal, 1*(3), 249–283.

Berdell, J. (2002). *International Trade and Economic Growth in Open Economies*. Cheltenham: Edward Elgar.

L. Hill, *Adam Smith's Pragmatic Liberalism*,
https://doi.org/10.1007/978-3-030-19337-9

Berg, M., & Eger, E. (2003). *Luxury in the Eighteenth Century*. New York/ Basingstoke: Palgrave Macmillan.

Bernstein, J. A. (1978). Adam Ferguson and the Idea of Progress. *Studies in Burke and His Time, 19*(2), 99–118.

Berry, C. J. (1992). Adam Smith and the Virtues of Commerce. *Nomos, XXXIV*, 69–88.

Berry, C. (1994). *The Idea of Luxury*. Cambridge: Cambridge University Press.

Boucoyannis, D. (2013). The Equalizing Hand: Why Adam Smith Thought the Market Should Produce Wealth Without Steep Inequality. *Perspectives on Politics, 11*(4), 1051–1070.

Bradley, J. E. (1975). Whigs and Nonconformists: "Slumbering Radicalism" in English Politics, 1739–89. *Eighteenth-Century Studies, 9*(1), 1–27.

Brewer, J. (1976). *Party, Ideology and Popular Politics at the Accession of George III*. Cambridge: Cambridge University Press.

Brewer, J. (1988). *The Sinews of Power: War, Money, and the English State, 1688–1783*. London: Century Hutchinson.

Brown, V. (1994). *Adam Smith's Discourse*. London: Routledge.

Buchan, D. E. (1791, June 8). *The Bee or Literary Weekly Intelligence*.

Buchan, B., & Hill, L. (2014). *An Intellectual History of Political Corruption*. Basingstoke: Palgrave Macmillan.

Campbell, W. F. (1966). Adam Smith's Theory of Justice, Prudence and Beneficence. *American Economic Review, LVII*(2), 571–577.

Campbell, T. D., & Ross, I. S. (1981). The Utilitarianism of Adam Smith's Policy Advice. *Journal of the History of Ideas, 42*(1), 73–92.

Carr, E. H. (1946). *The Twenty Years' Crisis 1919–1939*. London: Palgrave Macmillan.

Clarke, S. R. L. (1987). The City of the Wise. *Apeiron, 20*(1), 63–80.

Clarkson, T. (1808). *The History of the Rise, Progress and Accomplishment of the Abolition of the Slave Trade by the British Parliament in 2 Volumes*. London: Longman, Hurst, Rees and Orme.

Coats, A. W. B. (Ed.). (1971). *The Classical Economists and Economic Policy*. London: Methuen.

Cohen, E. W. (1941). *The Growth of the British Civil Service, 1780–1939*. London: George Allen & Unwin Ltd.

Cohen, E. S. (1992). Justice and Political Economy in Commercial Society: Adam Smith's "Science of the Legislator". *The Journal of Politics, 51*(1), 50–72.

Corrigan, P., & Sayer, D. (1985). From Theatre to Machine: Old Corruption. In P. Corrigan & D. Sayer (Eds.), *The Great Arch: English State Formation as Cultural Revolution* (pp. 87–113). Oxford: Basil Blackwell.

Crane, V. W. (1950). *Benjamin Franklin's Letters to the Press*. Chapel Hill: University of North Carolina Press.

Cropsey, J. (1957). *Polity and Economy: An Interpretation of the Principles of Adam Smith*. The Hague: Martinus Nijhoff.

Cropsey, J. (1975). Adam Smith and Political Philosophy. In A. S. Skinner & T. Wilson (Eds.), *Essays on Adam Smith* (pp. 132–153). Oxford: Clarendon Press.

Curtis, L. A. (1979). *The Versatile Defoe: An Anthology of Uncollected Writings*, edited and Introduced by L. A. Curtis. London: G. Prior.

Dickey, L. (1986). Historicising the 'Adam Smith Problem': Conceptual, Historiographic, and Textual Issues. *The Journal of Modern History, 58*, 579–609.

Dunn, W. L. (1941). Adam Smith and Edmund Burke: Complementary Contemporaries. *Southern Economic Journal, VII*(2), 330–346.

Edelstein, L. (1966). *The Meaning of Stoicism*. Cambridge, MA: Harvard University Press.

Emerson, R. (1967). Peter Gay and the Heavenly City. *Journal of the History of Ideas, 28*(3), 383–402.

Eriksson, B. (1993). The First Formulation of Sociology: A Discursive Innovation of the Eighteenth Century. *Archives-Europeennes-de-Sociologie, 34*(2), 251–276.

Erskine, A. (1990). *The Hellenistic Stoa*. London: Duckworth.

Fagerstrom, D. I. (1954). Scottish Opinion and the American Revolution. *The William and Mary Quarterly, 11*(2), 252–275.

Fay, C. R. (1930). Adam Smith and the Dynamic State. *The Economic Journal, 40*(157), 25–34.

Ferguson, A. (1792). *Principles of Moral and Political Science: Being Chiefly a Retrospect of Lectures Delivered in the College of Edinburgh, in Two Volumes*. Edinburgh: Printed for A. Strahan and T. Cadell, London, and W. Creech, Edinburgh.

Ferguson, A. (1816). *Biographical Sketch or Memoir of Lieutenant-Colonel Patrick Ferguson Originally Intended for the British Encyclopedia*. Edinburgh: Printed by John Moir.

Ferguson, A. (1834). *The History of the Progress and Termination of the Roman Republic*. London: Jones & Company.

Ferguson, A. (1995). *The Correspondence of Adam Ferguson*, V. Merolle (Ed.), with an Introduction by J. B. Fagg, in Three Volumes. London: William Pickering.

Ferguson, A. (1996 [1767]). *An Essay on the History of Civil Society*, edited and with an Introduction by F. Oz-Salzberger. Cambridge: Cambridge University Press.

Ferguson, A. (1996). *Collection of Essays*, edited and with an Introduction by Y. Amoh. Kyoto: Rinsen Book Co.

Fergusson, J. (1934). *Letters of George Dempster to Sir Adam Fergusson, 1756–1813*. London: Macmillan & Co.

Firth, A. (2002). Moral Supervision and Autonomous Social Order; Wages and Consumption in Eighteenth Century Economic Thought. *History of the Human Sciences, 15*(1), 39–57.

Fitzgibbons, A. (1995). *Adam Smith's System of Liberty, Wealth and Virtue*. Oxford: Clarendon Press.

Fleischacker, S. (2002). Adam Smith's Reception Among the American Founders, 1776–1790. *The William and Mary Quarterly, 59*(4), 897–924.

Fleischacker, S. (2004). *On Adam Smith's Wealth of Nations: A Philosophical Companion*. Princeton: Princeton University Press.

Flynn, D. O., & Giraldez, A. (2004). Path Dependence, Time Lags and the Birth of Globalisation: A Critique of O'Rourke and Williamson. *European Review of Economic History, 8*(1), 81–108.

Forbes, D. (1967). Adam Ferguson and the Idea of Community. In D. Young, A. J. Youngson, G. E. Davie, D. Forbes, The Hon. Lord Cameron, & A. Frazer (Eds.), *Edinburgh in the Age of Reason: A Commemoration* (pp. 40–47). Edinburgh: Edinburgh University Press.

Forbes, D. (1976). Skeptical Whiggism, Commerce, and Liberty. In A. S. Skinner & T. Wilson (Eds.), *Essays on Adam Smith* (pp. 194–201). Oxford: Clarendon Press.

Forman-Barzilai, F. (2000). Adam Smith as a Globalisation Theorist. *Critical Review, 14*(4), 391–419.

Forman-Barzilai, F. (2005). Sympathy in Space(s): Adam Smith on Proximity. *Political Theory, 33*, 189–217.

Forman-Barzilai, F. (2006). Smith on 'Connexion', Culture and Judgment. In L. Montes & E. Schliesser (Eds.), *New Voices on Adam Smith*. Abingdon: Routledge.

Forman-Barzilai, F. (2010). *Adam Smith and the Circles of Sympathy*. Cambridge: Cambridge University Press.

Furnisss, F. S. (1920). *The Position of the Labourer in a System of Nationalism*. Boston: Houghton Mifflin.

Gascoigne, J. (1991). The Wisdom of the Egyptians and the Secularisation of History in the Age of Newton. In S. Gaukroger (Ed.), *The Uses of Antiquity* (pp. 171–212). Amsterdam: Kluwer Academic Publishers.

Gee, J. M. A. (1968). Adam Smith's Social Welfare Function. *Scottish Journal of Political Economy, 15*(1), 283–299.

Gellner, E. (1994). *Conditions of Liberty: Civil Society and Its Rivals*. London: Penguin Books.

Gilpin, R. (1971). The Politics of Transnational Economic Relations. *International Organisation, 25*(3), 398–419.

Griswold, C. (1999). *Adam Smith and the Virtues of Enlightenment*. Cambridge: Cambridge University Press.

Guttridge, G. H. (1933). Adam Smith and the American Revolution. *The American Historical Review, 38*(4), 714–720.

Haakonssen, K. (1981). *The Science of the Legislator*. Cambridge: Cambridge University Press.

Haakonssen, K. (1998). *Traditions of Liberalism*. St Leonards: Centre for Independent Studies.
Hadas, M. (1943). From Nationalism to Cosmopolitanism in the Greco-Roman World. *Journal of the History of Ideas, 4*(1), 105–111.
Halevy, E. (1934). *The Growth of Philosophical Radicalism*. London: Faber and Faber.
Hall, C., McClelland, K., & Lang, R. (2014). *Legacies of British Slave-Ownership: Colonial Slavery and the Formation of Victorian Britain*. Cambridge: Cambridge University Press.
Hamowy, R. (1987). *The Scottish Enlightenment and the Theory of Spontaneous Order*. Carbondale: Illinois University Press.
Hanley, R. P. (2008). Enlightened Nation Building: The Science of the Legislator in Adam Smith and Rousseau. *American Journal of Political Science, 52*(2), 219–234.
Hanley, R. P. (2009). *Adam Smith and the Character of Virtue*. Cambridge: Cambridge University Press.
Hanley, R. P. (2014). The "Wisdom of the State": Adam Smith on China and Tartary. *The American Political Science Review, 108*(2), 371–382.
Hardin, R. (1986). The Utilitarian Logic of Liberalism. *Ethics, 97*(3), 47–74.
Harling, P., & Mandler, P. (1993). From 'Fiscal-Military' State to Laissez-Faire State, 1760–1850. *Journal of British Studies, 32*(1), 44–70.
Heilbroner, R. L. (1973). The Paradox of Progress: Decline and Decay in the Wealth of Nations. *Journal of the History of Ideas, 34*, 243–262.
Hellmuth, E. (1999). Why Does Corruption Matter? Reforms and Reform Movements in Britain and Germany in the Second Half of the Eighteenth Century. In T. C. W. Blanning & P. Wende (Eds.), *Reform in Great Britain and Germany 1750–1850*. Oxford: Oxford University Press.
Herzog, L. (2013). *Inventing the Market: Smith, Hegel, and Political Theory*. Oxford: Oxford University Press.
Herzog, L. (2016). The Normative Stakes of Economic Growth; Or, Why Adam Smith Does Not Rely on "Trickle Down". *The Journal of Politics, 78*(1), 50–62.
Hewins, W. A. S. (1903, June 5). The Fiscal Policy of the Empire. *The Times*.
Hill, L. (1996). Ferguson and Smith on 'Human Nature', 'Interest' and the Role of Beneficence in Market Society, *Journal of the History of Economic Ideas*, Adam Smith Special Edition, *IV*(1–2), 353–399.
Hill, L. (1998). The Invisible Hand of Adam Ferguson. *The European Legacy, 3*(6), 42–65.
Hill, L. (2000). The Two Republicae of the Roman Stoics. *Citizenship Studies, 4*(1), 65–79.
Hill, L. (2001a). The First Wave of Feminism: Were the Stoics Feminists? *History of Political Thought, 22*(1), 12–40.

Hill, L. (2001b). The Hidden Theology of Adam Smith. *European Journal of the History of Economic Thought, 8*(1), 1–29.

Hill, L. (2004). Further Reflections on the Hidden Theology of Adam Smith. *European Journal of the History of Economic Thought, 11*(4), 629–635.

Hill, L. (2006). Adam Smith and the Theme of Corruption. *Review of Politics, 68*(4), 636–662.

Hill, L. (2007). Adam Smith, Adam Ferguson and Karl Marx on the Division of Labour. *Journal of Classical Sociology, 7*(3), 339–366.

Hill, L. (2009). Adam Smith's Pragmatic Liberalism. *Proceedings of the Santiago 2009 World Congress of Political Science*, IPSA Online, pp. 1–34, https://www.ipsa.org/system/files/node/conferenceproceeding/109858-adam-smiths-liberalism.pdf.

Hill, L. (2011). Adam Smith on *Thumos* and Irrational Economic Man. *European Journal of the History of Economic Thought, 17*(4), 1–22.

Himmelfarb, G. (1985). *The Idea of Poverty: England in the Early Industrial Age*. New York: Faber and Faber.

Hirschman, A. O. (1977). *The Passions and the Interests*. Princeton: Princeton University Press.

Hont, I. (2005). Free Trade and the Economic Limits to National Politics: Neo-Machiavellian Political Economy Revisited. In I. Hont (Ed.), *Jealousy of Trade: International Competition and the Nation-State in Historical Perspective* (pp. 185–266). Cambridge, MA: Harvard University Press.

Hont, I. (2009). Adam Smith's History of Law and Government as Political Theory. In R. Bourke & R. Geuss (Eds.), *Political Judgement: Essays for John Dunn* (pp. 131–171). Cambridge: Cambridge University Press.

Hont, I., & Ignatieff, M. (1983). Needs and Justice in the Wealth of Nations: An Introductory Essay. In I. Hont & M. Ignatieff (Eds.), *Wealth and Virtue: The Shaping of Political Economy in the Scottish Enlightenment*. Cambridge: Cambridge University Press.

Hume, D. (1932). *Letters of David Hume*, J. Y. T. Greig (Ed.). Oxford: Oxford University Press.

Hume, D. (1983). *The History of England*, 6 Vols., William B. Todd (Ed.). Indianapolis: Liberty Classics.

Hume, D. (1987). *Essays Moral Political and Literary*, E. F. Miller (Ed.). Indiana: Liberty Classics.

Hume D. (2003). *A Treatise of Human Nature*, D. F. Norton (Ed.). Oxford: Oxford University Press.

Hundert, E. J. (1974). The Achievement Motive in Hume's Political Economy. *Journal of the History of Ideas, 35*(1), 139–143.

Ignatieff, M. (1984). *The Needs of Strangers*. London: Chatto and Windus.

Innes, J. (2002). Changing Perceptions of the State in the Late Eighteenth and Early Nineteenth Centuries. *Journal of Historical Sociology, 15*, 107–112.

Jary, D., & Jary, J. (Eds.). (1991). *The Collins Dictionary of Sociology*. Glasgow: Harper Collins.

Johnston, M. (1996). The Search for Definitions: The Vitality of Politics and the Issue of Corruption. *International Social Science Journal, 48*, 321–335.

Kennedy, G. (2005). *Adam Smith's Lost Legacy*. New York: Palgrave Macmillan.

Kettler, D. (1965). *The Social and Political Thought of Adam Ferguson*. Indiana: Ohio State University Press.

Kittrell, E. R. (1965). The Development of the Theory of Colonization in English Classical Political Thought. *Southern Economic Journal, 31*(3), 189–206.

Kleer, R. (1995). Final Causes in Adam Smith's "Theory of Moral Sentiments". *Journal of the History of Philosophy, 33*(2), 275–330.

Knorr, K. E. (1944). *British Colonial Theories, 1570–1850*. Toronto: Toronto University Press.

Lamb, R. (1973). Adam Smith's Concept of Alienation. *Oxford Economic Papers, 25*(2), 275–285.

Langford, P. (2002). The Management of the Eighteenth Century State: Perceptions and Implications. *Journal of Historical Sociology, 15*(1), 102–106.

Lee, A. (1764). *An Essay in Vindication of the Continental Colonies of America from a Censure of Mr Adam Smith in his Theory of Moral Sentiments*. London: Printed for the Author.

Lehmann, W. C. (1974). Review of P. Salvucci's Adam Ferguson: Sociologica e Filosofia Politica. *History and Society, 13*(2), 163–181.

Letwin, W. (1988). Was Adam Smith a Liberal? In K. Haakonssen (Ed.), *Traditions of Liberalism* (pp. 83–104). St Leonards: Centre for Independent Studies.

Liu, G. M. (2018). The Apostle of Free Trade: Adam Smith and the Nineteenth-Century American Trade Debates. *History of European Ideas, 44*(2), 210–223.

Lovejoy, A. O. (1964). *Great Chain of Being: A Study of the History of an Idea*. Cambridge, MA: Harvard University Press.

Mandeville, B. (1924). *The Fable of the Bees or Private Vices, Publick Benefits*, F. B. Kaye (Ed.). Oxford: Oxford University Press.

Marcus Aurelius. (1964). *Meditations*, translated and with an Introduction by M. Staniforth. London: Penguin.

Marshall, M. G. (2000). Luxury, Economic Development, and Work Motivation: David Hume, Adam Smith, and J.R. McCulloch. *History of Political Economy, 32*(3), 631–649.

Marx, K. (1969). *The Poverty of Philosophy*, with and Introduction by F. Engels. New York: International Publishers.

Marx, K. (1977). *Capital*, 3 Vols. Moscow: Progress Publishers.

McLean, I. (2006). *Adam Smith, Radical and Egalitarian: An Interpretation for the Twenty-first Century*. Edinburgh: Edinburgh University Press.

McLean, I., & Peterson, S. M. (2010). Adam Smith at the Constitutional Convention. *Loyola Law Review, 56*(1), 95–135.

Merton, R. K. (1934). Durkheim's Division of Labor in Society. *American Journal of Sociology, 40*(3), 319–328.

Mingardi, A. (2018). Adam Smith and the Vocabulary of Liberty: Two Views. *Economic Affairs, 38*(3), 447–455.

Minowitz, P. (1989). Invisible Hand, Invisible Death: Adam Smith on War and Socio-Economic Development. *Journal of Political and Military Sociology, 17*(Winter), 305–315.

Minowitz, P. (1993). *Profits, Priests, and Princes.* Cambridge: Cambridge University Press.

Mizuta, H. (1976). Towards a Definition of the Scottish Enlightenment. *Studies in Voltaire, 154,* 1459–1464.

Mizuta, H. (2000). *Adam Smith's Library: A Catalogue*, edited and with an Introduction and Notes by H. Mizuta. New York: Oxford University Press.

Montesquieu, C. L. (1989). *The Spirit of the Laws* (A. M. Cohler, Trans. and Ed.). Cambridge, B. C. Miller & H. M. Stone.

Moore, J. (2000). Hutcheson's Theodicy: The Argument and the Contexts of a System of Moral Philosophy. In P. Wood (Ed.), *The Scottish Enlightenment: Essays in Reinterpretation* (pp. 239–266). Rochester: University of Rochester Press.

Morrison, J. A. (2012). Before Hegemony: Adam Smith, American Independence and the Origins of the First Era of Globalization. *International Organisation, 66*(3), 395–428.

Mossner, E. C. (1969). *Adam Smith: The Biographical Approach.* David Murray Lecture, University of Glasgow.

Mossner, E. C., & Ross, I. S. (1976). Introduction. In A. Smith, *The Theory of Moral Sentiments,* D. Raphael & A. L. MacFie, (Eds.). Oxford: Clarendon Press.

Muthu, S. (2008). Adam Smith's Critique of International Trading Companies: Theorizing 'Globalization' in the Age of Enlightenment. *Political Theory, 36*(2), 105–139.

Nicholson, J. S. (1909). *A Project of Empire, a Critical Study of the Economics of Imperialism, With Special Reference to the Ideas of Adam Smith.* London: Macmillan.

Nussbaum, M. (1995). *Poetic Justice: The Literary Imagination and Public Life.* Boston: Beacon Press.

Nussbaum, M. (2000). Duties of Justice, Duties of Material Aid: Cicero's Problematic Legacy. *Journal of Political Philosophy, 8*(2), 176–206.

Nye, J. (1989). Political Corruption: A Cost Benefit Analysis. In A. J. Heidenheimer, M. Johnston, & V. Levine (Eds.), *Political Corruption: A Handbook.* New Brunswick: Transaction Books.

Ogborn, M. (2002). Wherein Lay the Late Seventeenth-Century State? Charles Davenant Meets Streynsham Master. *Journal of Historical Sociology, 15,* 96–101.

Oldenquist, A. (1982). Loyalties. *The Journal of Philosophy, 79*(4), 173–193.

Otteson, J. (2002). *Adam Smith's Marketplace of Life*. Cambridge: Cambridge University Press.

Oz-Salzberger, F. (2003). The Political Theory of the Scottish Enlightenment. In A. Broadie (Ed.), *The Scottish Enlightenment* (pp. 157–175). Cambridge: Cambridge University Press.

Pack, S. J. (1991). *Capitalism as a Moral System: Adam Smith's Critique of the Free Market Economy*. Aldershot: Edward Elgar.

Pack, S. (1996). Slavery, Adam Smith's Economic Vision and the Invisible Hand. *Journal of the History of Economic Ideas, 4*, 1–2.

Palen, M. W. (2014). Adam Smith as Advocate of Empire, c. 1870–1932. *The Historical Journal, 57*(1), 179–198.

Peck, L. L. (1979). *Court Patronage and Corruption in Early Stuart England*. Boston: Unwin Hyman.

Perelman, M. (1989). Adam Smith and Dependent Social Relations. *History of Political Economy, 21*(3), 312–329.

Phillips, J. A. (1979). The Structure of Electoral Politics in Unreformed England. *The Journal of British Studies, 19*, 76–100.

Phillipson, N. (1981). The Scottish Enlightenment. In R. Porter & M. Teich (Eds.), *The Enlightenment in National Context* (pp. 19–40). Cambridge: Cambridge University Press.

Phillipson, N. (2010). *Adam Smith: An Enlightened Life*. New Haven: Yale University Press.

Philp, M. (1987). Defining Corruption: An Analysis of the Republican Tradition. *International Political Science Association Research Roundtable on Political Finance and Political Corruption*, Bellagio.

Pitts, J. (2005). *A Turn to Empire*. Princeton: Princeton University Press.

Pocock, J. G. A. (1972). Virtue and Commerce in the Eighteenth Century. *Journal of Interdisciplinary History, 3*, 119–134.

Pocock, J. G. A. (1975). *The Machiavellian Moment*. Princeton: Princeton University Press.

Prest, W. (1991). Judicial Corruption in Early Modern England. *Past and Present, 133*, 67–95.

Pullen, M. J. (1981). Malthus' Theological Ideas and Their Influence on His Principle of Population. *History of Political Economy, 13*(1), 39–54.

Rae, J. (1895). *Life of Adam Smith*. London: Macmillan and Co.

Rashid, S. (1980). The Policy of Laissez-Faire During Scarcities. *The Economic Journal, 90*, 493–503.

Rasmussen, D. C. (2013). *The Pragmatic Enlightenment: Recovering the Liberalism of Hume, Smith, Montesquieu, and Voltaire*. Cambridge: Cambridge University Press.

Rasmussen, D. C. (2016). Adam Smith on What Is Wrong with Economic Inequality. *American Political Science Review, 110*(2), 342–352.

Rawls, J. (1971). *A Theory of Justice*. Cambridge, MA: Harvard University Press.
Reesor, M. E. (1951). *The Political Theory of the Old and Middle Stoa*. New York: J.J. Augustin.
Reinert, S. A. (2011). *Translating Empire: Emulation and the Origins of Political Economy*. Cambridge, MA: Harvard University Press.
Robertson, J. (1985). *The Scottish Enlightenment and the Militia Issue*. Edinburgh: John Donald.
Robertson, J. (1997). Introduction, to A. Fletcher, *Political Works*. Cambridge: Cambridge University Press.
Rosanvallon, P. (2006). The Market, Liberalism and Anti-Liberalism. In S. Moyn (Ed.), *Democracy Past and Future* (pp. 252–282). New York: Columbia University Press.
Rosenberg, N. (1960). Some Institutional Aspects of the Wealth of Nations. *Journal of Political Economy, 68*, 557–570.
Rosenberg, N. (1965). Adam Smith on the Division of Labor: Two Views or One. *Economica, 33*, 127–139.
Rosolino, R. (2018). Resisting Economic Conspiracies: Adam Smith, the (Labour) Market, and the Moral Basis of Antimonopolistic Resistance. *History of Political Thought, 39*(2), 297–324.
Ross, I. S. (1972). *Lord Kames and the Scotland of His Day*. Oxford: Clarendon Press.
Ross, I. S. (1975). Political Themes in the Correspondence of Adam Smith. *The Scottish Tradition, 5*, 5–22.
Ross, I. S. (1995). *Life of Adam Smith*. Oxford: Oxford University Press.
Rothschild, E. (1992). Adam Smith and Conservative Economics. *The Economic History Review, XLV*(1), 74–96.
Rothschild, E. (2001). *Economic Sentiments: Adam Smith, Condorcet and the Enlightenment*. Cambridge, MA: Harvard University Press.
Rothschild, E. (2004). Global Commerce and the Question of Sovereignty in the Eighteenth-Century Provinces. *Modern Intellectual History, 1*(1), 3–25.
Salter, J. (2012). Adam Smith on Justice and the Needs of the Poor. *Journal of the History of Economic Thought, 34*(4), 559–575.
Samuels, W. J., & Medema, S. G. (2005). Freeing Smith from the "Free Market": on the Misperception of Adam Smith on the Economic Role of Government. *History of Political Economy, 37*(2), 219–226.
Schumpeter, J. A. (1952). *Ten Great Economists: From Marx to Keynes*. London: George Allen and Unwin.
Schuyler, R. L. (1921). The Climax of Anti-Imperialism in England. *Political Science Quarterly, 36*(4), 537–560.
Schuyler, R. L. (1945). *The Fall of the Old Colonial System: A Study of British Free Trade* (pp. 1770–1870). Oxford: Oxford University Press.
Schwoerer, L. (1974). *'No Standing Armies!' The Anti-Army Ideology in Seventeenth Century England*. Baltimore: John Hopkins University Press.

Sen, A. (2009). *The Idea of Justice*. London: Belknap.

Shariff, I. (2003). Global Economic Integration: Prospects and Problems. *Economic Development Review, 1*(2), 1–25.

Sher, R. B. (1985). *Church and University in the Scottish Enlightenment*. Princeton: Princeton University Press.

Sher, R. B. (1989). Adam Ferguson, Adam Smith, and the Problem of National Defense. *The Journal of Modern History, 61*(2), 240–268.

Silver, A. (1989). Friendship and Trust as Moral Ideals: An Historical Approach. *European Journal of Sociology, 30*, 274–297.

Singer, B. (2004). Montesquieu, Adam Smith and the Discovery of the Social. *Journal of Classical Sociology, 4*(1), 31–57.

Skinner, A. (1976). Adam Smith and the American Economic Community: An Essay in Applied Economics. *Journal of the History of Ideas, 37*(1), 59–78.

Skinner, A. S. (1977). Adam Smith and the American Revolution. *Presidential Studies Quarterly, 7*(2/3), 75–87.

Skinner, A. S. (1996). Adam Smith: The Demise of the Colonial Relationship with America. *Cahiers d'Economie Politique, 27–8*, 113–130.

Smith, A. (1976 [1759]). *The Theory of Moral Sentiments*, D. D. Raphael & A. L. MacFie (Eds.). Oxford: Clarendon Press.

Smith, A. (1978). *Lectures on Jurisprudence (A and B)*, R. L. Meek, D. D. Raphael & L. G. Stein (Eds.). Oxford: Oxford University Press.

Smith, A. (1979 [1776]). *An Inquiry into the Nature and Causes of the Wealth of Nations*, R. H. Campbell & A. S. Skinner (Eds.). Oxford: Clarendon Press.

Smith, A. (1980a). *Essays on Philosophical Subjects*, I.S. Ross (Ed.). Oxford: Clarendon Press.

Smith, A. (1980b). Letter to the Edinburgh Review. In I. S. Ross (Ed.), *Essays on Philosophical Subjects*. Oxford: Clarendon Press.

Smith, A. (1983). *Lectures on Rhetoric and Belles Lettres*, J. C. Bryce (Ed.). Oxford: Clarendon Press.

Smith, A. (1987). *The Correspondence of Adam Smith*, E. C. Mossner & I. S. Ross (Eds.). Oxford: Oxford University Press.

Smith, A. (1987 [1778]). Smith's Thoughts on the State of the Contest with America, February 1778. In E. C. Campbell & I. S. Ross (Eds.), *The Correspondence of Adam Smith* (Appendix B). Oxford: Oxford University Press.

Smith, C. (2013). Adam Smith: Left or Right? *Political Studies, 61*(4), 784–798.

Stabile, D. (1997). Adam Smith and the Natural Wage: Sympathy, Subsistence and Social Distance. *Review of Social Economy, 55*(3), 292–311.

Stevens, D. (1975). Adam Smith and the Colonial Disturbances. In A. S. Skinner & T. Wilson (Eds.), *Essays on Adam Smith*. Oxford: Clarendon Press.

Stewart, D. (1980 [1793]). Account of the Life and Writings of Adam Smith, LL.D, I.S. Ross (ed.). In W. P. D. Wightman & J. C. Bryce (Eds.), *Adam Smith: Essays on Philosophical Subjects*. Oxford: Oxford University Press.

Stigler, G. (1975). Smith's Travels on the Ship of State. In A. S. Skinner & T. Wilson (Eds.), *Essays on Adam Smith* (pp. 237–246). Oxford: Clarendon Press.

Strasser, R. (1976). *The Normative Structure of Sociology: Conservative and Emancipatory Themes in Social Thought*. London: Routledge and Kegan Paul.

Teichgraeber, R. F. (1987). 'Less Abused than I Had Reason to Expect': The Reception of the *Wealth of Nations* in Britain, 1776–90. *The Historical Journal, 30*(2), 337–366.

Tribe, K. (1995). Natural Liberty and Laissez-Faire: How Adam Smith Became a Free Trade Ideologue. In S. Copley & K. Sutherland (Eds.), *Adam Smith's Wealth of Nations: New Interdisciplinary Essays* (pp. 23–44). Manchester: Manchester University Press.

Viner, J. (1958). *The Long View and the Short*. Illinois: The Free Press.

Viner, J. (1977). *The Role of Providence in the Social Order*. Princeton: Princeton University Press.

Wagner, D. O. (1932). British Economists and the Empire I. *Political Science Quarterly, 46*(2), 248–276.

Waltz, K. N. (2001 [1959]). *Man, the State and War*. New York: Columbia University Press.

Waterman, A. M. C. (2002). Economics as Theology: Adam Smith's *Wealth of Nations*. *Southern Economic Journal, 68*(4), 907–921.

West, E. G. (1969). The Political Economy of Alienation: Karl Marx and Adam Smith. *Oxford Economic Papers, 21*(1), 1–23.

West, E. G. (1976). Adam Smith's Economics of Politics. *History of Political Economy, 8*(4), 515–539.

Whelan, F. (1996). *Edmund Burke and India: Political Morality and Empire*. Pittsburgh: University of Pittsburgh.

Wight, M. (1991). *International Theory: The Three Traditions*. London: Leicester University Press.

Winch, D. (1978). *Adam Smith's Politics*. Cambridge: Cambridge University Press.

Winch, D. (1997). Adam Smith's Problem and Ours. *Scottish Journal of Political Economy, 44*, 384–402.

Witzum, A. (2013). Utilitarianism and the Role of Utility in Adam Smith. *The European Journal of the History of Economic Thought, 20*(4), 572–602.

Witzum, A., & Young, J. T. (2006). The Neglected Agent: Justice, Power and Distribution in Adam Smith. *History of Political Economy, 38*(1), 437–471.

Wolin, S. (1960). *Politics and Vision*. Boston: Little, Brown and Company.

Wootton, D. (1993). David Hume "The Historian". In D. F. Norton (Ed.), *The Cambridge Companion to David Hume* (pp. 447–479). Cambridge: Cambridge University Press.

Wyatt-Walter, A. (1996). Adam Smith and the Liberal Tradition in International Relations. *Review of International Studies, 22*(1), 5–28.

Xenakis, I. (1969). *Epictetus: Philosopher-Therapist*. The Hague: Martinus Nijhoff.

Index[1]

A

B

[1] Note: Page numbers followed by 'n' refer to notes.

L. Hill, *Adam Smith's Pragmatic Liberalism*,
https://doi.org/10.1007/978-3-030-19337-9

The manufacturer's authorised representative in the EU is Springer Nature Customer Service Centre GmbH, Europaplatz 3, 69115 Heidelberg, Germany. If you have any concerns regarding our products, please contact ProductSafety@springernature.com

Printed and bound by CPI Group (UK) Ltd, Croydon, CR0 4YY
30/09/2026
02225216-0003